Praise for *The Copyselling System*

"You'll think you're learning to write copy. Joanna's actually teaching how to build a business that scales."

—Dan Martell, *Wall Street Journal* bestselling author of *Buy Back Your Time*

"Positioning tells you what to say—this book tells you how to say it. It's the bridge between knowing your value and communicating it in a way that generates sales."

—April Dunford, author of *Obviously Awesome* and *Sales Pitch*

"In this excellent and practical book, Joanna shows you how to craft copy from real customer voices, constraints, and the exact progress they're after. Every product marketer needs to master this."

—Bobby Moesta, author and cocreator of Jobs to Be Done innovation methodology

"This is a must-read for any business that wants to make more money with copywriting. Joanna's book shows you how."

—Wes Bush, founder and author of *Product-Led Growth*

"A step-by-step system for writing messages that get people to buy—based on real customer words, not guessing."

—Peep Laja, founder of Wynter and CXL

"This book will forever change how you think about marketing copy. I predict it will become required reading for teams everywhere. Read it before your competition does."

—Andy Crestodina, speaker, founder, and author of *Content Chemistry*

"I loved this book. Joanna taught me pretty much everything I know about copywriting, beginning over a decade ago when she was helping 'hackers' like me sell software without sounding like engineers. *The Copyselling System* is a must-read for anyone who wants to learn how to sell at scale, and without the sleaze."

—Brennan Dunn, founder of RightMessage and author of *This Is Personal*

THE COPYSELLING SYSTEM

Write to Sell with the Secret Formula for **MAXIMIZING REVENUE**

JOANNA WIEBE

BENBELLA

BenBella Books, Inc.
Dallas, TX

This book is designed to provide accurate and authoritative information about copywriting, marketing, and entrepreneurship. Neither the author nor the publisher is engaged in rendering legal, accounting, or other professional services by publishing this book. If any such assistance is required, the services of qualified professionals should be sought. The author and publisher will not be responsible for any liability, loss, or risk incurred as a result of the use and application of any information contained in this book.

BenBella

BenBella Books, Inc.
8080 N. Central Expressway
Suite 1700
Dallas, TX 75206
benbellabooks.com
Send feedback to feedback@benbellabooks.com

BenBella is a federally registered trademark.

Printed in the United States of America
10 9 8 7 6 5 4 3 2 1

Library of Congress Control Number: 2026000655
ISBN 9781637748886 (trade paperback)
ISBN 9781637748893 (electronic)

Editing by Sarah Modlin
Proofreading by Jenny Bridges and Rebecca Maines
Indexing by Debra Bowman
Text design and composition by PerfecType, Nashville, TN
Cover design by Sarah Avinger
Cover image © Adobe Stock / Cagkan
Printed by Lake Book Manufacturing

CONTENTS

INTRODUCTION

Shortly after raising their Series A funding, GitPrime (YC W16), now PluralSight Flow, hired me to write their copy. A year later, they were acquired for $170 million USD.

My work with them started with a tagline, or a customer-facing *phrase that pays*. Then website copy. Then we crafted nurturing emails that drove leads to schedule and show up for sales calls. Then GitPrime realized that, as long as they were going to be marketing (forever), they were going to need not only good copy but freaking try-hard, sweaty copy. So they put me and my agency on retainer.

At the end of our first year together, GitPrime cofounder Ben Thompson sat me down to share some numbers. They attributed 337 percent year over year sales pipeline growth to the work I'd done with them.

That growth couldn't be attributed to just one message. It was a series of messages. It was the tagline—"Engineers Build Business"—that shaped the GitPrime brand and product messaging. It was the plan and copy for the welcome email through to the show-up sequence. It was the website, and each painstakingly crafted page on it. Growth didn't come from just one message on one asset, one time. It was all the messages across the assets, delivered and stacking upon each other.

The same was true when my agency worked, for several years, with the SaaS (Software as a Service) brand Follow Up Boss, which grew revenue

32 percent year over year and was then acquired by Zillow for half a billion dollars. It was also true when we worked, for several years, with what would become the ecommerce brand Resident (makers of Nectar, Dreamcloud, and Awara mattresses), who generated $250 million by the end of their first year with us, then doubled that by the end of their second year—and was later acquired for one billion dollars. In both cases, we helped guide their strategic messaging and executed and optimized their copy on an ongoing basis. Revenue wins rarely come from a single message or a single asset. It takes a lot of strategic messages, stacked and stacked, building on one another, to create an irresistible desire in the prospect to start a trial or buy a mattress—or sell the product or service *you're* trying to sell.

Over my twenty-plus years in messaging, I've helped marketing teams at a variety of companies—Bitly, British Telecom, Doodle, Egnyte, Nectar, Glowforge, Intuit, LaunchDarkly, Prezi, Shopify, Sprout Social, and more, along with a dozen or so entertainment and fashion brands I can't mention by name—increase their leads and revenue two-, five-, and even tenfold.

I've helped Catholic Company sell more rosaries. I've helped Evo sell more snowboards. I've helped Glowforge sell multiple $5,000 machines into schools with tight budgets. (The students *love* those machines!)

Throughout this book, you're going to see examples of one-off copy projects—strategically crafted pages or emails—that led, like a straight arrow, to killer business wins. What will not appear on the page are these three things, so let me share them with you now:

First, you've gotta have product–market fit. If you've built a product that no market wants, the most rigorous copywriting process won't help you sell it. The market needs to need it.

Second, it takes wildly strong leadership to make big results possible. What I'll show you is what can happen when all levels of marketing and product align around the fundamentals of the copyselling system, like GitPrime did. Ben Thompson was a wildly strong marketing leader, as was his senior marketer, Michael Smith. Ben and Mike cascaded the vision for marketing execution (copy, art, dev) to their team, and that empowered their crew and me, as a fractional team member, to take big swings. Everywhere

I've helped generate results, a wildly strong leader has cleared the way to make it possible; I think immediately of not only Ben Thompson but also Andrew Wilkinson of Metalab, Tara Robertson of Bitly, Hana Abaza of Shopify.

Third, marketing messages compound to "build customers" the way features compound to build products. The copy in Email A may convert more users than the copy in Email B, but it wasn't *only* the copy in Email A that drove the conversion. A series of struggling moments intersected with your acquisition messages, and that brought the prospect to Email A. You cannot "build a whole customer" with a single message or one block of copy.

At the same time, just one poorly executed email in a lead's journey can halt the production of a new customer. As my friend, the growth expert Matt Lerner, likes to say:

"Anyone with the power to fuck up your growth has the power to cause it."

I like to replace "anyone" with "any message." Any message your brand puts into the world can either grow your business or shrink it. An ad that can kick off the process of building a customer has an equal capacity to delay or destroy your chances of success. You get one message wrong—you get one asset wrong—and the customer creation system jerks to a stop.

HOW TO BUILD A CUSTOMER

I've mentioned that messages stack on each other, working together over time to generate stellar results. With that in mind, I often think and speak of acquiring customers as *building a customer on an assembly line.* You'll see the assembly line metaphor throughout this book. It doesn't mean customers are products, although we'd be wiser to think of marketing as creating customers than nurturing leads and selling products. You won't churn out mindless customers, mindlessly, like bots in a factory. Marketing is not a factory. That's not the idea.

Rather, when we think of marketing—and messaging in particular—as a system, illustrated as a step-by-step assembly line, the

guesswork (and its resulting chaos) starts to go away. There's no guessing on an assembly line. You don't just dump a bunch of messages on a factory floor then wait for something to happen. You architect everything—you engineer the whole system. We, as marketers, need to engineer the flow of messages to produce customers step-by-step, not chaotically (which is hard to track and measure).

Here's why I like the assembly line metaphor: One, my mind is systems-oriented, so I naturally seek out repeatable and efficient methods of solving messaging and marketing problems and generating results. And two, the visual is a great word picture—the stakes of a broken or underperforming assembly line are so easy to imagine! Think of an assembly line, like the one on reruns of *Laverne & Shirley*. At any stage along the assembly line, something can mess up, harming overall production. If you manage the factory floor of, say, Shotz Brewery and you see that bottles of beer keep stacking up, toppling over, and breaking at the part of the line run by Laverne DeFazio, you know that you've got to chat with Laverne; you know Laverne's performance is the most pressing constraint to getting bottles of beer off the line.

I would argue that a lot of messages are the Lavernes of your business. The message might feel lazy and disinterested; or the message might be stellar but placed at the wrong part of the assembly line. As a result, the assembly line is *constrained* where those messages are placed. The flipside is that, when you have your messages flowing in the right order, your assembly line produces better results.

A marketing "factory," if you will, exists to build a customer from zero to completion. And it does so with strong, strategic messages that move the customer along. All great copy has always done this. Message one kicks off the customer creation system. Message two moves them to message three, and message three continues moving them forward. If they don't see message three, they should not see message four because they're not ready for it yet. With the copyselling system, we map messages, one after the other, like stations on an assembly line; a prospect must consume one message before they see the next; a prospect must fully move through one stage before they are presented with messages for the next stage.

This message-first approach is different from the standard in digital marketing, which typically is channel-first, or funnel-first. The standard approach typically goes like this: *run ads that drive to landing pages that drive to emails that drive to sales or product pages, and then add in retargeting ads and emails along the way.* The marketing world is accustomed to starting with channels, not with the message. The marketing world is accustomed to drawing funnels with arrows between boxes, not drawing assembly lines with arrows between messages. And that might be okay, if it's working. But is it?

A SaaS client approached me about their brand's underperforming email flow. Their very smart, very engaged marketing team had drawn a funnel with eight boxes, representing eight emails, in a row, plus two additional boxes—one representing an in-product landing page and the other representing an upgrade-to-paid page. Ten boxes were connected by arrows. What went into the boxes? God bless 'em, they couldn't tell me. They didn't know what message went into Box Four, Box Seven, or, frankly, any of the boxes. After I applied the message-first approach (the copyselling system) to a new set of emails and tested them against the control, the message-first email flow converted 350 percent better than the control; that's three and a half times the paid conversions, with statistical confidence. (More on this example later!) All I had to do was start with the message.

The message-first approach is actually a *customer*-first approach—and that's why it works. At least, that's true when you follow the process I'm about to teach you, which finds **the world's highest-performing messages in the hearts and minds of your customers.** Customers tell you what to tell them. You just have to listen.

With the copyselling system, those messages coming from your customers get mapped, in sequence, along an assembly line. Some lines are longer than others. The stronger your messages, the faster the line can advance the customer to the end.

I've been told that there's just one hitch with the assembly line metaphor. An assembly line can turn out thirty thousand identical Converse high-tops or one reusable SaaS feature, but the journey to "make" a customer is not so repeatable. Customers are not created equal or equally. One lead may drop from the sky and land on your assembly line right at the very end of that line, while another may veer off the line, only to return later. Customers-in-the-making do not typically hit Point A followed by Point B followed by Point C with the linear regularity of machine assembly. If a universal difficulty in attribution tells us anything, it's that building a customer is chaotic!

Is it though? Or does it just feel that way because you aren't following the copyselling system yet? After all, a customer never drops out of the sky and lands in your checkout—the easy-won customers typically arrive via referral, which means that, although your marketing didn't expose them to the messages on the assembly line, someone else talked them through those messages. And THAT means that, if you can get your messages out into the world in a clean, repeatable way, it's easier for others to talk about you and send good referrals to you—everyone from Bob next door to ChatGPT can send you more quality prospects that you can convert much faster when your messages are clear and deliberate (not chaotic).

SPEND TIME WITH YOUR FUTURE CUSTOMERS

It takes more copy—not less—to create a customer. I ask you to be okay with that. After all, it can take some four to six weeks for a product team to ship one software feature. And here we are, trying to build a whole freaking customer! And then scale that process!

When I say "more copy," I don't mean that you need to be wordy or always write long copy. I mean you need to take your time hitting more key message notes along their journey, instead of trying to keep things as short as possible. Please stop rushing your customers; they want a solution, but a pithy headline with a short sentence is not going to be enough. Instead, let's create the assembly line and then make it infinitely more efficient. You need a full assembly line—you cannot shorten it just because you wish it were shorter.

Most teams are guessing their way through copywriting. Guessing is fast! Guessing takes as long as it takes to generate a guess. Three seconds? Five? Twelve minutes? Exactly one hour, aka the length of the Copy Brainstorm your associate added to your calendar? Guessing also gets crappy results. We shouldn't be surprised by that. After all, it took three seconds to produce the guess. How good could it possibly be?

My system takes longer—and it works.

I started to develop this system when I was in-house at Intuit. By the time I started my consulting business in 2011, I'd refined my system into what's now known as *conversion copywriting.* I moved from split-testing messaging for QuickBooks and TurboTax to split-testing messaging for a range of clients at Conversion Rate Experts to split-testing messaging with my own clients. When I ran a test worth talking about, I talked about it on my blog, on podcasts, on YouTube, and on stages all over the world, like Business of Software and Turing Fest. When more people asked me to teach them conversion copywriting, I created Copy School—the go-to training program for digital marketers and copywriters who get high on getting results. At the time of this writing, more than five thousand individuals have taken or are taking Copy School, and over 250 marketing or sales teams—from Calendly to Ramsey Solutions to AWS—are enrolled in it.

But even as marketers adopted conversion copywriting, I kept coming up against one problem: the word "copywriting" itself.

People mistake copywriting for a writing exercise, which makes it a creative exercise, which makes it a *guessing* exercise. This line of thinking, which I call The Guesswork Trap, happens at all levels of organizations. As I've been writing this intro, I've been in talks with a $16 billion tech brand that needs me to teach their SVPs, VPs, and directors how to develop messages; they currently develop messages by sitting around a literal boardroom table and brainstorming how to make X product *sound good*. They're guessing.

Sounding good is not the goal. Selling is the goal. To quote Steve Martin in *The Jerk, It's a profit deal.* If you don't believe THE key performance indicator for a marketing team is revenue generated, you're not gonna like this book. Selling is our goal. Not at the *expense* of brand building or community engagement or other secondary, possibly softer goals. But alongside those, and—when we're being honest—prioritized first above those. Except for rare unicorn situations with massive funding, a business cannot solve for customers, employees, and shareholders without revenue. So your copy needs to sell because you need sales.

So say it with me: *It's not writing. It's selling.*

I wrote this book because I am on a mission to replace the confusing term *copywriting* with a term that more accurately captures both our goals as marketers and the end we seek: *copyselling.* If you can see the written word, along with your video scripts and captions, as sales tools rather than creative tools, you will explode your business and love me forever. Both of those things seem good to me.

Introducing *The Copyselling System*. You're about to discover exactly how to plan, write, and *think about* copy the way my team and I have done for brands from LaunchDarkly to Huel, Nectar to Shopify, to get measurable, high-impact conversion wins. This system is how I planned and wrote lifecycle emails for Wistia that brought in that 350 percent increase in paid conversions I mentioned earlier. It's how I reduced churn for Canva by optimizing their lifecycle emails. It's how my team has generated seven-figure campaigns for little-known ecommerce brands. It's how my students increase Return on Advertising Spend (ROAS), decrease churn, increase Average Revenue per User (ARPU), decrease bounce, grow lists, increase show-up rates and otherwise—you guessed it—create more, happy customers for brands from L'Oréal to Land Rover, HelloFresh to Johnson Controls.

But before we were able to achieve strong results with those brands, we first needed to kill a few problematic ideas and establish some rules.

KILL THESE IDEAS

The following three phrases represent some of the more limiting ideas in marketing organizations. For a brand's copy to perform, we need to kill these ideas.

"Just take a stab at it."

Stabbing things hurts those things. Do not use any euphemism for guessing, and do not use the word *guessing.* Don't guess. Don't stab. There may, in fact, be a tiny amount of what looks like guesswork involved in planning and writing copy that gets results, just like there's a tiny amount of what looks like guesswork involved in choosing the best line of code when engineering a feature; however, that is less *guesswork* and more *drawing on years of experience and expertise.* And it too must be set aside if the data and system say otherwise.

"It's just words."

Programming languages are just words. Beautiful user interfaces are just pixels. A brick is just hay. An ocean is just water droplets. A bullet, flying through the sky, a millisecond from the consequences of impact, is just lead.

To avoid failure, we need to avoid reducing complex things to their building blocks. Copy is not *just words.* If it were, you could throw your dictionary at the screen and watch your screen crack but your business flourish. The *words* are not the point. They are just the delivery mechanism for the message.

"I know what my customers need to hear."

Sure, we've all guessed and gotten it right. But, with the exception of Jason Fried, one day every founder stops writing copy for their business. Someone else writes it. And they are unlikely to be able to guess accurately at what customers need to hear.

I know this because, in my early years as a copywriter, before I developed conversion copywriting or architected the copyselling system, I was tasked with guessing at what prospects needed to hear. And I was wrong far more often than I was right. Picture a twenty-seven-year-old writer-type trying to sell accounting software to a small business owner. That was me. I had never used accounting software. And I had never owned a small business. But I was going to craft compelling messages, dreamed up in my mind? No. When we have not stood in the shoes of our many customers, we cannot accurately guess what they need to hear.

WHAT THIS BOOK IS (AND IS NOT)

This book is not about your brand story or your founder story. There's no chapter on finding your tagline or value proposition. It's not about punctuation or grammar. It's not about positioning your business, finding the right market, or developing a persona. It's not a list of persuasion principles or biases. We won't dive into analytics, generative search optimization, or user experience design. It's not about content marketing or social media posts.

All of those things are necessary for messaging that builds businesses, but they're not part of this book. You can find them, well covered, in time-tested books by Donald Miller (*Storybrand*), April Dunford (*Obviously Awesome*), Robert Cialdini (*Influence*), Andy Crestodina (*Content Chemistry*), and Ann Handley (*Everybody Writes*), among other greats.

So . . . what is this book about, then?

It's about **finding your message** and **turning it into copy that converts**. The fact is, copywriting and messaging—labeled often, in house, as "content strategy"—are huge topics. So I'm focusing on what founders and marketers have paid me to help them nail for decades: the words on the page.

In a world of day-trading attention, marketers have given up on excellent on-page copywriting that drives sales. But brands need *both* attention *and* conversions. You need to continue your investment in your top of funnel demand generation, while adding back an investment in your middle and bottom of funnel revenue generation. That's what the copyselling system will help with.

We're going to nail copyselling because it is the most direct line to transforming your brand's hard-won attention into leads and revenue . . . at scale.

REPLACE GUESSWORK WITH SYSTEMS & TOOLS

This book is divided into two parts: understanding the system and applying the system.

Part I: Understanding the Copyselling System will provide you with an overview of the system as a whole, its parts in general and then its most unexpected part: the Message Matrix. We'll start by addressing a few key myths: that copy needs to be short to work, that you can guess your way through it, and that a brainstorming session is the best copywriter. We'll dig into critical concepts, like "List, Offer, Copy," which alone could transform your marketing strategy and execution. We'll break down the myths that prevent messaging wins, draw on old-school copywriting principles, like stages of awareness and unique principles, and begin to think like copysellers, not copywriters. Because the message matrix is so critical to understanding the system and needs to be nailed down, as a mechanism, before you can apply the system, we're covering it in detail in Part I—in two of the four chapters, in fact.

Part II: Applying the Copyselling System gets very practical, with overviews and examples galore. We'll discuss how to identify growth constraints using tools in your marketing tech stack. We'll walk through my three favorite ways to find your message in voice of customer (VOC) data. We'll complete a solution design, which is how you show the work behind what you're thinking of writing or creating. Then we'll move into assembling your copy and turning that into gorgeous, try-hard, persuasively crafted copy your Head of Brand and CFO alike will be high-fiving you over.

Truly, my objective is to get flooded by emails from readers complaining that their hands hurt from so many high-fives.

At every turn, you'll see examples and supporting data. My promise to you is that I will help you remove 90 percent of the guesswork from your business's messaging.

ALL COPYWRITING TODAY IS AI-SUPPORTED

Part of removing guesswork is adding great tools, like a large language model or AI in general, to your work. You'll see my techniques for using AI throughout this book, and I hope you'll feel free to use AI to suit your tastes, whether that be using it more or less than I do. Once we get the system down and the strategy sorted, tools like AI can be an incredible help.

Throughout this book, you'll find embedded insights, techniques, and notes on how I use AI to help with the work we used to slog through manually, in virtual isolation. There's no separate AI chapter. There's no tacked-on AI section. AI came to party, and we're gonna party with it.

Expect to see notes on using AI to help you implement what you'll learn inside this book. When I reference using AI, **I'll use projects in Claude almost exclusively** because that's what I use, daily, to get the most informed results for myself and my clients. However, please don't expect to see too many actual prompts. AI changes rapidly, and this book is printed in ink. The principles I'm going to teach you are largely evergreen, but if I include sections on how to prompt AI to write a stellar homepage headline, those prompts will feel outdated almost as soon as I type them. Everything I learned about prompting AI well comes from either Christopher S. Penn or the fantastic book *The AI-Driven Leader* by Geoff Woods.

I'm confident you'll find that AI can help you and your team identify strong messages more efficiently, map them across a customer assembly line, transform them into compelling arguments, and finalize them as copy. Note my use of the word "help" here. AI will *help* you find messages; I have not yet seen that it can find those messages on its own. AI will *help* you map them on the message matrix taught in this book; it should not be asked to map messages without your oversight. AI will *help* you craft arguments; you'll need to work with it to determine the most-likely-to-win arguments for your persona at their particular stage in the journey. And a great GPT can even *help* you validate and finalize your copy.

By the time you're reading or listening to this book, chances are you will already know that AI is a thought partner, not a replacement for your brain. It is a good doer, but it shouldn't do alone. (Just like an airplane shouldn't fly without an actual pilot in the driver's seat.) Read the book, share it with your team, and power it all with AI.

COPYSELLING, LIKE COPYWRITING, IS A TEAM SPORT

The final chapter of this book is dedicated to integrating the copyselling system into your team's workflows. Chances are, you have a team you involve in copy reviews. At many points throughout this book, you'll see notes about how you and your team can work together to implement a new idea I've just introduced.

That doesn't mean you absolutely do have a team, though. I wrote this book for people who "grow businesses," which, to me, means everyone from a tech founder writing their startup's copy in a coffee shop; to SVPs of Product who've got a hundred PMMs under them, all of whom are struggling to get copy out the door, and who want to be empowered to do their job more successfully by guessing less at it; to CMOs of fashion conglomerates, who have creative copywriting nailed but can't seem to crack how to sell more soccer cleats in a red ocean of sports apparel retailers; to the farmer in Idaho with a monthly shipment subscription to sell and no idea how to sell it. All of those people are in my mind as I write this book because I have worked with all of those people and then some. Founder, farmer, or CFO, everyone's ultimately trying to craft copy that grows the business.

Everyone in your organization who can influence a message should know and follow what you're about to discover in *The Copyselling System*. That's because it only takes one well-intentioned but under-informed person in a copy doc "taking a stab at" a new way to phrase a headline for team morale to slump. *Anyone with the power to cause your growth has the power to fuck it up.*

That said, I don't expect that everyone from the CEO to the front-line customer success rep is going to read this book and run fireside chats to discuss it. But I will recommend that the people on your team who develop messages, craft copy, and approve (or reject) copy *study and discuss this book.* For everyone else, we've created handy cheat sheets and resources you can distribute to facilitate better, shorter copy reviews. You can find those at copysellingbook.com.

Now, before diving in, let's agree on a few key terms.

KEY TERMS

CUSTOMER

I use the word "customer" as a catch-all for people who pay you money in exchange for the value your product or service provides. When you see the word "customer," think client, paid user, buyer, patron, or even persona. In some cases, where a distinction between leads and customers is unnecessary, I default to "customer" (instead of "leads and customers") for simplicity.

CUSTOMER JOURNEY

A customer journey is the A to Z path a person takes to become a customer, stay a customer, refer other customers to your brand, and upgrade to the next tier or return for the next purchase.

DIRECT RESPONSE

This form of marketing creates a 1:1 feeling between the customer and the brand and drives action in a manner that mirrors in-person sales experiences. Direct response marketing includes emails, ads, mailers, landing pages, and real-life encounters like trade shows. Due to its focus on driving action for leads and customers, direct response is at the heart of the conversion copywriting process and the copyselling system.

FUNNEL

A funnel is a representation of the journey a customer takes with your brand. Typically, a funnel means a marketing funnel, which is a series of assets that work together in a timed or evergreen campaign; for example, an evergreen webinar funnel is an ongoing campaign made up of assets including ads, landing pages, a webinar, a sales page, and several email flows.

LEAD

I use the word "lead" as a catch-all for everyone interacting with your business who has not converted to a paying customer yet. When you see the word "lead," think contact, email subscriber, free subscriber, prospect, or trial user.

VOC

The abbreviation for "voice of customer" data, VOC or VOC data means anything of significance that you hear from leads and customers. With this term, we conflate leads and customers for simplicity's sake. Know that VOC also means VOL, or voice of leads, as well as VOS, or voice of sales, and other qualitative data that does not come from a marketing brainstorm or the imagination of a copywriter.

VOP

The abbreviation for "voice of product" data, VOP or VOP data refers to the qualitative data you collect when listening to your product team. VOP is not what your product team tells you to write; rather, it's what they say or write naturally when having unscripted conversations about your product or service and its features.

VOS

The abbreviation for "voice of sales" data, VOS or VOS data refers to the qualitative data you collect when listening to your sales team and, sometimes, to the customers they're speaking with during sales calls. VOS is not what your sales team tells you to write; rather, it's what they say or write naturally when having unscripted conversations with leads.

PART I
Understanding the Copyselling System

CHAPTER 1

First, a Reset

"Advertising is salesmanship in print."

John E. Kennedy, early 1900s copywriter
at Lord & Thomas agency

So, you've picked up a book about copywriting. (Are you okay? Should we send help?) Chances are, you're here because you fall into one of two camps:

1. You mistakenly thought this book was about "copyright" law (whoops), or,
2. You are frustrated by how little revenue growth you can attribute to your marketing efforts.

If you're in the second camp, you're in the right place. And you're not alone. Every founder, marketer, or CXO reading this book wants more—a lot more—out of marketing. And because every good marketing plan comes down to its execution, marketing results often come down to the copy on the page. Very few people understand what copy exists to do. So almost nobody does it well. Which is pretty bad news, if marketing results come down to copy on the page.

In this book, we're going to establish the following fact, which will liberate you and your marketing team: copywriting is selling. The "writing" part of the word "copywriting" can cause confusion—successful copy is not about "writing well."

If you write copy right, your marketing produces results in the form of good leads and customers. It maximizes revenue. It sells.

If you write copy wrong, your marketing can still *appear* to produce results, but those results typically come in the form of no-money metrics like engagement, views, trial starts, and downloads. It's good to track those metrics, of course, alongside money metrics like leads generated, revenue generated, cost to acquire a customer (CAC), average order value (AOV), and average revenue per user (ARPU). But I'd like to draw your attention to the fact that engagement, views, trial starts, and downloads all have one thing in common: they're tracking clicks. And clicks are easy to manipulate.

If you put a big noticeable button in front of people, they'll click it. My team and I have tested this repeatedly. When we changed a button's color from black to green, clicks increased by 81 percent. When we changed a button's color from black to orange, clicks increased by 95 percent. When we added buttons where there previously weren't any, and added an image next to those buttons, we saw 104.5 percent more clicks. *But we did not get more sales.* Add more things to click, and you'll get more clicks, which means engagement goes up, views go up, trial starts go up, and downloads go up. Clicks look good on a click-tracking visualization, which looks good on a slide. But where are all the sales?

Here is the problem as I see it, after twenty years of optimizing copy to improve money metrics. Very well-intentioned marketing teams want to present monthly and quarterly results that show numbers going up and to the right; sales are very difficult and slow to generate, but clicks are not. Marketers are incentivized to get more clicks so they can report good numbers. And what gets in the way of clicks? Copy!

I have been in the room when growth leaders, screensharing a click-tracking image for a high-converting landing page, pointed at the big, unclicked blocks of copy and said, "Well, let's cut those." Why? *Because no one is clicking the copy*. All the clicks are coming *around* the copy! Their teams then removed the copy, and the page's conversion rate dropped. Did they add the copy blocks back? No. Why not? Because no one was clicking it, so it couldn't have been important. I sit in these rooms and I wonder, *When did copy become the enemy?*

SHORT COPY IS THE ONLY ACCEPTABLE COPY TODAY. AND THAT'S THE PROBLEM.

It is a truth universally acknowledged that a marketing team, in want of growth, must keep copy short. "People don't read online," they say. That's why the six-word value proposition homepage headline is not only ubiquitous but almost *required* for B2B and B2C tech companies. Consider these headlines.

Monday.com (six words): Discover why 225K+ customers choose monday.com
Asana.com (three words): Where work connects
Nvidia.com (six words): What's Next in AI Starts Here[1]
ClickUp.com (five words): The everything app, for work.[2]

But long before marketers had websites, emails, and super-short SMS campaigns, we relied on television ads, radio ads, and print, such as direct response mailers, and quarter-page or full-page magazine ads. In the 1950s and '60s, TV and radio ads were sixty seconds long; they shrunk to thirty seconds in the 1970s not because attention spans were shortening, but because cigarette ads had been banned and networks, losing ad revenue, needed to increase the number of advertisers. In print, direct response mailers, also called junk mail or lumpy mailers, were (and still are) composed of multiple inserts, which rely heavily on the reader's likeliness to read double-sided letters as well as buck-slips, postcards, and more. And then there were print ads. Print ads appeared in magazines and newspapers from the early 1900s to today, but most print ads today look nothing like those of the 1940s.

The best-performing early print ads were what we would today call "copy heavy." They used big, long headlines, a dozen or more paragraphs, and hundreds of words to hook the reader, draw them in, keep them reading line after line, and compel them to take action. We'll talk more about these later in the book. But there's one we need to discuss right now: "Lemon."

"LEMON" CHANGED EVERYTHING

Consider "Lemon," the old-school Volkswagen ad that every new-school creative director references in arguments about copy. The ad first went to print in 1960 in America, and it made VW a household name. It was an ad unlike anything the United States had seen.

Ever since that ad hit newspapers and magazines, advertisers, marketers, and leaders have referenced the Lemon ad as the gold standard in modern advertising (and marketing). And what do they like most? The short headline. It's as short as a headline can get: *Lemon*. One word. Plus a period. That headline turned the advertising world on its head.[3] The ad as a whole helped to increase VW's business in America tenfold.

Today, we don't see the ad in the context in which people in the 1960s saw it; we don't see it as a new kind of ad in a sea of magazine pages thick with copy. Today, we see it in the context of studies that tell us, repeatedly, that nobody reads online and, as such, short copy is the only way to go. So we look at the Lemon ad, with all its accolades, and tell ourselves we must keep our copy short just like that headline. (But don't look under the headline!)

THE "NOBODY READS ONLINE" STUDY

In 1997, the world wide web was brand-spanking new. Jakob Nielsen, who has done incredible work in user experience, was an early expert on websites. He is a cofounder of Nielsen Norman Group, now known as NN/g, the body behind a 1997 study that was intended to teach us how people read in this brave new world of digital, not print. *Print is dead; what do we do now?*

In the study, Nielsen and his team presented participants with copy to read on a computer screen. Different variants in the study had differently formatted copy. The results of the study are summarized like so on nngroup.com, under the article headline "How Users Read on the Web":

> *Summary:*
> *They don't. People rarely read Web pages word by word; instead, they scan the page, picking out individual words and sentences.*[4]

"People don't read online." That's the sound bite, repeated by digital marketers everywhere from 1997 to today. The implication for us is huge. If people don't read online, and online is where we do most of our marketing, then our digital marketing can't require people to read, can it?

But before we start sending blank sales emails, check out the copy that people in the NN/g study didn't read online. I'll share it here with you now.

Nebraska is filled with internationally recognized attractions

Wake up! We're just getting started!

Nebraska is filled with internationally recognized attractions that draw large crowds of people every year, without fail. In 1996, some of the most popular places were Fort Robinson State Park (355,000 visitors), Scotts Bluff National Monument (132,166), Arbor Lodge State Historical Park & Museum (100,000), Carhenge (86,598), Stuhr Museum of the Prairie Pioneer (60,002), and Buffalo Bill Ranch State Historical Park (28,446).

If we put ourselves in a lab with a 1997 (or older) monitor on the shaky table in front of us, and we fire up that monitor, and all 800 x 600 pixels per inch buzz into grayscale beauty, and we squint to see, on the screen, the above text about Nebraska, do we want to read it? Nebraska is the 46th most visited state in the United States.[5] Do I want to know about the Stuhr Museum of the Prairie Pioneer, and do I care to hear exactly how many people crowded its presumably dusty halls?

It seems to me we're operating on some slightly bad data. The study may have been good, but I'd argue the takeaway, or that which got published and distributed, was bad. It's not that people don't read online; it's that **people don't read boring, irrelevant stuff anywhere—online or off**. People will read interesting things. They'll read them a lot, or Reddit wouldn't be what it is and ChatGPT would push out video-only answers.

But here we are. We've got the short-copy celebration that is the one-word headline "Lemon." And we've got the copy-denigration that is the NN/g "nobody reads online" study. We're measuring marketing success by clicks, which are easier to manufacture than sales, and copy is getting in the way of clicks. Are you starting to see where the appetite for short copy comes from?

PEOPLE READ IF YOU HOOK 'EM AND KEEP HOOKING 'EM

Let's take a closer look at what makes the Lemon ad work so well. The headline is a helluva hook, but it's not working alone. It's accompanied by a photo of a car that looks unlike any car Americans had seen at the time. VW Beetles had been selling in the US since the mid 1950s, but fewer than thirty thousand had sold each year before this ad came out, so it's not like you'd see a ton of them driving through your neighborhood. You'd be more likely to see a Chevrolet Impala or other boat-sized cars produced on a Detroit assembly line.

The 1960 Chevy Impala

The 1960 VW Beetle

With the Lemon ad, the advertising agency that created it, DDB, turned the VW business around in America. At the time, VW was effectively Hitler's car trying to sell in post–World War II America—not an easy sale. Americans weren't buying foreign cars. Nearly 90 percent of car sales in America were domestically built by one of the Big Three automakers: GM, Ford, or Chrysler.[6] Buyers were loyal to American brands. The Big Three had well-established nationwide dealer networks, and tariffs on imported cars made imports the more expensive option.[7] To buy a VW, you had to really, really, really, really, really, *really* want a VW.

Yet not only did this ad (together with similarly styled and written VW ads) change US consumer perception of the VW brand, establish it globally, and make big pop-culture waves, it also helped VW go from 118,000 annual sales in 1960 to just under four hundred thousand annual sales in 1968,[8] a CAGR of more than 13 percent. The Beetle became the first import car to achieve mass-market success in America.[9]

And we marketers—everyone from interning social media coordinators to CMOs—have all been trying to replicate *Lemon* since, largely without ever reading a word of the body copy or understanding how the ad copy worked. So let's read it now:[10]

> *This Volkswagen missed the boat.*
>
> *The chrome strip on the glove compartment is blemished and must be replaced. Chances are you wouldn't have noticed it; Inspector Kurt Kroner did.*
>
> *There are 3,389 men at our Wolfsburg factory with only one job: to inspect Volkswagens at each stage of production. (3000 Volkswagens are produced daily; there are more inspectors than cars.)*
>
> *Every shock absorber is tested (spot checking won't do), every windshield is scanned. VWs have been rejected for surface scratches barely visible to the eye.*
>
> *Final inspection is really something! VW inspectors run each car off the line onto the Funktionsprufstand (car test stand), tote up 189 check points, gun ahead to the automation brake stand and say "no" to one VW out of fifty.*
>
> *This preoccupation with detail means the VW lasts longer and requires less maintenance, by and large, than other cars. (It also means a used VW depreciates less than any other car.)*
>
> *We pluck the lemons; you get the plums.*

That is 165 words about quality assurance. It's nearly three times the length of the ill-fated Nebraska copy—and people read it. In fact, in the years in which the "Lemon" and related VW ads were in circulation, those ads were reportedly more read than the articles in the magazines in which they were published.[11] The American consumer was reading them and then going into the dealerships, waving torn-out ads, to have sales conversations that led to 13 percent annual growth for the VW brand.

Do you want results like that? Every marketer and entrepreneur I've worked with over the last twenty years has sought a messaging strategy and copy that would result in 10 times sales and directly result in 13 percent annual growth for their brand. *Lemon* did just that. Remember: the ad was more frequently read than the articles that people actually bought the magazines for!

Lemon influenced all advertising and marketing that followed. And although the vast majority of the ads we study and reproduce today are top of funnel (or meant to generate brand awareness), the problematic takeaway for marketers, who are responsible for all parts of the funnel, is the same: keep it short. What I believe *Lemon* and NN/g alike can teach us is this: not to keep all copy short, but rather to hook people fast and draw them in with copy relevant to them. (The NN/g study might have been more useful if its participants had been people considering touring Nebraska or avid Nebraska tourists—that is, if the copy had been relevant to them.) If you hook them fast, they'll start reading; however, if what they start reading doesn't engage them, they'll stop.

BUILD ASSEMBLY LINES

Is there a difference between reading online (Nebraska copy) and reading in print (Lemon copy)? Sure. And is there a difference between attention spans in the 1960s and attention spans in the early 2000s? Sure. Are those differences so stark that we believe nobody reads online today? Even if you answered "sure," we'd still need to account for the preferred content medium today: video. Scripted videos. Persuasively written video scripts. And we'd also need to be willing to scrap all copy from our emails, ads, and pages, which I think we agree is not reasonable; we agree it's not reasonable because we know our prospect needs to consume content about our brand, products, and business, and they can and will consume that content in written form.

If we are to build customers with our marketing, we need to agree that people of all shapes, sizes, backgrounds, interest levels, intent, sophistication, and awareness will read copy if that copy does the right work. Work we're about to start uncovering. Work that begins with being relevant and makes it to a final draft only when it's *also* interesting.

And if you're not satisfied with the idea that people will read marketing copy—online or off—consider the direct response (DR) mailer mentioned earlier in this chapter. DR mailers are "junk mail." They're envelopes stuffed with marketing assets and built around a central piece: the sales letter. *Real prospects read the sales letter.* Here's the data to prove it. The average mailer lives in a person's house for seventeen days—you may have one on your kitchen counter now—and the average response rate is 4.9 percent for a purchased list and a whopping 9 percent for an owned list. These mailers generate paid conversions, on average, of 2.5 percent. All the pieces in a DR mailer work together to build a customer on a message-first assembly line. *People really do read!*

YOUR PROSPECT WILL READ YOUR SALES COPY

To round out this reset, let's bust some myths. Chances are you've heard a few great snippets about writing copy, which you should retain, and a shitton of horrible, conversion-killing generalizations, myths, and lies, which we need to dispense with swiftly.

I know you know that copywriting is selling (true). You may also have heard that people who read are people who buy (true). That people who spend time are people who spend money (true). That people only care about themselves (true). That people don't buy products—they hire products to do jobs (true). That copy is a conversation with the customer (true). That we should join the conversation happening in their head (true).

You've also heard copywriting is creative (false). Copywriting is a writing exercise (false). Great writers make great copywriters (false). Copy should be short (false). Nobody reads online (false). People only scan online (false). Direct-response copy is too salesy for modern brands (false) and for sophisticated buyers (false).

You've heard that people have shorter attention spans than ever (true). People prefer video over text (true). People prefer captions with their video (true). A great demo sells better than any copy (true). The purpose of a line of copy is to get you to read the next line of copy (true).

And of course: our customers don't read (false). No, really, our customers don't read (false). No, seriously, Jo, you have no idea what tests we've run or what our data shows (true) so you are wrong to say that our customers will read because they won't (false).

If you believe and continue to believe that your customers have not, do not, and will not read copy, then I invite you to put down this book and remove every single word from your website, emails, ads, social posts, video captions, and video scripts (because scripts are copy too).

Strip those marketing assets down to visuals and music, maybe, and see what happens. I'm gonna bet that your earlier concerns about how little growth you can attribute to your marketing will spike hard.

Not about to do that? Of course you're not! So we agree: businesses need copy. Now what?

Now let's align on this: it's time to reset your approach to copywriting. Start by relaxing your idea about what great copy looks like. Although you do not have to write big, long sales letters, you also should not *resist* big, long sales letters. Simply keep your mind open to the fact that your customers need to see details before they can convert and refer. The less you write here, the more you have to write there. A relentless focus on cutting copy is really just an exercise in kicking the can down the road—eventually your customer needs the information they need, presented with the emotion that will move them. And once you have the messages in place, you can make the assembly line more efficient. Fast results come slow.

"BUT WHAT IF MY TEAM HATES OUR NEW COPY?"

Some of them will! For this book to pay off for you, your business, and your customers, you need to get your team on board with copywriting as *copyselling*, a revenue-driving initiative. If they're not on board, it won't work.

That means everyone in the creative department, marketing, product, customer success, management, leadership—every single person with a say in what gets written—needs to agree that:

- We no longer guess at what we should write. We follow this system.
- We no longer brainstorm messages. We swipe from customers.
- We no longer edit to the shortest form. We use "VOC," frameworks, and formulas.

No one's title has to change, there's no reorg, and no one's getting promoted or demoted. What changes is:

- We no longer guess at what we should write. We follow this system.
- We no longer brainstorm messages. We swipe from customers.
- We no longer edit to the shortest form. We use "VOC," frameworks, and formulas.

Now let's flesh out those three statements by diving into the system behind maximizing revenue . . . using little ol' words.

CHAPTER RECAP

A reset

- ✓ It's not that people don't read online. It's that people don't read boring things that are irrelevant to them.
- ✓ A short headline may be great, but that doesn't mean all copy must be short to be great.
- ✓ Forget most of what you think you know about copywriting. The "best practices" you and your team have learned may be getting in the way of breakthroughs.

CHAPTER 2
The Copyselling System

"A copywriter should construct an ad the way an engineer builds a bridge."

Claude Hopkins, legendary copywriter and author of *Scientific Advertising*[12]

In a vast audience is a single person who's looking at you, nodding with you, interested in hearing more. She is your reader. You are going to write your copy for her. Finding her is the essential first step.

Once you've found her, the second step is to listen to her and mirror her words back to her, lightly reshaping those words so they're even more persuasive.

Next, you observe her response. And you optimize what you've written to better attract her, to get her to nod more passionately, to keep her all the more interested in you. This is step three.

These three steps make up the traditional conversion copywriting process:

1. **Listening**, including research and discovery.
2. **Writing**, including wireframing, or persuasive architecture, and editing.
3. **Optimizing**, including validation and experimentation.

For years I taught that three-step process as a way out of what I called *The Guesswork Trap*, in which too many marketing teams were stuck. But although it reduced some guesswork, it didn't actually help those teams escape the trap. The Listening step was useful, but it was a big leap from Listening to the next step: Writing. And teams struggled with knowing what to optimize, when or how.

Behind the scenes, I would help teams organize, in a spreadsheet, what they heard and discovered during the Listening step. I would steer them away from jumping too quickly into the Writing step; I told them they needed to synthesize what they heard and carefully plan their messages before writing copy, but they'd point at the conversion copywriting process like, *Jo, writing is literally the next step after listening.* And they were right. The three steps, though convenient to remember, didn't cover enough.

Over time, I fleshed out the three-step conversion copywriting process, and the copyselling system was born. It looks like this:

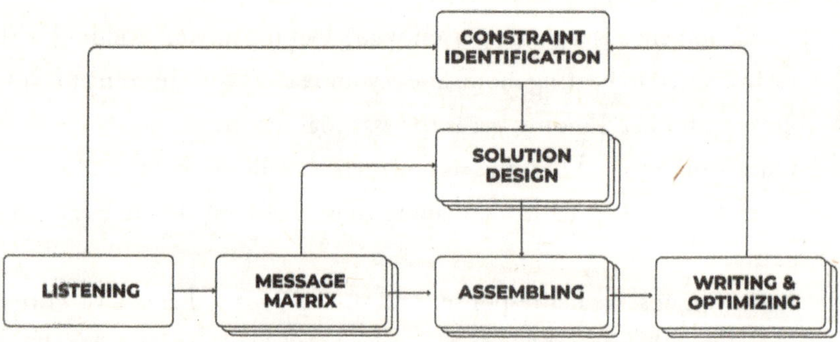

You can find a copy of the system diagram at copysellingbook.com, along with many other resources. Let's walk through it at a high level now; the rest of the book will address the parts of the system, and how to use them, in detail.

A HIGH-LEVEL LOOK AT THE SYSTEM

The copyselling system helps you maximize revenue using these three interconnected elements:

1. The identification of a performance **constraint**.
2. The plan to relieve that constraint, or the **solution design**.
3. The **conversion copywriting process**, which is modified from what I shared earlier to leave less room for guesswork.

Constraint Identification Feeds the System

The performance of every marketing funnel, campaign, or asset is hindered by constraints—such as not enough traffic, poor quality traffic, a dull offer, the wrong channels, high cost per click, low average order value, and so on. First, we identify the constraint or constraints that are preventing optimal performance of our marketing, against business goals. We do so at the business, finance, or analyst level. We also surface constraints during the *Listening* phase, when the people we listen to can reveal constraints, and the *Writing & Optimizing* phase, when the performance of a funnel, campaign, or asset is measured and constraints stand out.

The Solution Design Establishes the Plan

What will we do to relieve an identified constraint? That's covered in your solution design. And it's influenced by something called a *Message Matrix*. A message matrix is so critical to the copyselling system that the next two chapters are dedicated to explaining not only what it is but also how to complete, update, and continually use one.

A solution design is like a brief. But briefs are often too focused on what a campaign manager wants a creative team to produce. What the creative team really needs is to be unleashed on a business problem, like relieving a growth constraint.

The Conversion Copywriting Process Produces the System's Output

The updated conversion copywriting process starts with *Listening* and finishes with *Optimizing*. But I've divided the broad category of *Writing* into multiple parts that reflect the actual process you'll go through.

The message matrix organizes the marketing messages you identify during *Listening*. You'll then take pieces from the message matrix and assemble them into a first draft, persuasively architected (*Assembling*) and ready to be refined with writing techniques (*Writing & Optimizing*). Now let's explore each part of the system in greater detail.

CONSTRAINT IDENTIFICATION

Like the best salespeople, all the best copywriters are problem-solvers first. We respond well to clearly articulated problems. For the copyselling system to work, we start with a clear articulation of the constraint we've identified in our marketing or business. What are customers, employees, and/or shareholders struggling with? What is the data indicating? What is the business, quite simply, trying to do, and what's not working or is working well but could be further improved? What is getting in the way of generating more leads? Or more sales? At scale?

Note that, at the end of the conversion copywriting process, we return to constraint identification. If we've relieved the constraint, we can move on to relieving a different performance constraint. If we have not relieved it, we move through the system again, starting at constraint identification, moving to the solution design, and then moving into the conversion copywriting process.

Also note that what you hear during the Listening phase can reveal new opportunities. So *Listening* also helps us identify constraints.

THE SOLUTION DESIGN

You'll create a solution design for each constraint you identify. After you've documented the constraint, the rest of the solution design consists of three simple but important parts:

1. List,
2. Offer, and
3. Copy.

These three parts work together and are intentionally ordered from most important (List) to least important (Copy).

List, Offer, Copy comes from the early days of mailers, when a marketer would first create or buy a list of mailing addresses, then optimize an offer for the people on the list, and finally write copy to drive interest in the offer, for the people on the list. I did not coin the concept of *List, Offer, Copy*. It's always been under the surface of every conversation I've had with top copywriters over the years. I believe I first saw it, in writing, in the excellent *Great Leads* by Michael Masterson and John Forde.

List

When solving a business, marketing, or customer problem, we start with "list," which is a general term to describe the people we're targeting: readers, audience, visitors, leads, prospects, customers, segments, personae, journalists, product reviewers, whomever. We call them "customers" in this book.

Who are they? Where are they? Why did they come to us? What are they switching from? Who influences them? What are their jobs to be done? I'm speaking in the plural, but I am thinking of the woman I mentioned at the start of this chapter—that *one* person in the audience you're going to write for.

Offer

We consider the people on the list and go, *Hmm, how can we make our offer sound extremely appealing to these particular people?* This is offer optimization, and you need it in order to sell well. Now, in my experience with SaaS and ecommerce, most businesses either have no true offer or equate *offer* with *discount.* We'll dig into offers and offer optimization in chapter eight, but let me warn you that you always need an offer, and let me celebrate with you: offer does not have to mean discount.

Copy

Copywriting and copy optimization happen only after an offer is optimized, which happens only after a list is pinpointed. You should never hop straight into writing the copy. You are more likely to generate leads and revenue at scale by refining your list than by refining your copy and by refining your offer than by refining your copy. Copy comes third.

In the previous chapter, I cited the Nielsen "nobody reads online" study of copy about tourism to Nebraska. I offered this rationale for its low engagement: The NN/g study might have been more useful if the copy had been relevant to the study's participants. That's *List, Offer, Copy* at work. Nielsen's study focused on writing style—on *Copy.* It ignored *List,* to its detriment. I would hypothesize that, had the study copy been about top rides at Disneyland and the study participants been parents planning their child's first trip to Disneyland, engagement would have been much higher and we might have seen that, in fact, people do read online. You just have to match the copy to the reader.

Feeding *List, Offer, Copy* in our solution design is the message matrix. That's part of the conversion copywriting process. Let's dive into that process now.

THE CONVERSION COPYWRITING PROCESS

The process kicks off with *Listening* because all high-converting copy starts with listening to our "List." All great messages are sourced from related, relevant third parties. You should be listening not only to your leads and customers (voice of customer, or VOC) but also to your sales team (voice of sales, or VOS), your product team (VOP), as well as journalists, your founders—everyone who might have something interesting to say that you can swipe and use.

You organize what you hear during *Listening* in your message matrix, which you then use (along with a solution design) to start the *Assembling* stage, where you are assembling your copy. And finally you make it sound great and work harder with the *Writing & Optimizing* stage.

Listening

Listening helps us execute copyselling principles and understand our customer more wholly–it's both strategic and practical. When you deeply understand your customer, you can better activate your customer-driven mission. If your mission is to turn five thousand startup founders into happily exited millionaires, you can do that more effectively if you know those founders wholly. You're already listening. Now let's listen; document what we're hearing; and use it to craft, write, and optimize high-performing messages.

Most brands brainstorm their way to a message. That ends today.

Instead of brainstorming, we are going to swipe our copy directly from VOC, VOS, VOP, and other unscripted spaces, like articles and Reddit comments. You may think of this work as research. This isn't a book on qualitative research because—*and this is going to freak some purists out*—listening to customers for copyselling purposes isn't the job of a qualitative researcher. We're listening to customers because we're focused marketers on the hunt for two key things that will help us write stellar copy:

1. frequently repeated messages, and
2. standout statements or insights.

Frequently repeated messages become the *What* of your messaging strategy, at the brand, product, or campaign level. Standout statements or insights become the *How*, or the copy that appears on the page in a first draft.

NOTE: If your team is used to rejecting language that is not used frequently, it'll take some practice to get them to see that the most interesting messages—those with the greatest potential for impact and even virality—are typically expressed just once, by just one person, who had no idea they were saying something unexpected.

Now let's pause for the people in the room who don't want to listen to their customers.

Do you long for an easier or different customer?

I was standing in a swimming pool in Mexico with fifty or so entrepreneurs. The water was up to my elbows. I'd just delivered a talk about how to find your message in what your customers say. And I'd done so while standing in a bathing suit, in a pool, with no slides or resources to show. It was an unusual environment for a growth conference, but the question an entrepreneur shouted from the other side of the pool was tragically common:

"What if the customers I want aren't the customers I've got?"

If you don't want to build a business around the customers you have, should you listen to them when crafting messages? When your new messaging is based on old customers, how do you ensure you're speaking to your next customer, not just your last one?

The simple answer: Instead of listening to your current customers, listen to the ones you want. Invest more to better target leads who match your ideal customer profile (ICP). Listen to them. Put their words on the page. Done.

The better answer was the one I gave the gentleman who asked me that question: **Start with the customers you've got.** Most businesses will barely scratch the surface of their serviceable obtainable market (SOM); little wonder nearly 40 percent of US businesses fail in the first two years. In your current customer base are more customers waiting to be activated. Serve those customers, generate revenue from them, and then use that revenue to explore other markets.

I'm not a business analyst, but if your SOM or your total addressable market (TAM) is a reasonable size for you to grow, and if you haven't captured a significant share of it yet, then maybe it's too soon for you to move on. That said, to the entrepreneur on the other side of the pool, I also offer this: Instead of going upmarket, go up-problem. What if you listen to your customers who've shared, in VOC, their most expensive problems? Your customers—current and future—will always buy a stellar solution to a costly problem. So find the costlier problem.

Listen to Current (and Future) Customers, Instead of Brainstorming

There's a saying in copywriting: Think like a fish, not a fisherman. We can catch more fish when we:

- Listen to what "fish" (customers) say and how they say it.
- Find our hook in their words.
- Choose a framework based on the hook (and the business goal for the asset).
- Paste their exact words into the framework.
- Use formulas to make each line work better.
- Layer on better practices in copywriting and persuasion.
- Edit out the extra, and edit in the awesome.

Wait, Are We Allowed to Do This?

In listening to our customers, are we stealing copyrighted material? I used to get that question a lot. And then AI came and stole every damn thing anyone had ever published anywhere ever, and now I don't get that question much. But when I did, I would shrug. And here's why.

The results of swiping copy are wonderful. When I was writing a new homepage for a product called Sweatblock, I swiped copy from some of the five thousand or more Sweatblock reviews on Amazon. I combined "It doesn't even have to be hot out," from one review with "even when I'm cold, my armpits are always wet," to generate this headline:

> "It doesn't even have to be hot out. My armpits are always wet."

I used additional VOC from Amazon reviews for Sweatblock to write the rest of the page. And that page, when tested against the control, generated a 108 percent increase in revenue.[13] The results of swiping copy are quantifiably wonderful.

But is it ethical? Yes! For starters, you're listening to your customers. Isn't that exactly what they want us to do when they leave us reviews?

Do you need to ask permission? This isn't legal advice, but here's what lawyers have told me over the years. For anonymous reviews, you do not need to ask permission to use their words or phrasing as long as:

1. The review was posted publicly.
2. You don't misrepresent or change the meaning of what they were saying.
3. The terms of service for the platform on which it's posted allow you to reuse it.

You can add mice type to your footer that explains some messages are taken directly from customer reviews, to help cover your bases.

The bigger consideration is compliance with the policies of any platform you may swipe from, like Amazon reviews. Always look those up to be sure.

All this to say: by mirroring back what your customers say, you are more likely to attract more of them. The best businesses have always had a deep customer obsession, and the same is true for the best marketers. To sell with your copy, you must listen to your customer. They use the words and phrases that are more likely to convert more of them.

The Message Matrix

The *Listening* step produces tons of potential messages. We need to organize those potential messages so we can use them well. We organize them in a *message matrix*. We do so across four of the five key stages of awareness that your prospect moves through on the path to becoming a customer.

The Stages of Awareness

The late, great copywriter Eugene Schwartz articulated the five stages of awareness for a prospect on the path to becoming a customer:

1. **Unaware.** A person may have heard of your brand, product, or solution—or they may not have—but they're unaware of how it could fit into their life.
2. **Problem aware.** The moment a lead is born! The person has felt their problem, which your solution can solve—they just don't know it yet.
3. **Solution (or category) aware.** The person has passively or actively developed an understanding of possible solutions to their problems. These solutions can fit across countless categories.
4. **Product (or brand) aware.** The person has heard about your product and is learning about it.
5. **Most aware.** The person is in the best position to make a yes/no decision.

On the customer assembly line, we want to efficiently move our prospect through the earliest stages to Most Aware, which is where we'll pull out all the stops to get them to buy. The message matrix does not include the Unaware stage. Quite simply, marketing to Unaware prospects is often best done by brand marketers, not by people obsessed with copyselling. I've never written a Super Bowl ad, and I should never be hired to.

The next two chapters are dedicated to the message matrix. It will become the single source of truth for your messaging. It will fundamentally change the way you write copy for your business and experience other businesses' copy in the wild. And it puts an end to the least-fun game ever: the guessing game.

Assembling

Eugene Schwartz not only introduced us to the stages of awareness, but he also elicited a few mind-blown emojis with this statement: "Copy is not written. Copy is assembled."

To be fair, there is, of course, writing involved in copywriting. But more important than the writing—the prose, its rhythm, its many rhetorical devices—is what's behind it. What's it about?

After receiving a completed solution design, we assemble our first draft copy using the message matrix and copywriting frameworks. This becomes a copy-paste job: copy a line of VOC from the message matrix, and paste it into a framework on your copy doc. I know that sounds very unappealing to the writers in the room, but as I've said before, copywriting is not a writing exercise. You've got to assemble messages, in order, before you layer in writing techniques.

Writing & Optimizing

Now that I've just told you copywriting isn't about writing, let's talk about writing! Once your copy is assembled, you can't just publish it. You do, in fact, need to make it readable and persuasive. *Writing* happens with the use of formulas, better practices, rhetorical devices, and techniques like the seven sweeps. Applying those techniques—with and without the help of AI—transforms your first draft into a strong second draft.

You then validate your second draft internally, with copy reviewers, and externally, with people who are a proxy for or lookalike audience of your actual audience.

You hit send or publish. And that kicks off the *Optimizing* part of the *Writing & Optimizing* step. When your copy is in the wild, you measure its performance against your originally identified constraint. Is the copy performing well to relieve the identified constraint? Is the new variation beating the control?

HOW THE SYSTEM WORKS IN PRACTICE

Let's use an example to illustrate how the copyselling system parts work together. Because this system only works when you know how to use all of its parts, we have to pretend that you have completed this book in order for this example to make sense. So if something feels really new or unfamiliar, don't worry—it should. You're only on chapter two.

Here's the situation: You run an ecommerce brand called Daylight that sells infrared light devices to consumers. You've recently launched Powernap, an attachment for your most popular handheld device, called Daydream. You have several persona-segmented funnels in place to market the Powernap attachment. All funnels start with social ads . . . which drive to either a webinar landing page (for the webinar funnel) or an advertorial landing page (for the advertorial funnel) . . . which drive to product pages . . . which finally drive to cart and checkout. There's an abandoned cart flow. And there are retargeting ads.

Your analytics show you that one funnel in particular is underperforming: "Melissa's Powernap Funnel—Advertorial Version." This is the funnel targeting female customers over forty (known internally as the *Melissa* persona) who bought Daydream in the last two years. Of the one hundred thousand such customers in your database, which you've uploaded to your ads platform, fewer than a thousand of them have bought a Powernap—a less than 1 percent conversion rate. Your forecast was that five thousand of them would buy by now. You pause ads to this funnel while you try to fix it.

Here's how you fix it. You create a project in your preferred AI platform; I use Claude. You add these files to the project:

- The completed message matrix for the Powernap product and Melissa persona,
- The solution design(s) that drove the assets in the underperforming funnel,
- All data you've got on your Melissa persona (e.g., slides on Melissa's Jobs to Be Done),
- The Powernap product specs,
- The performance report (analytics) for the funnel and,
- The copy docs for all the copy across the funnel.

Now Claude will use those files—and any others you may add—to help you optimize this funnel.

First, identify the constraint. What is preventing Melissa from buying a Powernap in the advertorial funnel? Claude identifies that the biggest drop-off in the analytics for the funnel is not the advertorial page itself but the product page: nearly 90 percent of Melissas who click from the advertorial page exit the product page in under twelve seconds.

The assembly line is broken at the handoff between the advertorial page and the product page.

Next, complete your new solution design. Claude compares the message matrix, original solution design, advertorial copy, and product page copy against each other to help you diagnose the potential source(s) of the problem. You add the webinar deck and transcript to the files because they may help Claude see what's working for the Melissa persona.

Claude notices that both the advertorial copy and the webinar transcript join the conversation happening in Melissa's head at *Beat 3: Moments of Highest Pleasure, Longed for*—in keeping with the solution design—but the webinar continues all the way through *Beat 32: Risk & Uncertainty Reduction*, only after which does Melissa see the offer and how to get it, while the advertorial page both 1) includes calls to action starting in the hero section, and 2) ends earlier than the webinar at *Beat 27: Uniquely Qualified.*

It looks like your advertorial page design, with buttons placed during Problem and Solution stages of awareness, and without the benefit of success stories (Beat 29), use cases (Beat 30), goal amplification (Beat 31), or risk reduction (Beat 32), may need some buttons stripped away and more copy added at the bottom. This is your initial hypothesis.

You open your click-tracking and scroll-mapping software, look at the advertorial page, and see that people are clicking on the buttons in the hero—which covers only *Beat 3: Moments of Highest Pleasure, Longed for.* That could be sending poorly qualified traffic through to the product page, where Melissas would see the price of the Powernap and exit quickly. You add the click-tracking and scroll-mapping images to your Claude files.

You've developed a hypothesis, which you ask Claude to challenge:

> *On the advertorial page, we will remove all calls to action that appear before Beat 27: Uniquely Qualified, and we will add copy that covers beats 28 through 32. In doing so, we will increase qualified clicks to the product page, lower the exit rate, and increase paid conversions for Powernap.*

Claude suggests you A/B test two variations of this page, one of which (Variation A) is the same advertorial page but with buttons removed early on the page (e.g., before *Beat 25: Proof of How*), and the other of which (Variation B) is the page built based on your hypothesis. Claude also suggests that, given how lengthy the new page will be, you consider adding a video sales letter (VSL) to the top of the page for those who will not read it all.

You agree that a VSL could help, but you don't have the resources to record and produce a video during this product launch phase. Instead, you decide to move forward with Claude's recommendation for an A/B test.

You ask Claude to create an updated solution design, which you then use to brief your copywriter and designer. The designer quickly creates Variation A.

For Variation B, your copywriter grabs the message matrix and the original advertorial page copy doc, and revises the bottom of the doc to incorporate beats 28 through 32. Then she applies formulas, writing techniques, and the Seven Sweeps during editing. She finishes by uploading the copy doc to Claude, along with the *Copyselling* validation rubrics, and gets it to identify areas of opportunity. She finalizes the copy based on Claude's feedback, gets the team to review it, implements their notes with the help of Claude, and hands it off to design.

You turn the advertorial funnel back on, this time with the A/B test. You immediately see a lower exit rate on the product detail page and an uptick in purchases. Variation B wins. But you spot the next constraint: fewer clicks from the advertorial page to the product page. And so the system goes.

At the heart of the system is the message matrix. Let's dig into that now.

CHAPTER RECAP

The Copyselling System

- ✓ The copyselling system is made of three key parts: constraint identification, solution design, and the conversion copywriting process.
- ✓ Inside each part are additional systems and practices that drive success.
- ✓ The system repeats until growth constraints are effectively relieved within an asset, in a campaign, or across a funnel.

CHAPTER 3
The Message Matrix

"Leaders start with the customer and work backwards."

Jeff Bezos, founder of Amazon

You're now ready for an introduction to the message matrix, which you'll come to see as the blueprint for your customer assembly line. It's available as a printable poster at copysellingbook.com. You can see what it looks like on page 50.

Your message matrix is the single source of truth that integrates everything you've learned so far with everything you're about to do. It releases The Guessing Trap that your marketers and copywriters have found themselves in. With it, you can move a prospect from early consideration, at the start of the assembly line, all the way to purchasing, at the end of it, *without guessing at what to say to them to move them along.*

There are 36 beats, or points, along a message matrix. These beats represent the stops on a customer journey. You'll use a message matrix to map voice of customer (VOC) and voice of sales (VOS) data across the beats.

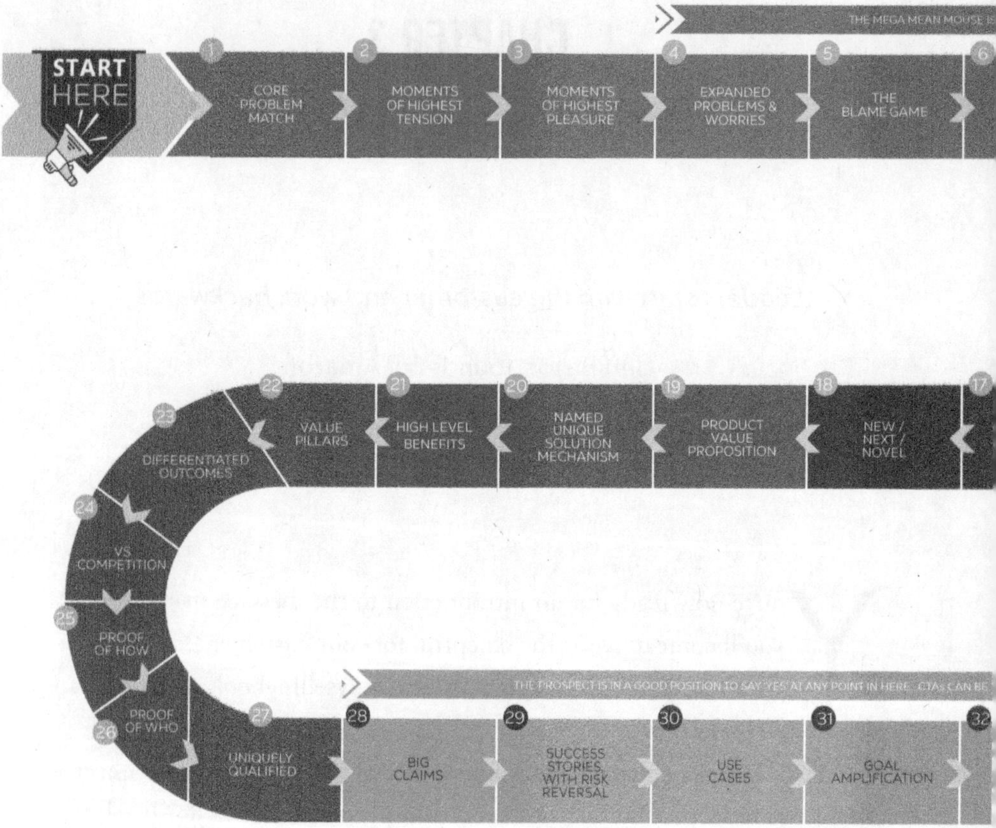
THE MEGA MEAN MOUSE IS
START HERE
1 CORE PROBLEM MATCH
2 MOMENTS OF HIGHEST TENSION
3 MOMENTS OF HIGHEST PLEASURE
4 EXPANDED PROBLEMS & WORRIES
5 THE BLAME GAME
6
17
18 NEW / NEXT / NOVEL
19 PRODUCT VALUE PROPOSITION
20 NAMED UNIQUE SOLUTION MECHANISM
21 HIGH LEVEL BENEFITS
22 VALUE PILLARS
23 DIFFERENTIATED OUTCOMES
24 VS. COMPETITION
25 PROOF OF HOW
26 PROOF OF WHO
27 UNIQUELY QUALIFIED
THE PROSPECT IS IN A GOOD POSITION TO SAY 'YES' AT ANY POINT IN HERE. CTAs CAN BE
28 BIG CLAIMS
29 SUCCESS STORIES, WITH RISK REVERSAL
30 USE CASES
31 GOAL AMPLIFICATION
32

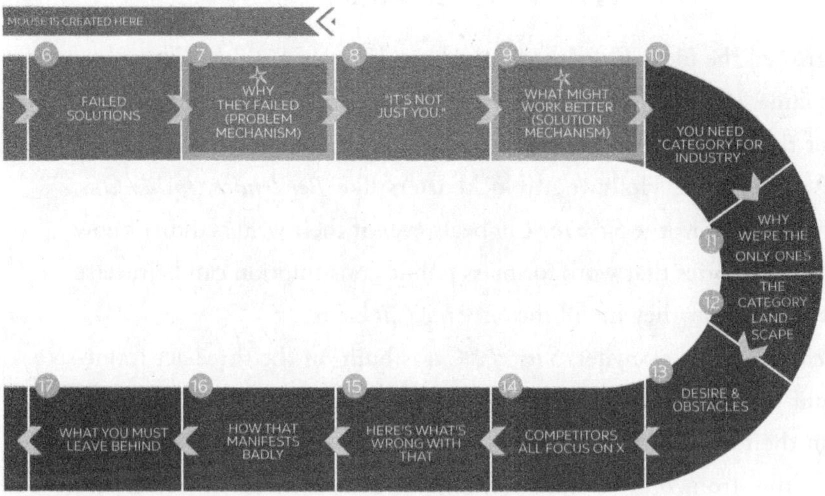
MOUSE IS CREATED HERE
6
FAILED SOLUTIONS
7
WHY THEY FAILED (PROBLEM MECHANISM)
8
"IT'S NOT JUST YOU."
9
WHAT MIGHT WORK BETTER (SOLUTION MECHANISM)
10
YOU NEED "CATEGORY FOR INDUSTRY"
11
WHY WE'RE THE ONLY ONES
12
THE CATEGORY LAND-SCAPE
13
DESIRE & OBSTACLES
14
COMPETITORS ALL FOCUS ON X
15
HERE'S WHAT'S WRONG WITH THAT
16
HOW THAT MANIFESTS BADLY
17
WHAT YOU MUST LEAVE BEHIND

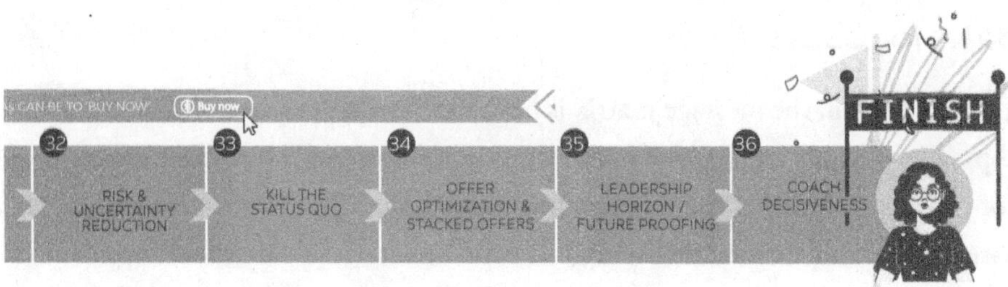
CAN BE TO 'BUY NOW'
Buy now
32
RISK & UNCERTAINTY REDUCTION
33
KILL THE STATUS QUO
34
OFFER OPTIMIZATION & STACKED OFFERS
35
LEADERSHIP HORIZON / FUTURE PROOFING
36
COACH DECISIVENESS
FINISH

That will give you everything you need to write killer copy—both what to say and how to say it—from the moment a prospect enters the assembly line to the moment they say yes to your offer.

WHAT IS A BEAT?

I've borrowed the idea of beats from the beat sheets of *Save the Cat* screenwriting fame. If you're not familiar with a beat sheet, it's effectively a breakdown of the main points in a narrative arc that will take the reader from Point A to Point Z. Hollywood blockbusters like *Beetlejuice*, *Inside Out*, and *Deadpool* follow the *Save the Cat* beats even if their writers didn't know it—nearly all stories that work for mass public consumption can be reverse engineered to show they hit all the *Save the Cat* beats.

Created by Blake Snyder, *Save the Cat* is built on the three-act framework and hero's journey most storytellers know and follow. Snyder adds detail in the form of 15 beats that all the best movies and even television episodes hit—from *Beat 1: Opening Image* to *Beat 10: Bad Guys Close In*, through to the last, *Beat 15: Final Image.*

Beats for Copyselling

Created by moi, the message matrix is built on the stages of awareness most copywriters know and follow. I add detail in the form of the 36 beats your copy needs to hit, and the order to hit them, along the customer journey, based on what's worked across digital experiments and old-school direct response copywriting. The 36 beats are:

1. Core problem match
2. Moments of highest tension, lived
3. Moments of highest pleasure, longed for
4. Expanded problems and worries
5. The blame game

6. Failed solutions
7. Why they failed (problem mechanism)
8. "It's not just you."
9. What might work better (solution mechanism)
10. You need category for industry (positioning statement)
11. Why we're the only ones who can do this
12. The category landscape
13. Desire and obstacles
14. Competitors all focus on X (the old way)
15. Here's what's wrong with that
16. Here's how that manifests badly for people like our persona
17. What you must leave behind
18. New/next/novel
19. Product value proposition ("The Only")
20. Unique mechanism and its value
21. High level benefits
22. Value pillars
23. Differentiated outcomes
24. Versus the competition
25. Proof of how ("The Promise")
26. Proof of who
27. Uniquely qualified
28. Big claims
29. Success stories, with risk reversal
30. Use cases
31. Goal amplification
32. Risk and uncertainty reduction
33. Kill the status quo
34. Offer optimization and stacked offers
35. Leadership horizon/future proofing
36. Coach decisiveness

PRODUCT				______________				
PERSONA				______________				
VALUES				______________				
				Beat sheet	**What (The Message)**	**How (The Copy)**		
PROBLEM AWARE	**Early**	HOLD UP A MIRROR	1	**Core problem match**			Why our persona needs this product	**WHERE CONSIDERATION HAPPENS** (ads, social, content, partner workshops)
				For this persona / buyer, what is the core problem that drives them to start looking for new solutions?				
			2	**Moments of highest tension, lived**				
				Bring the problem to life across 2-3 buckets; search VOC for frequency of mentions of time loss, money loss, social standing loss, success stolen, embarrassment, frustration . . .				
			3	**Moments of highest pleasure, longed for**				
				Compound the agitation of the Moment of Highest Tension by showing what they can't have–the Moment of Highest Pleasure that they seek, that others have, that they should have.				
	Mid	DIMENSIONALIZE THE MEGA MEAN MOUSE	4	**Expanded problems and worries**				
				List 2-3 additional problems, stacked on top of the core problem. You are starting to create a bigger mouse with sharper teeth and destruction on the brain.				
			5	**The blame game**				
				It's never the prospect's problem! What is the world, the category, the competition, the ***mouse*** *doing to cause these problems? These are the reasons for the problems. (Eliminate threat to their ego or pride. Focus on the good in even searching for a solution.)*				
			6	**Failed solutions**				
				Our wonderful prospect has tried valiantly to solve this problem. Those solutions failed them. List them. They were no match for the Mega Mean Mouse!				
	Late		7	**Why they failed (problem mechanism)**				
				Identify the core reason for the failure across the solutions they've tried. Give that "problem mechanism" a name.				
		REVEAL THE HERO	8	**"It's not just you."**				
				Without killing their belief that they're special and unique, help them see that they're not alone. The Mega Mean Mouse is ruining lives everywhere. (Implication: our customer can be a hero.)				
			9	**What might work better (solution mechanism)**				
				Begin to tease the solution mechanism you offer along with what they desire most. Make it clear that the solution mechanism will be hard to find but worth it. This solution will help them be heroic–even hearing about it now makes them more qualified to save the day.				

PRODUCT ________________

PERSONA ________________

VALUES ________________

			#	Beat sheet	What (The Message)	How (The Copy)		
SOLUTION / CATEGORY AWARE	Early	BE THE TRUSTED VOICE OF REASON	10	**You need CATEGORY for INDUSTRY, and the solution should champion PERSONA**			Why our persona chooses this category of solution over the others	**WHERE CONSIDERATION HAPPENS** (ads, social, content, partner workshops)
				Your fundamental positioning moment. This is your one thing, the thing you're known for. For example, "the CRM for banks."				
			11	**Why we're the only ones who can do this (category for industry serving persona)**				
				What uniquely qualifies you to be the best blank for blank serving blank? This may introduce or circle back to your unique solution mechanism.				
			12	**The category landscape**				
				List the options you know this persona is considering (without introducing new ones for them to go research). Your objective will be (but isn't yet) to show how they're all inately flawed.				
	Mid	SHOW FLAWS IN THE STATUS QUO / THE CATEGORY	13	**Desire & obstacles**				
				In a world with so many options that should give your prospect X desire, why are they still coming up short? What obstacles are preventing them from reaching that desire?				
			14	**Competitors all focus on X (the old way)**				
				Agitate what competitors are all getting wrong. Show how they're missing the point. Arouse a desire to find someone who gets it right.				
			15	**Here's what's wrong with that**				
				Demonstrate how and why their mousetrap is wrong for the Mega Mean Mouse.				
	Late		16	**Here's how that manifests badly for people like our persona**				
				Show and tell the failures that our prospect will recognize and wish to avoid. Consider manifestations across functional, social, and personal jobs.				
			17	**What you must leave behind**				
				Finish your fight with the old way or competing solutions, reducing the pull of the now / status quo. (By now, the death of the old way should be obvious.) For example, to get into Harvard, you have to abandon the myth that you can do so without a college coach.				
		INTRODUCE YOUR PRODUCT	18	**New / Next / Novel**				
				Introduce the new, next, or novel thing happening in the space. This is at the heart of the right mousetrap to catch Mega Mean Mouse TODAY (not yesterday, not with other solutions)! And your solution just so happens to nail it.				

PRODUCT		________________			
PERSONA		________________			
VALUES		________________			

Awareness	Stage	Section	#	Beat sheet	What (The Message)	How (The Copy)	Why our persona should buy	WHERE BUYING HAPPENS (site, emails, retargeting, workshops)
PRODUCT / BRAND AWARE	Early	INTRODUCE YOUR PRODUCT	19	**Product value proposition ("The only")**				
				What's the big win your customers can expect to lock in when they use your solution? State your core value proposition for your product in customer-facing language. This is often the "phrase that pays." It should reflect the primary JTBD for this persona.				
			20	**Named unique solution mechanism**				
				Express and unpack the value of your core unique mechanism–the one that neutralizes the Mega Mean Mouse and brings happiness. The UM is ***how*** *your value prop gets delivered. Effectively this beat is How It Works.*				
		ESTABLISH ITS VALUE	21	**High level benefits**				
				The benefits of your solution for your prospect. Where these can be tied to features or systems, make those clear to eliminate skepticism.				
	Mid		22	**Value pillars**				
				Beyond the value prop, mechanism, and benefits, what does your product or brand stand for that's in keeping with what your persona stands for?				
			23	**Differentiated outcomes ("Unlike ever before")**				
				These are the outcomes of the previous 5 beats. Because the competition doesn't have this stuff, they can't deliver these outcomes. Hence, differentiated outcomes. In this beat, try completing the phrase "Unlike ever before."				
			24	**Vs. competition**				
				Answer the question, "If it's so easy for you, why aren't all your competitors doing it?" This is also where you clear up category confusion.				
	Late		25	**Proof of how ("The Promise")**				
				Reduce skepticism and increase optimism by giving evidence of ***how*** *your product gets those differentiated outcomes. Dig in with demos, feature walk-throughs, algo insights, secret sauce stuff.*				
		CONNECT THE PERSONA WITH THE PRODUCT	26	**Proof of who**				
				Fill the prospect's eyes with nothing but proof that your product generates differentiated outcomes for the persona in question.				
			27	**Uniquely qualified**				
				Bring it back to your customer! What have they already done that uniquely qualifies them to move forward with this buying decision? Show them the milestones they've hit. Help them overcome friction regarding whether they have enough info to make this decision (they do!), and strike from their mind any concerns about other places they could put their resources, what they may lose if they continue on (gains only!). Align this purchasing decision with their efforts to date, their goals, and even their worldview				

PRODUCT ______________

PERSONA ______________

VALUES ______________

			#	Beat sheet	What (The Message)	How (The Copy)	Why our persona will buy now	**WHERE BUYING HAPPENS** (site, emails, retargeting, workshops)
MOST AWARE	**Early**	DIMENSIONALIZE THE VALUE	**28**	**Big claims** *Make your product iconic! What is it #1 at in the world? Why should your prospect buy into your brand, your team, your future? This beat reduces reputation risk, particularly if your buyer feels unqualified to recommend any solution to other decision makers.*				
			29	**Success stories, with risk reversal** *Ensure your prospect sees and understands at least three success stories when they're in this decision-making stage. Make it easy to advocate.*				
			30	**Use cases** *Neutralize risk of limited use (and misused resources) by fleshing out additional use cases for your product that solve problems for your prospect and/or the people in their sphere.*				
	Mid	EMPOWER THE YES	**31**	**Goal amplification** *Remind them of their goals, and amplify your solution's ability to get them there. Use calculators and other amplifiers of goal attainment / value.*				
			32	**Risk & uncertainty reduction** *Guarantees, trial periods, white-glove support, account managers, support forums, live events—remove the risk of saying yes by showing you have skin in the game. Ideally match these to the persona's biggest friction points at this stage, such as learning curve or fears of bait and switch, being burned, being abandoned, being embarrassed.*				
			33	**Kill the status quo** *Eliminate all historical allegiance! Why the old way is not good enough, how this change is low risk, and what makes the new way, which they're so close to getting, magnetic (Jobs progress-making forces). If your product / solution makes it easy to kill the status quo—like you offer migration services or contract buyouts—highlight these now.*				
	Late	BUY OR BYE-BYE	**34**	**Offer optimization & stacked offers** *Move the prospect to act now. Limited time offers, bonuses, pre-filled forms, even free t-shirts if that'll get the deal closed.*				
			35	**Leadership horizon / Future proofing** *Your prospect is buying your product and buying INTO your brand. Assure them there's plenty more where this came from! Make it clear you're a future-proofed business so they're future-proofed, too. If they haven't bought into the company, they won't buy.*				
			36	**Coach decisiveness** *Encourage a yes or no—eliminate the possibility of no decision. Name the stakes of inaction, and normalize decision making.*				

I recognize that 36 beats feels like a lot. The reality is that your marketing already has to hit all of these beats; your crew just hasn't seen this yet, so they've likely been randomly hitting most of these beats in a scattershot way. With the message matrix, we're gonna organize the work. Layer a system behind it. And document and share it within your organization. This will make everyone's lives easier. It will help your team produce copy that's more likely to be the marketing equivalent of a Hollywood blockbuster.

"I THINK I'LL JUST BRAINSTORM THIS STUFF, JO."

If you're not yet sold on writing copy with VOC and VOS—instead of brainstorming or going on gut—check this out. Appcues, a product experience SaaS, used the VOC of their ICP (product managers and marketers) to generate a 73 percent increase in visit-to-trial conversions.[14] Strata Identify, a B2B tech company, saw a 16.3 percent conversion rate lift and a 72.8 percent boost in organic search traffic when they used VOC in their site content.[15] And Learn Visual Studio, an online learning space, used VOC on their homepage to increase course signups by 9.2 percent and increase curriculum views by 23.9 percent.[16] VOC and VOS data help you *clone your customers* successfully simply by mirroring their words instead of trying to dream up new ones.

Further, in an AI-driven marketing landscape, a common complaint is that copy is sounding less human, more impersonal. People can spot AI-written copy. Using VOC to write your copy helps ensure it sounds more human. It adds in the rawness—the humanness—that an LLM can't collect from a world of existing messages and try to replicate.

The message matrix I use and recommend is a spreadsheet. A GPT or other AI solution can automate this process, but we're not in the business of automating customer insights. If you're going to mirror back what customers say, in their words, then you need to listen to what customers say, in their words. Be there to hear them. Don't let an LLM get all the rich data when you and your team can benefit from it instantly.

FILLING IN THE MESSAGE MATRIX

You won't actually begin filling in a message matrix until you've been through the *Listening* step. But before we dive into listening activities, know this: you and your team will be organizing your messages *with the highest potential for conversion* so that they're available for use at exactly the right point in a customer's journey. Map your messages. The money is in the matrix.

> **GET COPIES FOR YOU AND YOUR CREW**
>
> Download free copies of the message matrix template at copysellingbook.com. You'll also find example completed matrices and lessons on how to ensure you're filling your message matrices with the most useful data.

Here's an example of how mapping VOC can directly unlock revenue. When software brand Productboard was in its early days, cofounders Hubert Palan and Daniel Hejl interviewed hundreds of product managers and meticulously mapped what they heard in a spreadsheet. The result? They knew their personas and what to say to them, which made all of their messaging and marketing decisions infinitely more efficient. Today, Productboard is valued at over $2 billion.[17] It's not enough to listen; you must map what you're hearing in detail.

USING THE MESSAGE MATRIX IN YOUR MARKETING

Practically speaking, you and your team will use your message matrix to write ads, emails, and pages as well as any SMS, chatbot, social selling, in-app messaging, or other marketing you do across channels you use.

You will find that each of the 36 beats on a matrix can stand alone as an ad. So one message matrix gives you at least 36 ads.

In some cases, each beat can also stand alone as an email, so one message matrix can give you at least 36 emails. You can also use one beat to craft multiple ads. You can use one beat to script a video. You can use one beat a hundred times over, if your assembly line warrants you spend more time in that beat. You can stack multiple beats together to script a video ad, to write a meatier email, or to write a landing page. (Try using the eleven sections to guide you here.) You can use all 36 beats to craft a sales webinar. You can use all 36 beats to craft a long-form sales page.

But always present the assets to your customer in *order*. For example, Beat 14 should not appear before any of the thirteen beats that precede it on the message matrix. There's no bouncing around on a conveyor belt.

ONE PRODUCT, ONE CUSTOMER PER MESSAGE MATRIX

You'll create one message matrix for each product, and for each customer segment or persona for that product. *This message matrix becomes the single source of truth for all teams.*

If you have one product, like project management SaaS, and you serve one audience, like freelance creatives, you will need one message matrix. If you have four products with three audiences for each, you'll need twelve.

Some companies use Jobs to Be Done in place of personas. Cool. If that's what you do, then start by creating three Messaging Matrices—one functional, one social, one emotional. Note that you may need to reference all three simultaneously when assembling, writing, and optimizing copy.

"Uh oh. I think I need 300 matrices."

You have multiple products, multiple personas, multiple constraints. How do you prioritize which message matrix to put together first, perhaps as a test project?

Start with the most pressing growth constraint in your department or team. Then develop the solution design for *that* constraint. In the solution design, you'll identify the persona and product in question, under List and Offer, respectively. (See chapter eight.) You will prioritize creating the message matrix for the persona and product you've just identified.

Alternatively, start with AI. Let's say you know you have a ton of research for X persona and Y product. Grab a blank copy of the message matrix, grab your research, and pop it all into a project in an AI solution like Claude. Prompt it to complete the message matrix for you. For example:

> *I'm using Joanna Wiebe's copyselling system to write copy that converts. The system is heavily informed by a beat-based message matrix, which is a file in this project.*
>
> *I have many products and personas to write copy for. I'd like your help creating just one message matrix for ____ persona, a buyer of ____ product. This is a test of the concept of the message matrix.*
>
> *I've uploaded the persona profile, a product sheet, VOC data for that persona, and other survey information for that product. Using only those files, please fill in the How column for the message matrix with that VOC, adding the best-fit VOC data to the best-fit beat. Do not generalize, make up new data, or try to squeeze data that doesn't fit into any beat. Do not write copy.*
>
> *When you're done, we'll start identifying gaps in the data.*

THE ANATOMY OF THE MESSAGE MATRIX

The matrix is based on the stages of awareness. Along the side of the matrix, you'll see four categories matching these four stages:

- Problem aware
- Solution aware
- Product aware
- Most aware

Because a prospect doesn't bunny hop from stage to stage but rather moves through them as if going along a conveyor belt, within each of those four stages you'll find substages:

- Early
- Mid
- Late

That brings us to the eleven sections, inside of which are beats that your copy needs to hit. The eleven sections are as follows:

1. Hold up a mirror
2. Dimensionalize the Mega Mean Mouse (which will make sense soon)
3. Reveal the hero
4. Be the trusted voice of reason
5. Show flaws in the status quo/the category
6. Introduce your product
7. Establish its value
8. Connect the persona with the product
9. Dimensionalize the value
10. Empower the yes
11. Buy or bye-bye

To create a customer, your marketing needs to move each person through all eleven sections, in order. Over the last two decades, I've dedicated my waking hours to running experiments, studying marketing, and reverse-engineering high performing copy, which is how I developed and then fleshed out those eleven sections. The result is the message matrix, your template for building a customer.

"Jo, what if our product lineup is graduated?"

Many companies have graduated product lineups, or tiers. As your customer finds success with Product A, they graduate to Product B. This is common in SaaS and training businesses. Product A requires one message matrix per person; Product B requires one message matrix per person. Your marketers for Product B are switching your customer from Product A.

Now a question: because you're moving an existing customer from A to B, should your message matrix for Product B effectively pick a fight with Product A?

The answer: yes, but. Think about the straightest, cleanest assembly line for turning a Product A customer into a Product B customer. That customer needs to recognize the limitations of Product A in order to move to Product B; they also need to recognize the limitations of external alternatives to Product B (i.e., the competitive landscape) so that they don't abandon your brand for an actual competitor.

That means, on your Product B message matrix, you will incorporate the reasons to switch from Product A to Product B; you will do this in the Solution Aware stage, which you'll see covers Beats 10 to 18. However, you will not mention Product A during the Problem Aware stage. Your job is not to demonize Product A to move a person to Product B—not at all. Rather, in this scenario, you'll typically move rather swiftly through the Product Aware beats, noting only the limitations that they may be experiencing and how the better version of their lives—one without those limitations—is easy to switch to.

As you begin to learn more about the message matrix and its beats, keep in mind that one of your products may be a "competitor." *But nothing about your product lineup should ever be demonized*—not at all. To clearly move a customer to the next tier in your product lineup, however, you will need to message the experienced limitations of Product A; message that the competitive landscape does not tackle those limitations; and then message how Product B is the perfect solution to those limitations, in keeping with the beats of the message matrix.

What to Write and How to Write It

The final two parts of the anatomy are these: *What it is*, and *How it's expressed*. That's shortened to *What* and *How*. *What* is your marketing message, which is typically used internally rather than in customer-facing copy; *How* is the language that will become your copy.

Put simply: what is your message, how is your copy.

These are the two core columns you and your team will fill in.

You'll fill in the How column first. *How* is where you capture raw voice of customer data (VOC) from the customer, segment, or persona in question; raw voice of sales data (VOS) from your sales team; raw voice of product data (VOP) from your product or founding team; and sometimes you'll use language from other sources, like Reddit comments and articles that journalists write. Importantly, what you add to *How* is not marketing-approved copy. It's what you hear when you're *listening.* You don't edit it. You don't change it. You just hear it (or read it) . . . copy it . . . and paste it in the How column for the best-fit beat.

Let's say you're in marketing for Dale, a fictional solution that helps product managers bring features to market faster. You're watching a replay of a sales call between a VP of Product and a sales rep when you catch this line from the VP:

> *Our PMs were just always staying late at the end of every sprint, and I mean every sprint. Three PMs at a time, stuck at work on Friday—they called those meetings Pizza After Dark. Obviously there was pizza involved. They should have been at home with their families or out with their friends, but they're stuck in our games room eating Postmates, trying to make it feel fun, with their laptops on a Friday night because we just lost so many hours during the sprint.*

That VOC belongs in the How column, in unedited form—exactly as it's shown here. (And as you'll soon discover, it belongs in either *Beat 1: Core problem match* or *Beat 2: Moments of highest tension, lived.*)

Next, you'll fill in the *What* column. *What* is where you identify the message underlying the VOC, VOS, and VOP from the *How* column. For the previous Dale example, you might write this under *What*:

> *PMs lose hours each sprint*

Try to avoid interpretation when you're identifying the *What.* When I was coming up with the *What* for the above example, it took me some time. That's okay. It should take time. It's also okay if it feels imperfect and if you find yourself changing it.

Your objective is to keep the *What* tight. Go nuts with all the VOC and other data under *How.* But *What* should be a one-liner—a single line, fewer than ten words. *What* is going to turn into the single message that whole campaigns and assets may be built around. *What* is easy to memorize and repeat.

Think of completing each message matrix like a card sorting exercise. If you're unfamiliar with card sorting, it's a research method commonly used in user experience design (UX) where users categorize items, written on cards, based on what makes sense to them. In this case, your "cards" are spreadsheet cells filled with VOC, and your team must categorize them in the beat that makes the most sense to them; then they come up with a term to express the purpose of the card's content (i.e., the What).

The more frequently you hear a message, the more likely it is that the message will resonate with others who match the persona. The *What* column typically expresses a summarized take on several data points in the corresponding *How* column, not just one. For best results, wait until you have three or more phrases in *How* before you try to identify their *What.*

HOW YOU'LL USE THE MESSAGE MATRIX WHEN COPYSELLING

Every time you have a new revenue-focused asset to create, you'll start with two things:

1. A solution design, which is a document we'll discuss in chapter eight, and
2. Your completed product- and persona-specific message matrix.

Using the solution design, you'll pinpoint where on the message matrix the person you're writing for (i.e., your One Reader) is likely to be in their journey. This helps you know which beat to start at when you're writing. The solution design will also tell you what the goal of the asset is, which will help you know which beat you're going to end on. This is how we kill the chaos of guesswork . . . while actually getting into the heads of our prospects.

For example, let's say you're going to write a retargeting ad for people who attended your session at an online summit. Your session was heavy on problems and failed solutions, and it was very, very light on your brand and product. You crafted it by following Beats 1 through 11. So in your retargeting ad, you can reasonably assume that you are safe to pick up the conversation around Beat 11. Ad #1 might start at Beat 11, while ad #2 goes back to Beat 10 and ad #3 goes back to Beat 9. Trust me, this will all make sense very soon.

The 36 beats provide you with clean and clear entry points into the conversation with your prospect at each stage of the assembly line. This will come together once you see all 36 beats in detail, which is what's next.

CHAPTER RECAP

The Message Matrix

- ✓ The message matrix is the blueprint for your customer assembly line.
- ✓ It is based on 36 beats that span the four primary stages of awareness.
- ✓ You will fill it in using raw voice of customer and voice of sales data.
- ✓ You will use it, alongside a solution design, to identify the beat your prospect is at and join the conversation there.

CHAPTER 4
The 36 Beats

"You must increase the perceived value of what you are selling to at least 10 times the price you are charging."

....

Michael Masterson, author of *Great Leads* and *Ready, Fire, Aim*

Here's what you need to know to hit each beat successfully on the customer assembly line. Open a copy of the message matrix template, which you can find in the back of this book and at copysellingbook.com, and follow along. Note that I'll use the term "customer," but I mean lead, segment, prospect, persona—the person you're trying to convert. I'll also use the term "VOC" as a catch-all term for VOC, VOS, VOP, and all other snippets swiped from valuable spaces.

For the first three beats, I've included example products to give you an idea of what sort of message and copy might live in each beat on the message matrix. To get more sample beat sheets, with all 36 beats completed for your edification, head over to copysellingbook.com.

PROBLEM AWARE BEATS

Problems create customers. But people love to forget their problems. Our job is to bring them back to those problems so that they want to solve them.

In the Problem Aware stage, you'll make a convincing case for why your persona is going to become a customer, and it will start with identifying and agitating the problems that have driven them to look for solutions. You will not, in this stage, message your product.

Hold Up a Mirror

We are all biased toward self-interest. Any armchair psychologist can tell you as much. Because that's how we're built, lean into it on the page. You lure a prospect onto your customer assembly line by holding up a mirror, showing them not your product or your category or your offer—but themselves.

Beat 1: Core Problem Match

What is the core problem that drives this prospect to start looking for a solution? The core problem is the most frequently stated issue that surfaced during the *Listening* step. Critically, it should also be the problem that your product solves best for this customer. Don't introduce problems you can't solve.

PRODUCT	WHAT	HOW
Anbesol toothache gel	My tooth hurts	"I bit into an apple and felt lightning shoot across my face."
Stream Deck control panels	Clunky livestreaming	"I thought I was switching to my gaming screen–but it was my online banking."
Apollo sales software	My sales team hates prospecting	"I just fired another sales rep–where did all the great sales prospectors go?"

Beat 2: Moments of Highest Tension, Lived

How does that core problem manifest in their lives? What do the consequences of that problem look like, in the lived, real experience of your customer?

If you do Jobs to Be Done interviews, you may find that the problem manifests functionally, socially, and/or emotionally (personally) for them. It manifests as money lost and time lost. It manifests as embarrassment in front of their peers, their boss, their partner, their kids, their dad, strangers at the park, strangers on the train, friends at camp. It manifests as frustration with their team, which itself manifests as finally blowing up and being embarrassed, getting reprimanded, getting put on leave, dreading seeing your team again, having to look for a new job, telling your spouse why you're looking for a new job.

Be sure to listen and document what you're hearing, without interjecting. The natural inclination of most marketing teams is to take something raw and make it sound polished. Don't. Instead, do as my friend Ryan Schwartz recommends: document each moment of highest tension so vividly that even the worst actor on earth could come along, read what you documented, and act the scene out perfectly.

PRODUCT	WHAT	HOW
Anbesol toothache gel	Eating is painful	"Last night at dinner, I looked at my plate and wondered how I could mush this meal up without anyone noticing."
Stream Deck control panels	Viewers aren't subscribing	"I must look like I have no idea what I'm doing. They come to watch me play—I've got that down. But I look as underproduced—as unpolished—as I actually am. So viewers come and go without liking or subscribing. Which means I can't monetize my gaming."
Apollo sales software	Numbers of leads are down	"The business reps are staring *daggers* at the SDRs in our standups, and I can't say I blame them. We need more leads—at this point, we're desperate for any leads, good or not. And this is what the SDRs were hired to do. They were trained for it. We should have more leads coming in than ever."

This is the section of the message matrix where we begin to bring to life the idea of a Mega Mean Mouse™. And that means it's time to pause for a "Weapon of Mass Copyselling" exercise.

Weapon One: The Mega Mean Mouse.

Eugene Schwartz taught us this:

"Don't build a better mousetrap. Build bigger mice."

Most businesses are trying to sell a better mousetrap. What they're leaving off the page is the trouble that mice–and the wrong mousetrap–can bring.

My husband and I were in a very nice restaurant in London, and not one but three mice ran across the floor. Do you think we stayed? Was a mouse infestation perhaps the reason the otherwise beautiful space was empty of diners? Didn't the nearest seller of mousetraps owe it to that restaurant's owner to help them solve this costly mice problem? Didn't the local exterminator? Don't we owe the same to people experiencing problems our solution can easily remedy?

In your social media marketing, in your ebooks, in your blog posts, in your webinars and workshops–across the customer journey and in your sales copy–you have the space and your prospects have the time for you to increase the size of, the scariness of, and the damage caused by the mouse your solution eliminates. But here's why too few brands use The Mega Mean Mouse weapon: "It's fear mongering."

I heard that regularly when I worked in big tech and tried to get problem-based copy approved. What I've learned to hear when someone says, "It's fear mongering," is that it stirred feelings they didn't like . . . which is what it's supposed to do. The job of problem-based copy is, like all copy, to join the conversation happening in your prospect's head; for people dealing with problems, the conversation is one of *struggling with a real, lived problem*. It's only fear mongering if you make your reader feel like a fool or a jerk. Always stay aligned with your reader.

Unless you're selling a solution without a problem, you have a mouse you can make bigger, or "hulkify." Here's what to do.

1. Step 1: Find the problem or the problem behind the problem.
2. Step 2: Hulkify it.

For example, here's a problem that a prospect for a project management solution, like Asana, might have:

"We've got invisible bottlenecks that get in the way of hitting deadlines."

Good start. But I can't visualize it, and I'm not sure it really applies to me. So we hulkify that problem and pop it in a customer story embedded in a workshop, posted to LinkedIn, and shared on Instagram:

"We sat for our emergency meeting only to discover that the copywriter was still waiting on the brief, the UX designer was still waiting on feedback, and four team members were waiting on those two. The deadline didn't just get missed. The deadline will have to be moved out three months. And that's what I have to tell the CTO this afternoon. I can hear her now: 'Why didn't I know this earlier?' What am I gonna do–blame the project management tool? Blame the team? It lands on me."

An accountant is worth a thousand bucks if you want to avoid the pain of an audit. A prenup is an easier battle to undertake if you know someone who lost everything in a divorce. An unseen God is easy enough to obey if you want to avoid the fires of Hell.

To create a bigger, scarier mouse, we need to flesh out the problems that our prospect has just been suffering through. This is how we ensure our customer will move mountains to solve their problems.

PRODUCT	WHAT	HOW
Anbesol toothache gel	Canker sores that swell up. Receding gumlines that cause cold sensitivity.	"I bit my cheek on Tuesday. By Thursday I could barely talk. I looked like an idiot when I was bussing tables and a guest tried to joke with me."
Stream Deck control panels	Starting from scratch every livestream. Moving quickly between screens. Showing interactions and comments, then shutting them off without jarring the experience.	"Keep a checklist for all livestreams, but it's awkward to keep referring to throughout the stream."
Apollo sales software	The leads they're getting are wrong. They're doing cold outreach using their actual work addresses.	"One of them bought a list of teachers to target, even though teachers hold no sway in decision making for our product. Then they basically spammed all of the schools in New Jersey. We got flagged, and now it'll be a cold day in hell before a New Jersey school accepts an email or even a call from us."

Beat 3: Moments of Highest Pleasure, Longed For

The flipside of a moment of highest tension (Beat 2) is the moment of highest pleasure. This is something that your customer may not have experienced yet but can imagine vividly or may have experienced in the past and now longs for again. I'll use a common example that my friend Shane O'Quinn, who owns hair transplant clinics, gives: *A (straight) guy's on his second date, and once again he's wearing a ball cap. The woman he's dating reaches across the table, playfully grabs at the brim of the cap and says, "Let's see what's under there!"*

The moment of highest tension: she lifts his ball cap to find that his forehead just keeps going—he's nearly bald. He doesn't even have to look at her expression, and he couldn't if he wanted to. In this moment, he would pay a bajillion dollars to have the lush head of hair he is absolutely convinced she was expecting.

The moment of highest pleasure: she lifts his ball cap to reveal a tumble of thick curls. He laughs, she laughs, a third date is definitely on the horizon.

Side note: The above exchange can strike as unsophisticated. It is. People are. A great rule to follow when you think something is below you: Write for a Walmart reader, not a Bergdorf Goodman reader. Unless the data proves your prospect is the ultimate sophisticate, quoting Nietzsche and looking down on the plebes with their ball caps and bald heads, default to writing for everyday people as we are, not as we wish we could be.

Dimensionalize the Mega Mean Mouse™

On the message matrix, your customer is now at Mid Problem Aware. Your copy has had them confront their problem instead of ignoring it, which they'd prefer to do. And now we need to ensure they recognize:

- Their problems run deep,
- Their problems manifest in ways they can't afford to ignore, and
- Their problems are not about them—the real problem is the mouse!

A mousetrap exists to catch a mouse because of all the problems the mouse causes. The mouse chews holes in walls, letting other vermin and insects into your house. It defecates and urinates in your walls, soaking your house with unseen toxins. It chews both wires and gas lines in your walls—did you know that these problems cause a whopping 20 percent of house fires in America each year? And it reproduces quickly, multiplying the problem every time it brings six, seven, eight offspring into the big, itchy nest that it's continually expanding inside your walls.

Meanwhile, mice are completely cute. If you don't have a mouse problem, you think mice are adorable. They're not rodents—they're potential pets! Did you see all those cute Instagram reels where people set up tiny cafes for the potential pets taking shelter from the cold inside just a tiny part of the ample space of your walls? *Kawaii desu ne!*

If you don't describe the problems that the Mega Mean Mouse causes, you're not selling a mousetrap—you're selling a makeshift guillotine designed to end the life of Cinderella's own hero, Gus-Gus.

By Mid Problem Aware, your customer needs to agree with you: *the problem is real, it is big, it cannot be ignored, and it's not my fault. The real problem is the mouse.*

Beat 4: Expanded Problems and Worries

One problem begets more problems, and anxieties, and frustrations. A problem that strikes a teacher affects their students, their principal, other teachers in the breakroom, even the school's reputation. To say nothing of how it trickles into and can grow to dominate their home life. You will hear so many struggles during the *Listening* phase. Put the most emotive, experienced, expanded problems on the page, in keeping with your brand's voice and the required tone for the asset you're crafting.

If your product solves a very specific problem, such that you can't find other problems or subsequent worries in your VOC, then use this area to flesh out the core problem further.

Beat 5: The Blame Game

How did the mouse get this big and dangerous? Why are we here? Take the blame off your customer and put it where it belongs: somewhere else.

The world is the reason this is happening. The lies they've been told, the myths that surround them, the secrets kept from them. Unrealized dreams because they followed the rules and went to school for a job they ended up hating. Flunking grade ten math because the system prioritized standardized teaching based on systems built in the 1950s when "neurodivergent" wasn't even a word. Being told they have to use one operating system when it's clearly not the right fit for them.

It's important to note that naming an enemy doesn't have to take a dark turn. For starters, it doesn't have to be—and shouldn't be—a person or group of people. Your customers will tell you what (not who) the enemy is. Blame it like they do. Name it like they do. While, of course, staying on brand.

Beat 6: Failed Solutions

Our wonderful prospect has tried valiantly to solve this problem. Those solutions failed them—list the solutions. But try to keep it to category level, instead of naming names. What we're showing, by the end of this beat, is that there's an enemy (the Mega Mean Mouse) who is not to be ignored and who cannot be eliminated by using the same old solutions.

Beat 7: Why they failed (problem mechanism)

Our customer is now Late Problem Aware . . . and we, as copysellers, are getting into the REALLY good stuff. We're about to give a name to our Mega Mean Mouse; this will be the name we assign to the Problem Mechanism, which you don't know about yet. So allow me to introduce another weapon of mass copyselling!

Weapon Two: Mechanisms

When giving marketing leaders examples of strong conversion copy, I've learned never to make reference to the following two words.

The first word: Apple. Nobody wants to hear how Apple is doing everything right, as far as iconic brands go, in their copy.

The second: infomercials. Tech brands, makeup brands, luxury brands all have an allergic reaction to infomercials and direct sales . . . because they want to be more like Apple, who would never go in for such lowbrow shenanigans.

Meanwhile, Apple's copy truly is a masterclass in actively selling high-ticket, design-forward products to discerning consumers, on repeat, while building a world-class brand. And an infomercial truly is a masterclass in selling low-ticket, highly demonstrable products to bored brains while building brands that become the punchline in a *Saturday Night Live* skit. And I don't get to talk about either of them!

Except in this book, where I have the microphone, so you will listen to every word I say. (*The Wedding Singer* reference. No? Okay, moving on.)

Here's the reason I mention Apple and infomercials in the same breath: **both Apple and infomercials rely on the same weapon—the mechanism—in their copy.** This is true even though they're selling very different products to very different audiences at entirely opposite price points. So put aside what you don't want to hear about Apple's messaging excellence and an infomercial's unsophisticated supremacy. They both leapfrog objections and separate from the pack by messaging *mechanisms*.

What Do I Mean by "Mechanism"?

A mechanism is a secret that your copy reveals. There are two kinds of mechanisms:

1. The unique problem mechanism.
2. The unique solution mechanism.

The unique problem mechanism is the mechanism that holds your customer back or creates their problem; if a person experiences it, they are prequalified to buy your solution. The unique problem mechanism is the demonic driver of the Mega Mean Mouse.

The unique solution mechanism is the mechanism that makes your product solve the customer's problem uniquely. It's *your* mousetrap–the special, secret thing that makes your method of catching the mouse the *only* solution to the Mega Mean Mouse problem. It is a unique differentiator on overdrive. It is the most perfect form of proof. It replaces the horrible "just trust me" with the excellent "here's why it works like nothing else does!"

A solution mechanism is the team of aerospace engineers behind the Dyson vacuum. It is the hyper-elastic polymer grid in the Purple mattress. It is the specific type of MCT oil in Bulletproof Coffee. It is ShamWow's super-absorbent German technology. It is Scrub Daddy's FlexTexture® Foam. It is the M4 Max Chip in the 2025 Macbook Pro. Intel made its product–a core processor–a unique mechanism that relatively undifferentiated computer brands could borrow as their own mechanism. Just slap "Intel Inside" on your Dell, Lenovo, or HP laptop!

Let's use this book as another example.

The unique problem mechanism that prequalifies a marketer like you to buy my book is **The Guesswork Trap™**: the myth that copywriting specifically and marketing in general is an intuition-based practice best guessed at. The unique solution mechanism is **The Copyselling System™**: the hidden system at the heart of all repeatable lead- and revenue-generating activities. Inside each mechanism, you'll typically find more mechanisms, any or all of which you can name and claim.

Product	Problem Mechanism (For Customers)	Solution Mechanism (In Product)
Lucky Strike cigarettes	*I'm addicted to smoking, but chemicals in cigarettes will give me cancer. ("The Sick Stick")*	*Cigarettes made with toasted tobacco grown in warm, southern fields. ("It's Toasted.")*
TurboTax	*I have to force myself to do my taxes because it's such a confusing and expensive chore. ("The Tax Man Cometh")*	The Refund Calculator™ shows you in real time how much cash you can expect back.
The Jobs to Be Done method of innovation	*As a product manager, I should really know why people use and don't use products. ("Gut-Based Product Management")*	Identify a user's Struggling Moment™ that drives them to a new product.
eHarmony	*I want to find true love, but right now it's all just timing and luck. How can I find my perfect match? ("Love Takes Luck")*	Get matched across 29 Dimensions of Compatibility™ using a deep personality assessment developed by a clinical psychologist.
Headspace	*I can't meditate. ("Interruptive Thinking")*	Use Guided Meditation Packs™ to build the habit of meditating.

Product	Problem Mechanism (For Customers)	Solution Mechanism (In Product)
Le Labo	*I'm not interested in another scent. I don't want to smell like someone else. I want a scent that is uniquely me. ("My Name Is Not Susan")*	Personalized Scents™ made to order, blended fresh, and personalized with your name on the label.
Superhuman	*I will never maintain inbox zero. ("The Inbox Trap")*	Keyboard First UI™ means now your inbox works like a productivity tool.
Hermès Birkin	*My handbag should be a statement today and an heirloom forever. Why would I pay five figures for a bag anyone else can pick up in a store? ("Paying for Impersonal")*	Every Birkin bag is handcrafted by a craftsperson using the Artisan Saddle Stitch™ and must be custom ordered, exclusively by Hermès fans, so you never risk seeing your bag on the arm of someone at the mall.

How to Find Your Customer's Unique Problem Mechanism

The problem mechanism has been cropping up throughout the first beats of the message matrix! When it comes time to start the *Listening* step of the copyselling system, you'll find the problem mechanism in customer interviews, sales call replays, product reviews, online conversations, and surveys. Customers may not name it, but they will speak to it–and it's up to you to give it a name. (See chapter seven for questions to ask!)

How to Find Your Product's Unique Solution Mechanism

Start by getting crisp on what makes your product different *as a product*. Not the outcomes, not the benefits, not the customer. Think about the product (or service) itself. Who built it and what's special about them? How did they build it, and what's special about that?

Speak to your sales team, your customer onboarding team, your developers, your product managers, and your founders. Interview them. Get them to walk you through the product as they know it and, when they demo it, as they show it. Don't accept the surface walk-through–push for layers of detail. Watch recordings of their demos and pitches so you can see what stands out to prospects when talking about your product. Watch and listen for an interesting how–something with a story.

In most cases, your unique solution mechanism will either jump at you instantly or take a painfully long time to find; you may even identify that you do not have a unique solution mechanism, that a lack of such is holding your revenue back, and that it's time to build in the unique solution mechanism that eliminates your customer's unique problem mechanism.

The more concrete your mechanisms, the more likely they are to move leads to action. I like to coach teams with this question: "Does it pass the Name It test?" As in, can you give your mechanism a name and throw a ™ on the end of it? If you can't, you haven't found it yet. If you know you're stretching to call your mechanism unique, you haven't found it yet. It's okay; keep listening for it. You may find your solution mechanism is any of these:

- A rare ingredient
- A resurfaced ingredient that was used historically and then lost

- An exotic-sounding ingredient
- An ingredient only a small group of interesting people have been using (for a long time)
- A signature system
- A new system
- An old system made new
- A system borrowed from an unrelated but successful industry
- A superior enhancement to an otherwise dying system
- A chemical composition
- A new or better framework
- The uniqueness of the team (as one, not as individuals) that built it
- The uniqueness of the founder that built it
- An unexpected material
- An unexpected, but perfect, factory or development location
- A lightning-strikes brainwave (e.g., the Dr. Frankenstein founder's story)
- The brand's origin story
- The brand's creative philosophy

You're not just looking for general differentiators, like "we love design," or stuff that makes you a better place to buy. It's not about planting a tree for every shirt you sell. Rather, aim for something like this: *We import filtered, authentic tapwater from New York City to make your pizza taste like Lombardi's.* That! That is unusual and unique to you. It's a real solution mechanism that moves your prospective customer to stop thinking about the pizza they normally order from some chain on a Friday and instead make a snap call without hearing another word: *Um, hellz yes, we're ordering that NYC-style pizza tonight!*

Problem mechanism: Chain-Drain Pizza Boredom™

Solution mechanism: The Dough New Yorkers Know™

Importantly, the solution mechanism needs to address the problem mechanism *for your prospect*. If a person isn't bored by pizza chains, then they do not have the problem that your solution addresses. That's okay, as long as you're not relying on their patronage. Some people reading this book will go, "Ew, gross, New York water," and stick to their favorite pizza place; others will go "That's kinda cool," and invite their friends to join them for The Dough New Yorkers Know. Your job is to identify (or choose) who your customers are, and select the appropriate mechanisms for them. Are you competing with chains for a family's Friday delivery order, or are you serving a foodie customer who is hiring unique experiences to solve social jobs to be done?

When you think you might have a solution mechanism, ask yourself (or your team or AI) how to make the mechanism truly unique. You may find that what you thought was a somewhat rare ingredient in a plant-derived protein (solution mechanism) is actually sustainable moss-derived phytoproteinimides (which I just made up) originally sourced in Wisconsin and, due to supply chain issues, more recently sourced in Peru. Is it a coast in Peru? Is it a coast inhabited by rarely seen iguanas in Peru? Go look for a photo of a freaking iguana climbing a lush tree in that area! Now you've got yourself a Unique Solution Mechanism—a true copyselling upgrade. Brand storytelling at its clearest.

Once you've found a unique solution mechanism:

1. Give it a strong name.
2. Trademark or register the name, if possible. It doesn't take long for a popular mechanism to be reproduced by a competitor, and you don't want to invest in marketing for your competitors.
3. If it makes sense, replace "a" with "the" when you write about it.

You're aiming for a name like Scrub Daddy's FlexTexture® material. This may seem slightly ridiculous, but Scrub Daddy is a $220 million empire as of 2024, which doesn't feel remotely ridiculous to me.[18] Why would the Scrub Daddy team go to the trouble of registering the trademark on FlexTexture if they didn't have to?

Also, a product *feature* is not a solution mechanism. The Gantt chart you've built into your novel-writing software is not a solution mechanism. This may hurt, but I say it with love: don't bullshit yourself. Take the time to find your actual solution mechanism or to build one in.

Bring It Together

Here's a simple formula to help you solidify your two mechanisms and talk about them internally:

> [Product name] is made with [nameable solution mechanism] that solves [nameable problem mechanism] to [outcome promised].

The Ginsu Knife is made with our Full-Tang Japanese Blade that solves Dull Knife Drama to cut through a can then dice a tomato.

The Chrysler Cordoba has seats made with Genuine Corinthian Leather which means you'll never suffer from Pinching Plastic Seats—a luxurious difference your friends will envy.

Vancouver Island Flake Sea Salt is made with Hollow Pyramid Salt Flakes that eliminate Salt Assault to deliver pleasing pops of salinity.

OxiClean is made with Activated Oxygen that eliminates the possibility of Bleach Blotches to lift stains without chemicals.

Zapier is made with Codeless Connection Technology that solves Native Integration Irritation to seamlessly connect a world of disconnected apps.

Right now, concern yourself only with identifying and naming the problem mechanism that's making your prospect's life so difficult.

Reveal the Hero

Our customer has a chance to be the hero. In the next two beats, reveal to them that they can be the hero without explicitly calling them that. We're not trying to flatter or pander. Rather, this is where we are the sculptor, chipping away at the stone, *revealing* the hero inside. Our prospect didn't know the problem was so significant—this is their chance to save the day!

Beat 8: "It's not just you."

Increase the stakes by sharing stories of how the Mega Mean Mouse is wreaking havoc beyond the sphere of our customer. Our customer is more likely to step into the role of the hero—and eventual brand advocate—when they see the many ways that what you identified in *Beat 5: The blame game* is causing harm to others.

The more you know about the persona you're speaking to, the better you'll know how to use this beat. If they are prone to consider themselves extremely special, you may only touch on this beat lightly in order to prevent damage to their worldview. If they are unlikely to assume the role of the hero in their lives, you may use this beat more to dimensionalize the Mega Mean Mouse than to reveal the hero.

Beat 9: What Might Work Better (Solution Mechanism)

The solution mechanism you just discovered when searching for your problem mechanism goes in this beat. However, it's unlikely you'll name it yet unless you're trying to build hype for the solution mechanism as a category, such as during a product prelaunch. What you most want to do is increase interest in what masterful solution is required to trap our Mega Mean Mouse. You don't want—or need—to sell the product's unique solution mechanism yet.

SOLUTION AWARE BEATS

Our customer is still in the consideration phase of the buying process, and they're not ready yet to hear about our product by name. But we do want to start transitioning them from their problems through the murkiness of the many solutions they could consider toward the best solution for them, which we'll prove, in Product Aware, is our product.

Be the Trusted Voice of Reason

In every project I've worked on as far back as I can remember, when I'm writing copy, I think of the brand as the *advocate* for the person I'm writing to. With Wistia, I told myself, while writing, "They are the champion of DIY videographers." With GitPrime, I told myself, while writing, "They are the champion of engineers." The "champion lens" makes it easier to write with empathy and enthusiasm.

Your brand should be the champion of your customer from the moment they start to connect with it. That's why, as soon as we transition from Problem Aware to Solution Aware, we must help our customer see us as their advocate. We must be the trusted voice of reason as they navigate a potentially murky category.

Beat 10: "We are CATEGORY for INDUSTRY"

Although positioning is critical across the journey, it's when your customer is shifting from problem to solution aware that you need to be sure to express your position in the market. The best way? With this statement my friend and positioning expert April Dunford uses regularly: **"We are ______ for ______."** As in, we are the CRM for banks. We are the cooling gum for hot flashes. We are the French cookbook for American home cooks.

This is a good time to call out your persona. As in, we are the CRM for banks with one lifecycle marketer. Alternatively, you may position yourself as a champion for that persona without expressly stating it on the page; for example, you could run top of funnel ads showcasing your persona talking about your solution.

PS: Shout out to the legendary and always generous April Dunford for knocking this idea around with me on the message matrix.

Beat 11: Why We're the Only Ones Who Can Do This

What is it about your team, your location, your founder's experience that makes you the leader, or the hottest contender, in your category for X industry? Support what you stated in Beat 10. Tell your customer what uniquely qualifies you to be the ideal blank for blank serving blank.

Perhaps you have two cofounders, one of whom ran product at Klaviyo and the other of whom led marketing at RBC Royal Bank; they met each other in a hiking group, and the rest is history—that's why you're the best and only true CRM for banks.

Beat 12: The Category Landscape

What does the range of solutions look like, through the eyes of your customer? What solutions exist for a person trying to solve the problem your customer is trying to solve? If you sell blister pads for hikers, solutions to the problem (of blisters) could include bandages, duct tape, thicker socks, reinforced socks, new hiking boots, a different brand of hiking boots, a different terrain, a combination of all of the above, or simply sucking it up.

Mention only the solutions you know your customer is considering; avoid introducing anything they'll go off and research; avoid introducing anything that your prospect will find is superior to you. Unless you've tested doing so with success, don't introduce product names, just categories of solutions.

Show Flaws in the Category

The remainder of the Solution/Category Aware stage is largely dedicated to showing flaws in the category. Start by establishing what the customer wants most, then move them through the systems, processes, myths, ideas, and other underlying functions that get in the way of the customer getting what they want from other solutions in the category.

Some categories are complex, which allows you to spend more time really fleshing out the flaws in the space. But if your category is less complex, you can move more swiftly through these beats.

Beat 13: Desire & Obstacles

To help them reach their dreamstate, your customer has many options, most of which they already knew about. So what stopped them from using those solutions successfully? What are the obstacles keeping them from their dreamstate? Shouldn't it be as easy as just choosing one solution out of the landscape? (Of course not!)

Beat 14: Competitors All Focus on X (the Old Way)

How are your competitors' mechanisms keeping your customer stuck in a recurring state of pain? Speak directly to the problem mechanism, and bring it to life for the various competitors in the category landscape. Or, if you can't identify a single problem mechanism that runs through all the problematic solutions you wish to message, list the many problems that the various solutions create.

What you'll find, though, as you keep writing is that you'll get to a place where you want to have a big moment of presenting your solution as THE solution . . . and that may be impossible (or just super wordy) if all the solutions have their own problems. So for a more compelling message, identify and name the central problem mechanism, or the old way, that all solutions let them down.

Beat 15: Here's What's Wrong with That

Never imply! It's not enough to share that competitors are missing the point on X, Y, or Z. Now we spell out for our customer exactly what is wrong with what the competition is doing. How and why is a competitor's solution going to fail to trap the Mega Mean Mouse? Dig into the unique problem mechanism, and clearly tie it to competitors in the category landscape.

Beat 16: Here's How Misplaced Focus Manifests Badly

Show and tell the failures that your customer will recognize and wish to avoid. Be vivid. This is no place to cut back on hardworking words.

You'll find that a lot of what we do in copyselling is poking under the surface. Introduce a surface-level message, and then take the time (and words) to agitate or arouse deeper feelings—bring that moment to life for the customers. As we move toward the end of Solution Aware, we need to ensure that our customer is entirely aware of the good and bad of possible solutions. If you gave them a quiz on what the competition is doing wrong and how it manifests badly for people, could they answer it after reading your copy?

Beat 17: What You Must Leave Behind

By this point, your customer must recognize that there's a Mega Mean Mouse lurking, almost no mousetrap will do the trick, and the only thing that stands a chance of working is a solution that is made with the Unique Solution Mechanism messaged many times already. But that unique solution mechanism won't work if you hold tight to old ideas, limiting beliefs, so-called sacred cows, and myths; name those here, and pick a fight with them.

Introduce Your Product

Now we transition out of Solution Aware to Product Aware. As you introduce your product by name, focus your messaging around what uniquely qualifies your product to catch the Mega Mean Mouse today, what it does that no one else in the category does (as well), and how it does it.

Beat 18: New/Next/Novel

Y'know when you're shopping for a mattress and they've got an illustration that shows the seven different layers inside the mattress, and one layer in particular stands out. It's a cooling layer, for example. The tech used for that cooling layer is new, is next, is novel. That's where your brain should go when you're trying to determine what's new, next, or novel to move your prospect to be ready for Product Awareness—and the introduction of your product in particular.

Alternatively, what's happening in the world today that bolsters your solution in particular? Maybe someone got into power somewhere; a new tax incentive just got approved; a cheap copper alternative has put an end to copper wires; the ozone layer is in trouble again; AI just became illegal; climate change is driving desert conditions where your pinot grapes are grown; raccoons have learned to speak. This is happening now, you've jumped at it, only your customers will benefit from it.

PRODUCT AWARE BEATS

Welcome, at last, to the Product Aware stage, where most marketers feel most comfortable. Here we'll message features, benefits, and value of our product for the persona in question. This stage is all about why our persona should buy our product.

Beat 19: Product Value Proposition ("The Only")

What is your product's value proposition, in customer-facing language? It's your one-liner pitch. It is likely to reflect the primary job that your customer is trying to do by hiring your product, and it typically completes the phrase "The only way to" or "The only." The result is a stellar headline or a more tagline-esque *phrase that pays.*

For example, Kit is *the only way for* creators to automate their growth. On their homepage, that value proposition could read "How Creators Automate Their Growth." Another example: Dragonfruit Media is the only way to become a top voice on YouTube. On their homepage, that value proposition reads "Become a Top 1 Percent Brand on YouTube."

These are examples of value propositions that complete the phrase "The only." Stanley is the only fireproof insulated cup. Whims are the only anti-inflammatory vegan chocolates. Twigs are the only one-hundred-calorie snacks that taste like one-thousand-calorie snacks. Swingline is the only stapler for pop culture fans.

Just remember: your value proposition must hold value for your customer. It has to be something they value, and that value is amplified by the messages in the 18 beats that came before it.

Beat 20: Unique Mechanism and Its Value

Tie the unique solution mechanism you've been praising all along to your product, by name. State the value it brings for the customer in question. A product demo showcasing the unique solution mechanism goes a long way in this beat.

Establish Its Value

The next five beats are dedicated to establishing the value of your product by messaging benefits, outcomes, and value pillars. Let's define those so we can tell them apart easily.

A benefit is the answer to the question "So what?" when you're messaging a feature or a high-level benefit. When your product lead says, "This 15-button interface can be customized," and you say, "So what?" you're looking for the benefit. Benefits have layers. Behind each benefit is another benefit.

An outcome is a tangible result of using a feature or a product.

A value pillar is a concept usually at the core of your brand, the way design is a value pillar for Apple.

To illustrate the differences, consider AWS. Their *value proposition* is effectively to empower organizations to operate more efficiently, securely, and innovatively using cloud technologies. That value proposition is supported by five key **value pillars**: cost savings, increased productivity, operational resilience, business agility, and environmental impact. We find the benefits when we go deeper on each pillar (or just on features), by asking, "So what?"; this gives us a big list of benefits like *allocate resources to other business initiatives, drive a more efficient workforce*, and *thrive in changing landscapes*. There is going to be an overall **outcome** of using AWS, such as *save 14,600 hours per year with 99.99997 percent uptime*; and then there will be outcomes of using each of their features, such as *save 44 percent of your budget compared to using other solutions.*

With that understood, let's move on to filling this section in. Keep in mind that chapter seven will walk you through the filling-in process in greater detail. Some of the messaging for this section will come from VOC, but you may also use Voice of Product (VOP) and Voice of Sales (VOS) in this section. What's important is that you abandon messaging from a marketing playbook—nothing smooth, nothing slick. High-performing copy is about what the customer needs to hear, not what a creative director wants to say. Default to VOC. Listen to how your customers talk about the benefits they derive and what outcomes look like for them. Fill in VOC gaps with VOP and VOS.

Note that Beats 18 to 23 should all support one another and work together to create a convincing narrative about your product's value.

Beat 21: High Level Benefits

What benefits does your customer derive from using your solution? Think of these as soundbites, drawing people in rather than giving it all away. For example, easy onboarding, saves time, arrives fast, saves money, keeps kids busy without screens, simplifies integrations. Consider functional, social, and personal benefits.

Although the beat is called "High level benefits," in this beat you will also message what your product does to drive those benefits. If a high-level benefit is "saves time," then use VOC to write supporting copy about how it saves time. For example, the Basecamp product may have these three high level benefits:[19]

1. Organized teams.
2. Easy UI.
3. Never-annoying communication.

Basecamp fleshes these out like so:

1. Organized teams.

   VALUE: Hold everything and everyone in a tidy, predictably structured place.

   BENEFITS: Stay organized. Know who's doing what and who said what when. Hit deadlines because you always know what's due next. Never lose a file again. Keep people accountable so work gets done.

   FEATURES THAT CREATE BENEFITS/VALUE: Project page, To-dos, Schedule, Docs & Files, Reports, Timesheets

2. Easy UI.

   VALUE: Visual tools help you see where projects really stand.

   BENEFITS: Get ahead of delays by visualizing projects in six-week views. Instantly identify risk with red, yellow, and green dashboards. Pinpoint progress across a timeline.

   FEATURES THAT CREATE BENEFITS/VALUE: Lineup, Mission Control, Hill Charts

3. Never-annoying communication.

   VALUE: Keep work at work and conversations tied to projects.

   BENEFITS: Aggregate your notifications into a single menu, so you can stop looking everywhere from that lost message. Chat privately or in small groups.

   FEATURES THAT CREATE BENEFITS/VALUE: Hey, Pings

Beat 22: Value Pillars

Most brands have defined value pillars, or the core buckets of value that support the brand's value proposition, which are the sort of thing that gets written on the walls at HQ. In old school corporate docs, you'll often see this idea illustrated like so:

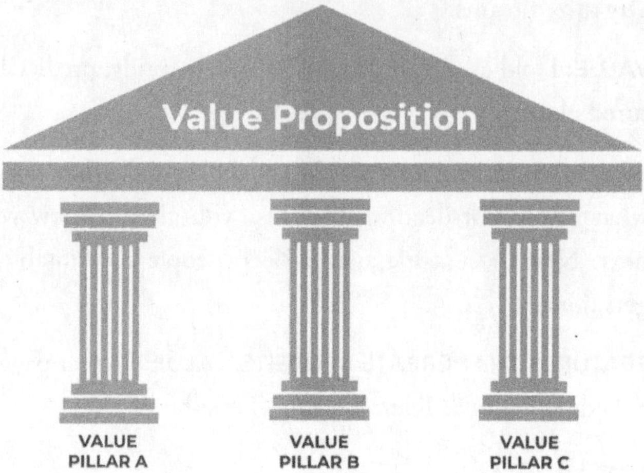

Your product, too, needs value pillars to support its value proposition and, in some cases, to support the brand-level value proposition. Value pillars are things like innovation, trust, value for money, scalability, ease of use, reliability, customer focus, and even very specific stuff, like developer first. They're based on and reinforced by features, systems, and sometimes people.

Consider AWS as a product of Amazon. Value pillars for AWS are scalability, security, and performance. A prevailing value pillar for Amazon (brand) is affordability. It makes sense, from a messaging perspective, that affordability would also be a value pillar for AWS because it is the product of a brand known for affordability.

These pillars work with your unique mechanism to help create differentiated outcomes.

A value pillar can underlie the brand and, by extension, the product. For example, if maximalist design underlies your brand, it may also underlie the product. A value pillar can underlie the product alone. For example, a luxury makeup brand introduces its first clean beauty concealer in compostable packaging; the value pillar for the product is eco consciousness, but that may not be a value pillar for the brand.

As always, your customers will tell you what your value pillars are. They will help you identify your value proposition based on those value pillars.

Beat 23: Differentiated Outcomes ("Unlike Ever Before")

When a prospect says yes to your solution, what will they now be able to do—unlike ever before? These are your differentiated outcomes. They come from differentiated features, built with unique outcomes, delivering desirable benefits.

The outcome is where your customer derives true value. The more differentiated your outcomes, the less desirable your competitors look. An outcome is a form of benefit, but it's different, and better, than a benefit because it is *lived* and *measured*. To illustrate:

- Tylenol's time release formula relieves tension headaches (benefit) in twenty minutes and continues to keep the headache away for eight hours (lived and measured outcome). Unlike ever before, you'll get back to life fast, knowing your headache won't interrupt you again.
- The Ginsu knife cuts through two hundred tin cans before it needs to be sharpened (lived and measured outcome). Unlike ever before, you can cut, chop, slice, dice anything and everything—without losing your edge.
- The Dreamcloud luxury hybrid core cools hot sleepers (benefit) by as much as 30 percent while reducing mattress movement by more than 90 percent (lived and measured outcome). Unlike ever before, you can fall asleep and stay asleep, right through the night.

Focus on the outcomes associated with your unique solution mechanism and value pillars. What outcomes can your customer expect from using your solution instead of the competition? What outcomes does your unique solution mechanism drive, including but not limited to eliminating the problem mechanism? It's on you to message these differentiated outcomes to be sure your customer is actually nodding along with you at this time—not clicking to open a new tab and searching for "alternatives to [your product name]."

Beat 24: Versus the Competition

Here we can answer this question: *"If it's so easy for you, why aren't all your competitors doing it?"* Maybe we already did answer that when sharing our unique solution mechanism. Great. Answer it again. But this time make it really clear why no competitors can do this or will do this like your product (mentioned by name at this point) does.

Is it cost prohibitive for others, but you have an exclusive deal with a supplier that allows you to provide this solution without charging more? Do you have a patent? Do you have a team of Swiss scientists in your back pocket? Is your factory next to a stream carved by arctic ice? Is your sommelier the only winemaker on the planet to have perfected this ratio of pinot noir and Cabernet Franc . . . because she is the sole descendant of a family of winemakers that goes back to fourteenth century France?

This beat is also a good moment to clear up any category confusion your brand or product may encounter if, to your persona or to someone who influences your persona, it seems to cross categories. You can distinguish your product or brand from a world of competitors by saying what it's not.

Take Lego for example. It's not a toy—it's Lego.

Or Ogilvy. It's not an agency—it's Ogilvy.

Jack Daniel's once ran an ad that went: *It's not scotch. It's not bourbon. It's Jack.*

Pro tip: You may want to use your competitor's name in your copy, and you may think that's a bad idea. It's only a bad idea if you're "smearing" the competition or telling falsehoods or exaggerations. In fact, the Federal Trade Commission, which is the group most American advertisers rightly live in fear of, actually encourages what they call "comparative advertising." (Visit them online at ftc.gov for details.) So you can mention your competitors by name. Just make sure it's truthful, accurate, and fair.

Beat 25: Proof of How ("The Promise")

You've heard of the why behind the why, or even the seven whys. This is the how behind the how—if you're the only CRM for creators, delivering differentiated value with X unique mechanism, it's time to share the how behind that mechanism and to prove it with:

- Video of the creation process,
- An image of the framed patent in your CPO's office, and/or

- Testimonials from people who've used the mechanism to realize value and achieve measurable outcomes.

Shipping in NYC water for your pizza dough is a cool, unique mechanism that can deliver differentiated value (social job to be done: I look like I know all the hippest trends, fellow kids!). Now let's dig into the *how* behind it. What happened that made your food scientist team realize NYC water was what made NYC pizza taste like no pizza anywhere else on the planet? Tell me that story. How did you ship in that water? Show me the extraction and freezing process. How did you get it approved to cross borders? How do you keep it fresh? Do you use any local water, or is there a perfect ratio of local to NYC water in your dough? Show me photos of the water arriving. Show me a video of the water sourcing system. Then show me real people taking a bite of that pizza and loving it. Prove the proof.

Connect the Persona with the Product

Thus far, we've avoided explicitly connecting the person we're talking to and the product we're talking about. We haven't said that this product is perfect for this person. For the next two beats, we do just that. We will leave no doubt that our product is made for our persona and that our persona is in the perfect position to buy our product.

Beat 26: Proof of Who

The best proof actually proves something. That's why you don't see any section on the message matrix that just reads "testimonials go here" or "now add your case studies." Proof has to prove a message or series of messages. And proof of who is all about proof that people *exactly like your persona* are successfully using your product.

Scrap any so-called proof that isn't directly provided by a person, or brand, that your customer identifies with. Use only (and lots of!) video testimonials, written testimonials, case studies, embedded user-generated content from social media, and even logo bars.

Because we're pushing hard to ensure the prospect sees themselves on the page, be careful of overlooking the seemingly little but actually very important things. Consider, for example, testing:

- The video testimonial thumbnail—does it look like our prospect?
- The photo alongside the written testimonial—is it big enough to clearly see the person who gave it?
- Whether logo bars for bigger—or smaller—brands impact results.

Ensure that the outcomes mentioned in testimonials and case studies are in keeping with the outcomes your customer seeks. If a testimonial speaks to how your product saves time but your customer is looking to save money and doesn't care about saving time, did your proof prove anything to your customer?

Beat 27: Uniquely Qualified

The actions our prospect has taken to this point uniquely qualify them to take the next action: buying our product. It's no mistake that they're here. Now turn the points that brought them here into reasons to buy, as if each thought they had and step they took was not accidental but was actually a milestone on the road to this moment, with this product.

This will seem silly, until you try it. What you do in this beat is effectively say, "You are uniquely qualified for this offer because you not only took X action, but instead of stopping there, you also did Y and Z." Then help them understand what that says about them. Reveal the hero. Remember, you are connecting the persona to the product here.

For example, if you're writing a sales email that goes out after a webinar to people who attended but did not buy during the webinar, you would want to express something like this:

> *You are uniquely qualified for this offer because you not only registered for the webinar but you also showed up for it live today. Consider all the steps that brought you here. You added it to your calendar, you made time in your day for it. These are not the steps of a person who's on the fence—these are the actions of a person who is ready to move*

forward. That you took these steps should tell you how important solving this problem really is. While others let these take-action, problem-solving moments come and go, your actions to date put you in the perfect position to move forward.

(Note that that is not copy. That's the message.)

MOST AWARE BEATS

We're at Most Aware! OMG! This is where money starts to happen! A Most Aware prospect needs to be tipped off the fence. The beats you're about to hit can happen in the usual channels—the emails, the SMS, the social chat, the website—but consider also unexpected channels. What about a lumpy mailer? What about a postcard campaign? Or just a good ol'-fashioned phone call?

Dimensionalize the Value

Earlier, you dimensionalized the Mega Mean Mouse. Now it's time to give your product, and the value it produces, its time in the spotlight. Dimensionalize the value.

Beat 28: Big Claims

Well-known brands that have been around a long time typically have big claims they can share to inspire confidence during closing. QuickBooks, for example, has long been the #1 accounting software in the world, a point that they can and do prove with objective third-party data. Big claims like that may not close a sale, but they can help move it along because they eliminate anxiety and increase confidence. After all, you don't usually get to be #1 by being hard to use, slow to load, glitchy, or lacking in features.

But what if you don't have any big claims? In Canada and the US, something called puffery is a legally protected way to make a big claim without objective support; for example, "The best profit and loss report ever," is understood at the time of writing to be puffery—it's subjective, opinion-based, un-testable, and unlikely to be interpreted by consumers as literal. A lot of big claims can fit under puffery. But claims like this cannot:

- Lose 30 lbs in 30 days
- Remove 100% of ground-in stains
- The cheapest and fastest
- Whitens teeth best

Those all require proof. I recommend that you think of all big claims as requiring proof, and opt not for puffery but rather for a more narrow big claim. For example, can you claim, and prove, anything that might better speak to your prospect, like the following:

- The #1 accounting software for florists making under $500,000 a year
- For florists with fewer than five employees, we're cheaper than QuickBooks Payroll
- 336 out of 400 florists tell us we're easier to use than QuickBooks

A big claim, and this beat, can be helpful during closing. However, of all 36 beats, this beat is the only one where I'd say, hey, if you've got nothing for this, move along. It can help close a sale, but its absence will not necessarily kill that sale.

Beat 29: Success Stories, with Risk Reversal

Success stories are not just for your prospect; they should also be easily shared with the people who help them make a decision. How deeply you dig into this beat depends on what you're selling and how important stories of success are for your prospect.

I recommend you share at least three fleshed-out success stories by this point in the customer journey. Ensure that each of those success stories so effectively speaks to the power of your solution that risk is neutralized or reversed; a compelling success story can neutralize the need for an expensive or lengthy refund policy.

Beat 30: Use Cases

One of my favorite survey questions is this: "Aside from [primary use case], how have you found yourself using [product name]?" When I was writing the Crazy Egg homepage test that beat the very strong control,[20] I used that question to develop a massive list of use cases.

Those use cases gave the prospect ideas for how they could use the product. Such a list can expand what is sometimes a narrow idea of the product. The use cases may not have brought your prospect to you, but they may help close them, particularly if your prospect is concerned that they will under-utilize your product and waste resources.

Here Are 30 Powerful Ways YOU Can Optimize Your Site's Usability & Conversion Rate During Your FREE 30 day Crazy Egg Trial...

- Discover "false bottoms" in your page design
- Know whether buttons are prominent enough
- Reorganize layouts to streamline UX
- Compare clicks before & after tweaks
- Generate new A/B test ideas
- See what style of banner ads get clicked
- Discover on-page distractions
- Know which messages to make prominent
- See how search traffic behaves on-site
- Reveal hotspots beyond the F-Pattern
- Make clickable elements easier to find
- Give HiPPOs proof of what's working or not
- Overhaul lead gen forms for different traffic
- Test if your visitors scroll beyond "the fold"
- Test if "one pager" designs work for your users
- Optimize for various screen resolutions
- Tweak your navigation copy
- Discover which graphics look disabled
- Make better sense of high bounce rates
- Inform user tests and further research
- Challenge "best practices" in design
- Replace or delete ignored content
- See if long-form sales pages get read
- Validate or question number for form fields
- Reveal anxieties about security or policies
- Compare clicks on buttons vs text links
- Learn whether users read or watch
- Determine if an image carousel gets views
- See what type of traffic is completing forms
- Be sure before you delete an element

Empower the Yes

As the advocate for and champion of your customer, you get to empower them to say yes to your solution, the absolutely right solution for them. Instead of thinking of this stage of the journey as closing or selling, remind yourself that you value and respect your customer—if your solution isn't right for them, they can stop paying attention at any moment, and if it is right for them, then it behooves you to ensure they don't walk away without it.

Avoid dodgy sales tactics by focusing on what they want, by eliminating their progress-preventing fears, and by finally separating them from the darkness of the problems they struggled with before they found you.

Beat 31: Goal Amplification

Remember back in Beats 1 through 9, when I said your customer loves to forget their problems and it's your job to remind them, because problems create customers? Well, customers also love to forget their original goals as they get closer to having to make a decision. So, in Most Aware, we will remind them of their goals the way that, the rest of the time, we remind them of their problems.

Here's an easy way to do this. It's a technique I learned from my friend Nathalie Lussier, founder of AccessAlly. Early in the customer journey, ask your prospect to state their goal in a form. Then pipe that goal verbatim into their contact details in your CRM. When it's time to message your prospect in this beat, dynamically populate their original goal in your emails or on your pages—or both—to let their former self re-inspire their current, fence-sitting self.

Beat 32: Risk & Uncertainty Reduction

You know about reducing risk with guarantees, trial periods, and refund policies. Those all belong here. I want to encourage you to add a **skin-in-the-game promise or guarantee**. This is a guarantee that proves, in real terms, how far you'll go to ensure your customer's success or happiness or both.

For example: "We guarantee you'll close enough business in the next thirty days that you'll be able to pay off your investment twice over. If not? We'll pay for four sessions for you to meet with our Presidents Club sales consultant, who will coach you through obstacles and challenges. We're so sure you will see results that we're happy to invest more than $2,000 if you don't. Because you will." Then add testimonials and data proof from those who have.

Be sure to match risk reducers to the biggest friction points at this stage for your prospect. If VOC tells you prospects are worried about a steep learning curve, now's the time to ensure they know about your academy, weekly live webinars, unlimited support, and three free calls with a trainer. If VOC shows they're afraid of a bait and switch, of being burned, of additional costs after the fact, of being abandoned once the sales process is over, message risk and uncertainty reducers that neutralize those fears.

Beat 33: Kill the Status Quo

Historical allegiance, or the habit of the present, is a powerful force that blocks change, as described by The Re-Wired Group in the popular Jobs to Be Done Forces of Progress diagram:

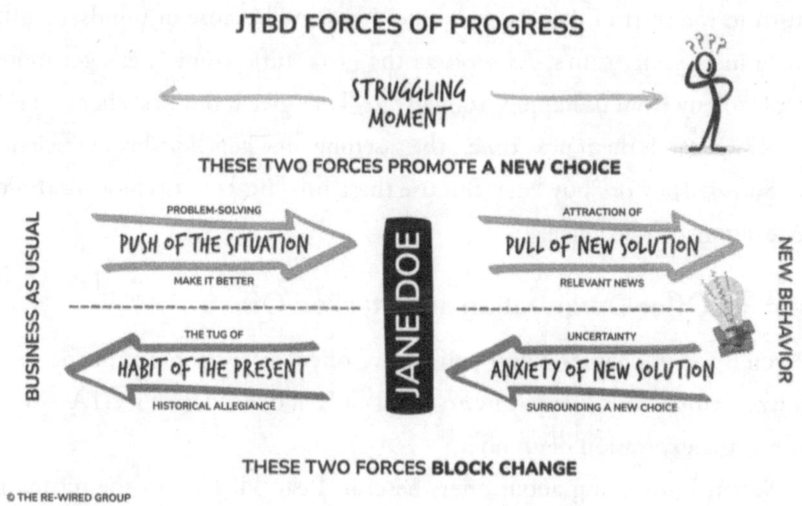

Earlier in the message matrix, we worked hard at picking a fight with the status quo, particularly in Beats 5 to 8, 12 to 17, and 24. Now, let's absolutely kill their historical allegiance. Repeat the most powerful messages from those earlier beats. Dig into the parts of your offer that make it easy to quit the old way, like migration services, contract buyouts, or anything that relieves sticky constraints.

*Buy or Bye-Bye**

Although we're architecting our assembly line to create customers on repeat, at scale, we know that some of the products are—wait for it—*lemons*. But just as Inspector Kurt Kroner at the Wolfsburg factory *fixed* every VW that turned out to be a lemon instead of tossing all two thousand pounds of it into a landfill, so do we continue to work on those people who do not turn into customers at the end of the line.

That's why "buy or bye-bye" comes with an asterisk. We want people to buy. But, if someone doesn't buy this time, they may buy next time or two years from now. We don't toss them out. There's no real "bye-bye" moment—just some retargeting, some segmentation, maybe some modified lead scoring.

However, I hesitate to suggest that this is the point at which they buy or return to the start of the assembly line. I hesitate because of mindset stuff. Not mine—your team's. As soon as the goal shifts from "Let's get more people to buy from us happily, sooner!" to "Let's give it our best shot and we can always catch them next time," the assembly line gets horribly inefficient.

So yes. They *can* buy later. But use these final beats to tip more of those fence-sitters off the fence.

Beat 34: Offer Optimization and Stacked Offers

As you'll see in chapter eight, you'll have offers at every point in the customer assembly line. Every time an email ends, it does so with a CTA—that CTA is the expression of an offer.

When I'm talking about offers here, in Beat 34, I mean the ultimate paid offer for the product you are moving your prospect to buy. This is when money confidently changes hands. In the solution design you will craft for copy that gets written at this stage, you should include your optimized offer as well as an offer stack, wherever possible.

And what, pray, is an offer stack? It's a revenue-boosting technique used constantly when selling courses and other digital products but which is used almost never when selling anything else. Offer stacking is the third and final weapon of mass copyselling in this chapter.

Weapon Three: Offer Stacking

Offer stacking is a technique where, immediately after a person has *just* bought something from you, you offer that new customer an additional, related product to buy. This offer is shown on a new page right after the first purchase is complete. It's an add-on, so the customer does not have to re-enter their payment information; the offer, if accepted, is billed to the card they just used in your system. The products on offer are directly related to the core offer the customer just said yes to, so you get to tap into the momentum they've built and make another sale, from the same customer, in the seducible moment that is post checkout.

You may know this technique as a post-order upsell. On its post-purchase pages, Instacart famously offers items you may have forgotten, which you can quickly add to cart, as well as recommendations for other products from other stores to add to your cart before the countdown timer runs out. Adding more products to cart post-purchase is a natural fit for ecommerce. SaaS is a little different. For SaaS, the stack is typically one or two of these secondary offers:

1. A done-for-you **setup offer** (e.g., book a call),
2. A monthly recurring **premium support offer** (e.g., $19/month), or
3. A **savings offer** to switch from monthly to yearly, or a two-year subscription plan.

You may have experienced an offer stack when checking out for a SaaS solution like SamCart or Typeset, each of which have seen massive growth under Brian Moran, their cofounder, thanks in part to his bold offer stacking strategies. SamCart's secondary offer stack is a done-for-you setup offer, where the SamCart success team will move your cart; this offer has resulted in additional revenue ranging from hundreds of dollars to as high as $20,000, to say nothing of the stickiness of retaining a customer who's set up for success with your product.

When Brian launched Typeset in 2024, he didn't use offer stacking, and the business grew well without it. But after nearly a year, its growth was on track to flatline around $1.5 million in annual recurring revenue (ARR). That's when Brian introduced this, his first stacked offer for Typeset: a monthly customer could save money by switching to an annual subscription or a two-year subscription.

(This isn't an unusual offer to make in SaaS. The legend Patrick McKenzie [patio11] has been touting the revenue-generating virtues of a save-with-annual email since he first stepped foot on a Microconf stage. The difference is that, with an offer stack, you put that optimized offer on the post-purchase page. Why? Why not wait? Because that post-purchase moment is a seducible moment, defined by Jared Spool as "the point in time when the user is most susceptible to being influenced–after they've achieved part of their goal, and before they move on to the next."[21] Dell taps into seducible moments by presenting financing options after you've built a PC and *before* you've checked out, while Airbnb, Expedia, Amazon, and other countless brands tap into revenue opportunities immediately *after* you've checked out. Pre-checkout is less ideal because an upsell offer could add a new friction point that can impede purchase.)

As a direct result of Brian's offer stack, Typeset went from $1.5 million ARR to $7 million ARR . . . within six months of implementation of the stack. How? It's not just about the uptake on the offer; it's what Brian can do with the revenue he receives on day one, instead of waiting month after month for more cash to dribble in. He reinvests it directly in ads. Typeset has gone from spending less than $100,000 a month on ads to more than $500,000 a month on ads, and from acquiring thirty users a day to 300. Each monthly subscription is offered an annual subscription in the post-purchase flow. And that's how Typeset found itself on track for $7 million ARR in six months.*

Offer stacking is an easy way to bring in more money faster, which can fund additional growth initiatives, customer advocacy initiatives, and great brand moments. If you're in SaaS, offer stacking is a particularly big opportunity, as it's so rarely done. Optimize your pricing plans and the page they're on. Get started with any of these offer stack formulas.

Primary offer: Core software on any monthly plan

- Secondary offer A: Weekly strategy calls for 60 days
- Secondary offer B: Switch to annual and save

Primary offer: Core software on any annual plan

- Secondary offer A: A year's access to a private community of practitioners
- Secondary offer B: Add a second year and save even more

Primary offer: Core software on Pro/Mid-Tier plan

- Secondary offer A: Add 20+ pre-built templates
- Secondary offer B: Book a call to see if you can save (and get) more on Enterprise

* Huge shout-out to Brian Moran for sharing his offer stacking story with me in detail.

Primary offer: Core software on any monthly plan

- Secondary offer A: Done-for-you setup, including ~~5~~ 10 integrations
- Secondary offer B: Free complementary software when you switch to annual

I'm going to break a cardinal publishing rule and invite you to stop reading now. Leave the book, audiobook, or ereader open, of course, but go make a note to yourself: *Create and execute a project to add offer stacks to all post-purchase flows.*

When it is time to present your offer to your perfectly primed prospect, don't miss out on additional revenue opportunities. Craft a one- or two-page post-purchase offer stack.

Beat 35: Leadership Horizon/Future Proofing

Your customer has been burned before. Let's give them a vision of not only a solved problem and an easier life but also of the company they're buying into. How is your brand advocating for the persona and/or the tribes to which they belong? Are you leading their tribe? Get them excited about it. What events are you speaking at, what panels will your leadership be on, when is their book coming out, what's their Netflix show called? How are you protected against the threats of wars, AI, pandemics, or larger, disruptive competition?

Prove to your prospect that you are future proofed so that their investment and growing allegiance to your brand are also future proofed.

Beat 36: Coaching Decisiveness

Our greatest competition is not a rival but indecision. Anywhere from 40 to 60 percent of qualified sales opportunities end with no decision.[22] Did you already know that? Cool, what are you doing about it?

If you visualize the customer assembly line, you can see a huge number of incomplete customers stacking up at the end of it—not falling off, and not ready to finish it. It may feel like we should leave the door wide open, let them sit in indecision for a while, they know where to find us when they're ready! And you can absolutely do that, if that's your strategy. This beat, inspired by my friend and copywriter Ry Schwartz, asks us instead to encourage a yes or a no. We do so by:

- **Naming the stakes of inaction.** Express the opportunity cost. Answer the question for them, "What happens if nothing changes?"
- **Normalizing decision making.** Message that they are uniquely qualified to move forward with this offer at this time, with phrasing like, "Most [persona] who [X quality] decide to [action] on a [today's day]." Such as, *Most new moms who attend our workshop live decide to join our community on the following Thursday.* Or take a chance with a very pointed email subject line like this: "I, %FULLNAME%, hereby reject this offer."
- **Making the action tiny and easy.** If you have a trial, message that they're saying a mini-yes by taking you up on this trial—that they're not committed. Commitment is scary. If you have a money-back guarantee, message that the onus is on your solution to prove its value—the only thing they need to do is say yes now. The rest is up to you!
- **Messaging the swiftness of knowing.** Will they know within five minutes of using your solution whether they'll stay with it or bail? Can you give them a rubric for identifying if your product is perfect for them within the first ninety seconds or ninety minutes or even ninety days? Can you name the rubric, give it a ™, and use it throughout their customer onboarding process so they're always in a state of reduced risk and anxiety?

My team and I have created and published example beat sheets online. Check them out to get a sense for how these matrices work across products and customers globally.

You're now fully introduced to the 36 beats of the customer assembly line. Next, we'll start filling in the message matrix using VOC, VOS, and other data from reliable sources.

GET SAMPLE BEAT SHEETS

We've created example beat sheets for a range of products and segments. Find them at copysellingbook.com

HOW, THEN WHAT

The Listening phase helps us populate a message matrix with "how" language. As in, how do customers, prospects, visitors, etc. talk about the subject of this beat, in their actual words, and how might we talk about it in our copy? On the message matrix spreadsheet, you'll paste interesting snippets of qualitative data into cells in the "how" column, adding more cells as you need them.

For example, let's say you're selling project management software for small businesses. In a customer review online, you see this line: *"It feels like all the task managers are made for certified PMMs and everyone out there is building in advanced management features when all business owners need is a way to organize tasks inside projects and assign people and deadlines."*

Because that's VOC data, it will go in the "how" column in your message matrix. But what is the right beat in which to organize it? Start by reading through each beat, from the top. And know that a line of VOC can live in multiple beats; know also that you may later realize that a line of VOC doesn't belong where you put it, and it's okay to delete it or move it.

Reading from the top, you realize the line of VOC could be a core problem match, so you paste it under How in *Beat 1: Core problem match* and keep reading down the list of beats. The next good fit is *Beat 14: Competitors all focus on X (the old way)*, so you paste it under How there, too. It doesn't seem to fit anywhere else, so you're done and ready to move onto the next line of VOC. Perfect.

When you've filled several cells in the "how" column, you may be ready to move to the "what" column. "What" is where a brand-level message for a beat will live. You develop this message using everything in the "how" column. Think of this as a more typical marketing message—it's a succinct statement that summarizes the message behind the raw data in the "how" column.

To use the project management software for small businesses example, let's say under *Beat 14: Competitors all focus on X (the old way)*, you also added the following lines of VOC under "how":

> *"I was using a really popular PM tool until it occurred to me that I only kept one view open—my task view with deadlines. I'd check them off and move on. So I canceled that bloated tool and just started using a checklist."*

> *"I never once used the reporting view. Who am I gonna report to? There are three of us on the team."*

Alone, with your team, or with AI, you'll workshop a powerful message that underlies all the VOC in Beat 14, and you'll put that in the "what" cell. When I workshopped this with ChatGPT, here's the line we came up with in about thirty-seven seconds:

> *Competitors all focus on adding features, like advanced reporting, that small business owners don't need.*

Now you have both what to say and how to say it for *Beat 14: Competitors all focus on X (the old way).* You'll repeat that process across all the beats.

CHAPTER RECAP

The 36 Beats

- ✓ The message matrix is made up of 36 beats, with nine beats per stage of awareness, that work together to transform a prospect into a customer.
- ✓ A prospect moves through all 36 beats to become a customer; you cannot pick and choose which beat you'd like to start messaging at (it always depends on where your One Reader is).
- ✓ Three weapons of mass copyselling are the Mega Mean Mouse, unique mechanisms, and offer stacking.

PART II
Applying the Copyselling System

CHAPTER 5
Identifying Constraints

"Any improvement not made at the constraint is an illusion."

Eliyahu M. Goldratt, developer of the Theory of Constraints management methodology

A marketer's ideal world is one in which a funnel looks like a cylinder: every lead that goes in the top of it comes out the bottom. If I get one hundred leads, all one hundred leads convert into paying customers. Perfect.

That is, of course, not the reality. That's why we have funnels in marketing—one hundred leads go in, many drop off along the way, maybe ten come out the bottom as paying customers. *Funnel.*

I like the assembly line metaphor for customer creation partly because it looks something like a curving pipe, where you can visualize clogs—particularly if you, like I, grew up watching a lot of TV with ads for products like Drano. Thanks to ad execs, I can easily visualize a pipe under a sink. I can visualize a clog in that pipe. And I can visualize a solution like Drano clearing that clog. *Constraint.*

The clog in the pipe is the constraint. The neck in the bottle is the constraint. The cinch that creates a funnel out of a cylinder is the constraint. We have to identify the constraint before we can relieve it. But first, here's where this whole constraint-relief idea comes from.

THE THEORY OF CONSTRAINTS

In 1984, Mr. Eliyahu Moshe Goldratt published a business novel (that's a thing) called *The Goal.* It's the story of a factory manager named Alex who is trying to save his factory from closing down. He's dealing with chronic delays, big expenses, and low productivity—those are the *symptoms* of a malfunctioning system. Just a few months before Alex's business will be shut down, a mentor named Jonah swoops in to teach him "the goal" and how to achieve it. Basically, Jonah teaches him the theory of constraints.

Jonah says the goal of business is to make money. Everything should serve that goal. A constraint impedes that goal.

With Jonah's help, Alex identifies two constraints to his factory's output: a machine called the NCX-10 and a machine used in heat treatment. With the constraints identified, Alex can relieve them (or as Goldratt calls it, *exploit* them). Once they're relieved, though, new constraints appear. This is normal. Alex's job is to continually improve the system by relieving constraints and then identifying new ones. Once the biggest constraints are relieved—spoiler alert—the factory is saved.

There are probably a lot of ways to save a dying factory. But if you think in systems, the theory of constraints Goldratt offers us will likely sit well with you.

We can see that a systems approach to problem solving increases the likelihood of solving an actual problem. Instead of pointing fingers, relying on what worked for so-and-so at their last company, or the dreaded Guesswork Trap, we objectively assess the assembly line, spot where the in-progress customers are stacking up or falling off, and fix the problem. It's efficient.

The theory of constraints allows us to increase profitability, shorten sales cycles, and gain control over an otherwise chaotic world of marketing. It focuses us on throughput—on getting more people through the funnel and into our customer database—which means we marketers bring more money in. Even marketers who don't believe their job is to directly generate revenue love the slide that shows how much money their efforts have generated.

IDENTIFYING CONSTRAINTS AND MAXIMIZING REVENUE

Roles like data analysts and tools like Google Analytics (GA) exist to, among other things, help growth leaders identify constraints on the digital assembly line. In conversion rate optimization (CRO), we use a variety of mechanisms to identify constraints.

One such mechanism is a funnel analysis in GA. The funnel view shows us conversion rates at each stage in a funnel, from landing page visit to product page visit to add-to-cart to checkout to completed purchase. The GA funnel report shows us the conversion rate and drop off at each stage in a funnel. The stage with the *highest drop-off* is likely to be the first constraint you should address in CRO for that funnel. So if, in a thirty-day period, you were to get ten thousand visitors to your landing page . . . and a thousand visitors (10 percent) continued to your product page . . . and 400 visitors (40 percent) added your product to cart . . . and 200 visitors (50 percent) completed the first page of checkout . . . and seventy visitors (35 percent) completed purchases, you'd likely identify two key constraints to growth in your business.

The first: with a 0.7 percent conversion rate overall, this funnel is underperforming against industry benchmarks (which hover, at this time, around 1 percent) and is, in itself, a constraint to the business's growth. **The**

second: with a 90 percent drop-off from landing page to product page, the first constraint to relieve in this funnel is the landing page.

The constraint identification step in the copyselling system does not require that you dig into the constraint itself. You don't yet have to ask what's going on on the landing page, what could be the problem with traffic driving to it, or any other such questions. You'll form those questions during your hypothesis development when completing your solution design. That's when you conduct heuristic analyses of the assets and dig deeper into the data.

The only thing we need to do during constraint identification is—quite simply—identify the most pressing growth constraint to relieve.

A TECHNIQUE FOR PRIORITIZING CONSTRAINTS TO RELIEVE

A popular contemporary marketer, Alex Hormozi, teaches a great model for entrepreneurs to prioritize what to work on: *More, Better, New.* The idea is that, to grow, you should prioritize your work by first identifying what works and doing *more* of that; then identifying what works and doing that *better*; and finally—only when you can't do more of a good thing or make that good thing better—you try something *new.* Although this model is taught to entrepreneurs, I find it applies at all levels in an organization and in almost every role. I use it daily.

For most of this book, I have focused on optimizing an existing asset or funnel—the *better* in the *More, Better, New* model. But copyselling also applies to doing more of a good thing and creating new things from scratch.

More

If you have a demo funnel in place, and that demo funnel is working like gangbusters, then you may identify that a constraint to growth is simply not getting enough people into that demo funnel—you need more traffic (*more*) in the funnel. If a particular style of abandoned cart emails has been working well for one category in your product lineup, apply that style to the abandoned cart emails for more categories (*more*) in your product lineup.

Better

If you have a demo funnel in place, and that demo funnel is working, but it's not working like gangbusters yet, then you may identify that a constraint to growth is that it needs to work *better.* It's a good thing. It could be great. So make it better.

New

Newer businesses will find that their biggest constraints to growth are simply not having certain funnels or assets in place; they need an evergreen webinar funnel (*new*), a nurturing email sequence (*new*), or ads (*new*). Sales-driven product companies switching to or integrating product-led growth (PLG) will find that a lack of lifecycle emails (*new*) is directly impeding their growth.

If you have a whole bunch of ideas, follow the *More, Better, New* model to help you prioritize all of your options. Start by doing more of what's working; then make what's working work better; and finally, when you've exhausted *more* and *better*, try *new* things.

MECHANISMS FOR CONSTRAINT IDENTIFICATION

Across every funnel, we use key performance indicators (KPIs) to spot constraints. At the full funnel level, low conversion rates signal a funnel problem; discrepancies between acquisition costs (CAC) and lifetime value (LTV) can signal problems with product lineup or retention; and high engagement but low revenue can signal problems with product–market fit or monetization strategies in general.

At the top of the funnel, KPIs to watch are low click-through rate (CTR), high bounce rate, high exit rate, low engagement rate, low branded search volume, and high cost per click (CPC) in ad spend. **In the middle of the funnel**, KPIs to watch are low CTR, low time on page, low time on site, and high scroll depth abandonment (i.e., people don't make it down the page). **And at the bottom of the funnel**, watch for high cart abandonment rates, low CTRs for abandoned cart emails, high pricing page exit rates, and low CTRs for sales emails.

Of course, you don't have to do any of this on your own. You can create a project in your preferred AI platform and add monthly analytics or performance reports to the project, then prompt AI to help you identify constraints by finding patterns across KPIs in a single period or over time. I like to work with AI to analyze exit intent pop-up responses/exit survey responses; customer relationship manager (CRM) reports showing opens, clicks, and complaints; attribution and path analyses from ad platforms, CRMs, or tools like Segment; transcripts from user tests, like those on Wynter or UserTesting.com; and performance audits showing page speed, like load time and technical errors. There's also good ol'-fashioned *looking at the thing.*

Let's Finish with an Example

Suppose you're a lifecycle marketer, and one of the assets you're in charge of is a trial-to-paid nurturing sequence for a fourteen-day trial. You open the sequence in your CRM and run a cohort report. You spot something curious: for a cohort that started their trial in the second week of October, trial users converted to paid not on the usual day fourteen of their trial but on days three and four. Why would they pay so early in their trial? The flipside: why aren't others paying early in the trial? Could be a constraint!

You hop into GA to cross-reference traffic sources for trial starts in the second week of October, in case a particularly influential but unusual referral source is to credit, but everything looks unremarkable.

Over lunch, you mention this anomaly to your coworker, who reminds you that the demand gen team ran a webinar the week in question. The webinar was a one-off, so they didn't set up a unique email flow for webinar attendees—they sent all trial starts into *your* trial-to-paid email sequence. Now you have a list of at least four possible constraints.

1. Webinar converts users to paid effectively (good) but does not actually prompt them to pay during the webinar (constraint).
2. Webinar converts users to paid effectively (good) but sends them into a generic trial-to-paid email flow (constraint).
3. Webinar converts users to paid effectively (good) but ran only one time (constraint).
4. Generic trial-to-paid email flow converts a small percentage of people on day three (good) but could convert more people earlier in the trial period (constraint).

You share the webinar-specific constraints with the demand-gen team. That leaves you, the lifecycle marketer, to relieve the fourth constraint: converting *more* people earlier in the trial period.

As you move into heuristic analysis of the existing flow and hypothesis development, you may find yourself wondering why the webinar converted people so successfully. That may show you that the webinar took more time moving people through the stages of awareness—through everything on the message matrix—such that webinar attendees were in Most Aware when they started receiving *your* trial-to-paid sequence. The emails you have may not be the constraint; the non-existent emails that need to come before those emails may be the constraint.

CHAPTER RECAP

Identifying constraints

- ✓ Using a systems approach to customer creation, we identify a growth constraint so we can then relieve it.
- ✓ Data will show you where constraints exist in your marketing generally and funnel specifically. Use AI as your thought partner to help you understand the data and see the opportunities you may be missing.
- ✓ Abandonment and drop-off are clear signals that a constraint exists.
- ✓ Use *More, Better, New* to prioritize constraints.
- ✓ Remember to *look at the thing*—use what you know across data sources and even within your team to spot and prioritize constraints.

CHAPTER 6
Listening

"If you don't listen to your customers someone else will."

Sam Walton, founder of Walmart

The listening phase is always on. As marketers, we're always listening; as AI-powered marketers, we're always listening and using AI to help us make sense of what we're hearing. Your team never stops listening to leads and customers (and updating each message matrix with the most interesting stuff you hear). Listening is never done.

Two notes as you begin listening. The first, slow down and take your time. Although you can luck into hearing the perfect VOC for that next landing page hook, and that can make you think everything in the *Listening* phase moves fast, recognize that it was luck. Take your time.

Second note: don't refer to this work as "research." Vast masses of resources vanish in what orgs call *research*. Listening looks a lot like research, but it's actually listening *in order to develop messages.* Listening is the most efficient form of message development. It is more efficient to interview a customer for an hour than it is to brainstorm for an hour. It is more efficient to pore over three thousand lines of survey responses for eight hours than it is to spend eight hours fiddling with tools you think *might* get you there.

You can listen via interviewing. Now valued at $1.6 billion, Vanta unlocked their product value proposition—automating SOC 2 for startups—only after they interviewed founders, engineers, and sales teams to discover their pain.[23] And thousands of companies, from Snickers to Toyota, have used Jobs to Be Done interviewing to drive product and messaging revelations.

You can listen via ethical eavesdropping, or mining online groups. Now valued at $3.2 billion, Retool mined LinkedIn groups to discover that their assumed ICP (i.e., FileMaker devs) was wrong and that their actual ICP was frontend/backend engineers at large enterprises needing internal tool solutions.[24]

In this section of the book, we'll focus on my three favorite listening techniques for finding copy that sells: confirmation page surveys, online mining, and sales call reviews.

WHAT LISTENING REVEALS

Voice of customer (VOC) data can tell us, in our customers' own words, everything they did, heard, and thought about along the customer journey. As you'll see in these next three chapters, customers (and prospects) will give you *everything* you need to fill in a message matrix.

- What core problem first set them looking for a solution like ours (Early Pain Aware);
- When they most sharply felt each problem (Early Pain Aware);
- How each problem manifested in their lives (Moment of Highest Tension);
- Who noticed they were experiencing the problem (Mid to Late Pain Aware);

- Who tried to help them solve the problem (Late Pain Aware into Early Solution Aware)
- What they did first to try to fix the problem (Early Solution Aware);
- Why they did that (Early Solution Aware);
- How that solution did or did not work (Early Solution Aware);
- What they did next to try to fix the problem (Solution Aware);
- When they backtracked or gave up (Mid Solution Aware);
- What or who brought them back to seeking a solution (Mid Solution Aware);
- What they liked and disliked about each solution they considered (Late Solution Aware);
- What their early reaction was to seeing our product (Early Product Aware);
- The dreamstate they desired our product to give them (Early Product Aware);
- What they learned wasn't true about our product (Mid Product Aware);
- What they were surprised to learn about our product (Mid Product Aware);
- The product differentiators that mattered most to them during consideration (Mid Product Aware);
- What drove them to start to use our product or a version of it (Mid Product Aware);
- Their first use experience (Mid to Late Product Aware);
- What they used it for first (Late Product Aware);
- How the product worked for them in general (Late Product Aware);
- What or who got in the way of using the product (Late Product Aware);
- How long it took them to derive value from our product (Late Product Aware);
- Their most common use cases (Late Product Aware);
- Their process for choosing a paid or upgraded product (Mid Most Aware);

- What or who got in the way of paying or upgrading (Mid Most Aware); and even
- When they announced they were using our product and to whom (Late Most Aware).

You'll hear what nearly got in the way of a conversion; the jobs your prospect is hiring your product to do; the precursors that need to be in place for a conversion to be possible. You'll hear if you actually need to optimize your offer, or if you just need to make it easier for your leads to communicate your value proposition to other decision makers. And of course, the real gold here is that you'll hear what message to put where in order to add more leads to your assembly line and keep them moving along efficiently.

ALWAYS START WITH QUALITATIVE DATA

My friend Els Aerts is an absolute conversion rate optimization (CRO) celebrity who focuses on user research. I was lucky to go on stage after she spoke at a CRO event; my oh my, did she warm that audience up! She gets on stage, and she asks the audience two questions.

"Who here prefers quantitative data over qualitative?"

There's a show of hands. Lots of people.

"Why?"

Someone tries to shout out an answer, and she stops them short. *"Ut tut tut! Answer in numbers only please."* The house goes wild.

Although we're not talking about research in the *Listening* phase, we are talking about qualitative VOC data, which helps us complete the How column on our message matrix. When we listen, we'll learn the *why* that drives everything our prospects do. Let's start with my favorite quick win method of listening: a confirmation page survey.

THE CONFIRMATION PAGE SURVEY

Over the last twenty years, I've refined one question that helps draw useful VOC data from leads and customers immediately after they've become a lead or a customer. I call this question *The Bridge*. It gets embedded on your confirmation, or thank-you, pages. And it goes exactly like this: What was going on in your life that brought you to ______ today?

The ______ (blank) is filled with what the lead or customer just did. You fill the blank when you're setting up the survey. Examples include:

- What was going on in your life that brought you to download this ebook today?
- What was going on in your life that brought you to want to lose weight today?
- What was going on in your life that brought you to join this Slack team today?
- What was going on in your life that brought you to start managing your team's projects with Asana today?
- What was going on in your life that brought you to order from StockX today?
- What was going on in your life that brought you to buy Kentucky bluegrass seed today?

I've intentionally selected each word in The Bridge. I'm telling you this because I've seen people go "Cool, Jo, so just ask people why they bought?" and then I have to book in with my therapist and it all gets very messy and expensive. You're not asking, *"Why did you buy ______?"* You're asking, *"What was going on in your life that brought you to ______ today?"* The only thing you should iterate on is what goes in that blank.

Crafting Your Question

As always, take a little extra time to fill in the blank for The Bridge in a way that will elicit the most useful responses. I like to engage an internal team of testers—people who play the part of the persona and answer the question as that persona might. By testing your question before publishing your survey, you increase your chances of getting useful responses.

Let's say that you're part of the growth team at David's Bridal. You're completing a message matrix for this persona: *mother of the bride*. The

Bridge will help you identify what mothers of the bride are looking for when dress shopping. So on the post-purchase confirmation page for any purchase in the category "mother of the bride," you embed The Bridge. But that blank in the question means you have a choice of ways you could ask The Bridge. The most obvious:

What was going on in your life that brought
you to David's Bridal today?

You set up this survey. But before you publish it, you get a team of testers to answer it for you first. They answer with things like the very literal "I was on my phone," and the more useful "I needed a dress for my daughter's wedding." K, you already knew that. In the tester responses, you don't see any fresh language or insights to use for a more compelling page. So you try again:

What was going on in your life that brought you to
choose the dress you purchased today?

Okay, perhaps better. Your testers reply with things like "It was the right price," or "It was in the right color." If you publish this question, perhaps someone will write something interesting. But are the answers worth the effort? After all, a post-purchase page could instead be an offer stack; you could be selling a matching trenchcoat or hat or pair of shoes or all of the above, but you're asking this question. So you try again:

What was going on in your life that brought you to
buy your dress at David's Bridal today?

This question elicits a variety of answers. Some testers lean on the "buy" part, telling you why they bought today instead of *browsing* today. Others pick up on the "at David's Bridal" and tell you why David's Bridal versus somewhere else. And others focus on the "going on in your life" part, telling you that they bought their dress here today *because the bride decided at the last minute to have a destination wedding and the dress that our fine customer had already bought for a Winnipeg church wedding can't be returned and will be horrible in Cancún's humidity so she needed something lightweight and affordable that shipped immediately.*

The way you fill that blank in The Bridge's structure will shape the quality of responses you get. Before you publish a survey, test it internally. And refine or replace it as you collect responses. Remember: this is a listening exercise, not hard-nosed research. If you have to change a survey question midway through collecting data, that's not the end of the world—as long as you don't report on your results in a quantitative way.

What the Bridge Reveals

The Bridge gives you pure VOC that you transfer directly onto your message matrix. I've seen responses to this question fill in almost all of the first twenty beats on the message matrix.

You'll learn core problems: the more frequently you see a message, the more likely it is to be a core problem. You'll see moments of highest tension brought to life in your customers' own words. They'll tell you their dream-state. They'll tell you about solutions that have failed them. They'll tell you about their lives and who participates in their decision making. And they'll also share stuff that can give you a sense for the sort of voice and tone you may wish to use; for example, when we asked new customers what was going on in their lives that brought them to join Copy School today, here's one reply:

> *Groping in the dark of uneducated purgatory destined to be chained to low wages and toxic work environments, yet unwilling to surrender, to the perils of loserdom . . .*

Now, we haven't yet used that VOC in our copy. But its value is that it shone a light on the possibility that we could push a little further with our brand voice, which we did successfully from then on.

Today, we have thousands of responses to that question, all from new Copy School students. And, with those, we've been able to continually update both our *What* and *How* columns almost across the entire Copy

School message matrix for each of our four core personas: the Struggler, the Skill Builder, the Career Optimizer, and the Results Generator. Because we hire freelancers and agencies, we're able to hand those matrices off to others, and they know what to say, how to say it, when and where in the journey.

You Do Not Have to Run the Bridge Eternally

A confirmation page is a terrible thing to waste. It's the perfect seducible moment, which is a point in time when the user, lead, or customer "is most susceptible to being influenced—after they've achieved part of their goal, and before they move on to the next."[25] They've just said yes to you. They're feeling successful, they don't have another high-priority task on their immediate list, and they're looking for "what's next." So we want to use this moment very well, forever.

You can turn off The Bridge on a confirmation page and turn on a new one-question survey. Whatever you're asking, be sure it helps you listen—not just "do research." So look at gaps on your message matrix, and ask questions that help you fill those gaps.

REVIEW MINING

Early in my career, I worked with a SaaS brand on identifying their value proposition, which we were testing as their homepage headline. We'd used all the frameworks, formulas, and tricks of the trade to find that value proposition. We had a scorecard. We'd run audits. Nothing was working. Our headlines tested flat, with neither a lift nor a drop in conversion and without a hope of reaching confidence. We were doing everything right, except the obvious thing: we were sitting around dreaming up value propositions instead of listening to customers and swiping their language.

Slightly desperate, I started poring over their testimonials page. Buried in a testimonial was this line:

"[Brand name] helped us eliminate 99% of paper files."

The next day, we launched a new homepage headline test with this headline:

Eliminate 99% of paper files.

Two weeks later, we had a statistically significant winner on our hands. We'd increased clicks to the next page, a conversion page, by 103.7 percent.[†]

How to Find Messaging Gold

Review mining is the process of digging into unbiased voice-of-customer data that's available online. The term review mining covers mining:

- Online reviews, like product reviews left on Amazon product pages;
- Online comments, like those at the ends of articles and videos;
- Online threads, like subreddits;
- Collected testimonials that have not been edited, like those on Reviews.io; and
- All the other forms of reliable sharing your leads and prospects do online.

Now, it wouldn't take more than a few seconds to come up with a giant list of problems with the idea of mining online comments and reviews to find unbiased VOC. You may be thinking, *But people get paid to leave fake reviews of their product online.* Or, *But people get paid to leave fake reviews of competitor products online.* Or, *But people get compensated for trying a product and leaving a review online, and that review is typically glowing even if the product didn't earn it.* Or, *Wow, there's a lot of junk online.*

And you're right! But there's also a ton of gold out there. I'll share an example pronto. But first, here's another problem that you may not have spotted yet: When you're mining reviews, you don't know who left the

† With statistical confidence of 98.9 percent achieved over a three-week online experiment, we increased clicks from the homepage to the key conversion page (i.e., plans and pricing).

review. Are they the sort of people you'd target? What segment are they in? Which message matrix should their data be pasted into? You can answer none of those questions!

So what should you do? Keep the data separate. Paste review snippets into a message matrix, and change the color of those snippets. That will help you capture the potential VOC without muddying the waters.

Why Review Mining Is Great Even If It's Imperfect

With review mining, I've surfaced messages that then turned into high-performing copy for ecommerce, SaaS, and services countless times. I include review mining in every project I take on.

For example, a conversion consultancy engaged me to help their client—a rehabilitation center—get more leads on their website. We started by optimizing the homepage. I went off to collect VOC data. But I couldn't do surveys or interviews because of the dramatic nature of the transformation of a person when they go into and come out of rehab. I was worried that if I talked to someone after they left rehab, I might somehow say something that could possibly send them reeling back.

So I decided to look at reviews on Amazon for books about addiction and recovery. The way I saw it, people hire a book to do the job they would hire a treatment center to do: help me or a loved one survive addiction. So, book reviews could give me insights into what people want, and may or may not get, from addiction and recovery solutions.

I found seven books about addiction and recovery, each with a few hundred reviews. Then I pored over those reviews, one by one. In one of the reviews, I came upon this phrase:

> ". . . but if you think you need rehab, you probably do."

I swiped that language verbatim. (Later in this chapter, I'll explain why a phrase like that stood out to me.) And here's what happened. We tested three homepage headlines against the control. One variation was a data proof point; another was a testimonial in quotes; and the third was this review-based headline:

If you think you need rehab, you do.

For fun, and because we're nerdy, the consultants, the clients, and I took bets on which variation would win. No one bet on the review-based headline. And as you can guess, yes, it was the winner. It produced unbelievable results. Not only did it increase homepage clicks by 400 percent, but it also saw 26 percent more lead forms submitted. And the lead form was *on the next page*. Which means that the headline was so powerful it managed to get people not only to click, but also to fill in a form down funnel. With statistical confidence.

There's gold out there. So stick with me. There are two paths you can take when mining to find your message; they are passive mining and active mining.

Passive Review Mining

Analyze what customers wrote at some random moment in history using passive review mining.

Yelp, Amazon, Sephora, and TripAdvisor all have more reviews than we can fathom. There's no good data showing what percentage of reviews can and cannot be trusted, so let's assume that approximately 10 percent of all online reviews are fake or embellished. That means somewhere in the vicinity of 90 percent of those millions of reviews may be trustworthy. Not perfect. But not hot garbage either.

When I'm mining reviews, I'm looking for two things. The first, what drives people to choose a solution or to switch solutions. And the second, what they desire most or wish for.

For years, I would open up Amazon on one screen and a spreadsheet on the other. I would block hours to read each review. Over the years, I learned to filter out five-star and one-star reviews. I learned to look for big, meaty reviews. I learned to eliminate any polished-sounding reviews, those that used the product name in Title Case (especially if the name is three or more words long) and those that appeared to be keyword stuffed.

And then along came Shane O'Quinn. He took my training, loved it, and decided to simplify my life as a thank you. He sent me this formula and told me that, the next time I wanted to go review mining, I should instead type it into my Google search bar:

site:website.com intitle: "category" "tired of"

All I had to do was replace 1) website.com with the actual dot-com I wanted to search and 2) the word category with the actual category of the product I was trying to mine reviews for. So if I was mining to find what people hate about yoga studios, I would enter:

site:yelp.com intitle: "yoga studios" "tired of"

I tried it. And I got three results pages filled with reviews, from Yelp, for yoga studios, that included the phrase "tired of." Here are a few.

I was really tired of going into gyms and participating in a supposed "yoga" class.

I joined because I was tired of paying excessive annual memberships to spend three hours a week on a cardio machine.

I had gotten away from yoga because I was tired of huge classes at clubs and gyms, noise at rec centers, pricey drop-in costs, etc.

In the same formula, I then replaced "tired of" with other phrases that speak to problem situations, such as "scared of" and "worried about." And boom! So many phrases pulled directly from online reviews. Some of those phrases were gold and belonged in the How column of a message matrix. We can use a similar formula to find what people desire most or wish for:

site:website.com intitle: "category" "really want"

The phrase "really want" typically appears in reviews and comments about what a person desires, in a way that phrases like "desire most," "desire," "want," and "want most" do not. I search this:

site:yelp.com intitle: "yoga studios" "really want"

And I get results like these:

really want to learn the poses and get comfortable first. I'm not one who likes to jump into things because of trend.

For people who really want to understand not just large but also small and incredibly important details of poses, Jay is kind of like Buddha.

really want to improve core strength. I've done weightlifting, yoga, cycling, and now I can cross Pilates off my list too.

Although this formula is imperfect, and review mining too is imperfect, what I've found is that the review mining exercise absolutely helps you surface messages you wouldn't otherwise find, and high quantities of them. Be sure to experiment with variations on the formula.

Active Review Mining

You don't have to wait around for random people to talk about their problems, your category, your competitors, or your solution to mine for reviews. Instead, seed a targeted conversation in a subreddit. This allows you to better target audiences that may match yours (i.e., a proxy for your customer) and to hear richer stories you can mine for copy that sticks. Just be careful not to overuse this method of VOC collection as the Reddit community is not terribly forgiving.

Start by identifying the messaging gap you want to fill. Is it a beat on your message matrix? Is it a way to optimize your offer on your solution design (chapter eight)?

Then make a list of the subreddits where a proxy for your customer is talking about solutions like yours. If you're not sure, solutions like SparkToro are the fastest, easiest way to pinpoint where on Reddit your ideal audience might be located. Go to the subreddit and check on the rules for posting; for example, r/finance has a Moronic Monday thread, which is where the most participation happens in that subreddit on Mondays—if you post a generic question there on a Monday, it ain't gonna fly.

Next, phrase your post strategically. Start with the title. My AI-supported analysis of original posts (OPs) that drove the highest engagement on r/business, r/finance, and r/software between 2023 and 2025 showed that the OPs that consistently drive meaningful engagement used open-ended questions that asked for advice, experiences, or predictions. Questions like:

What are your biggest challenges with X? (What are your biggest challenges with Teamwork?)
Any regrets about Y? (Any regrets about flying United to Maui?)
What do the new fans think will happen to Z? (What do the new fans think will happen to Claude now that ChatGPT117 is available?)

Also consider asking the community for ideas, like "What's the best protein for women?" You can ask a personal question, like "Do you regret buying a pilates machine?" You can prompt a debate, like "Is Ozempic better for men or women?" Or invite a critique of the industry, like "Should fast food be healthier?" Or even call out fakers, like "I lost 600 lbs in 20 minutes with organic honey."

Next, write your actual post. Because redditors are hyper-sensitive to marketers, make sure you either do not sound like a marketer or clearly state that you are a marketer for the brand. In your post, keep the tone conversational, and try to add a personal angle or story. The most successful OPs in B2B environments start with a relatable situation. So if your post title is, "Do you regret buying a pilates machine?" then your post might be:

Has anyone else tried one of those at-home pilates machines? I'm concerned about another lockdown and falling out of the habit of working out, but I'm not sure what to choose or if I should just stick with going to the studio and spending a ton of money there for now. Is a home stretcher a total waste of money? Does it just collect dust in the corner (like the pool table and Peloton!)? What are the worst machines out there, and any examples of at-home awesomeness?

Wait for a timely moment to post your question so that you see engagement. Use a Reddit handle or account that's not related to your brand. After you've posted, block time to engage in the comments. This is typically known as the Golden Hour—the first sixty minutes after you post are critical for engagement. Reply to comments to dig deeper, asking why, how, when—anything you need to flesh out their story.

Finish by returning to the post a day or two later to thank everyone. And then, let the mining begin!

WHAT NOT TO LOOK FOR

Customers will share a ton in the reviews they have, especially if those reviews are anonymous. But that doesn't mean that everything they say is gold. So when I'm teaching people to mine reviews, I remind them of the following.

If it punches down, don't use it. Homeaglow famously created an ad with the message being that you can fire your house cleaner when you choose Homeaglow services. The brand punched down. Maybe they found, in VOC, that people were firing their part-time house cleaner to save money with Homeaglow. And maybe that VOC was unexpected and raw. But what brand wants to pick a fight with a cleaning person who's working multiple jobs and making minimum wage without benefits?[26]

If it's off color or clearly off brand, don't use it. Real people say really weird shit, but that doesn't mean your brand needs to. Even if it's unexpected! Even if it's a reflection of the lived experience of the vast majority of your customers, making them understood! Even if it's unedited! If you don't want to build a brand that talks the way some of your customers do, don't use their VOC.

It can help to write this Peter Drucker quote over your desk: *"The most important thing in communication is hearing what isn't said."* When you're listening, be careful to listen with empathy. The best copy is based in empathy.

LISTEN TO SALES CALL REPLAYS

What better way to uncover what your ideal customer needs to hear in order to buy than to sit across the table from them and listen to them *tell you* what they need to hear in order to buy? This is why I love watching sales call replays and observing client game tape reviews. I have sat for nine straight hours without moving, watching sales call recordings on half speed so I could not only take notes but also observe the lead's reactions, watch their facial expressions, spot that moment when their eyes light up in a product demo, that moment when I realize the lead has just given me the hero image and messaging for a product page.

The messages you find by listening to the real-life voice of the customer—speaking candidly to a good salesperson—are game changers. That's why, of the myriad qualitative methods at our disposal in *Listening*, I'm focusing the third and final chapter of this critical step on sales call replays.

Marketing Needs to Watch Sales Calls

First, can we just pause to celebrate amazing salespeople? Watching a stellar salesperson work has helped me find killer lines and identify objections, worries, and even patterns that I would never have otherwise surfaced, the kind of stuff that has turned into high-performing email sequences for more than a few disruptive tech brands, like GitPrime and Shopify Plus.

Second, can someone tell me why sales and marketing are so far removed from each other? I think of the stepbrothers in the movie, um, *Step Brothers*. Two stepbrothers, played by Will Ferrell and John C. Reilly, are forty-year-old children forced to live together and share a bedroom. They hate each other. Then they have a breakthrough. Which leads to this classic exchange:

"Did we just become best friends?"

"Yup!"

Sales and marketing are stepbrothers who are, like, one conversation away from becoming best friends. Copywriters should sit in sales meetings, listening at the back of the room and asking questions. *Copywriters are salespeople.* Sales and marketing need to make up . . . because there is pure gold in sales call replays. When marketing watches those calls, we not only get better-performing messages but we also send more qualified leads into demos with sales. Everyone wins!

Sales Calls Are Basically Spoken Long-Form Sales Pages

The surprising value of a long sales cycle, with multi-threading and multiple sales calls, is that you can fill almost your entire message matrix by watching nine or ten sales call replays. Break this up over the course of a single week, and you've filled in everything, for each persona. In the first 12 minutes of a call, you'll hear everything from the core problem that drives them to seek solutions (Beats 1, 2, and 9) to what they blame for their problems (Beat 5) to the many, many, many solutions that have failed them (Beats 6, 12, 14, 15, 16, 17, 24).

In the intro to this book, I mentioned I worked with GitPrime for a little over a year and helped them realize a 337 percent increase in sales pipeline. When I was working with them, I pulled pages of VOC from leads in sales calls. GitPrime was a very technical solution that helped enterprise technology companies measure their engineering team's strengths and weaknesses using proprietary reporting. They sold into the Googles and Samsungs of the world. These buyers are tough. They are not a good marketing guess away from signing a seven-figure contract; they're not filling in confirmation page surveys after purchasing because that's not how they purchase; and it's hard as hell to mine reviews to find the worries and desires that the Global SVP of Engineering for VISA has when it comes to their distributed engineering team. Like, impossible.

But check out what I heard in sales call replays. Here's a verbatim from one call (anonymized), which was the first of three sales calls:

> "I'm worried about the overhead—the overhead and the upkeep. Where does the data come from that GitPrime reports on? How much attention are my guys gonna have to focus on this? Are the inputs intuitive? Do they make sense? Or is it gonna be a real drag? If you take for example a timekeeping system—they sound great in theory and everyone thinks the outputs will be useful . . . but then people spend more time trying to figure out how to record their time than they actually do working. If this takes more than 5 to 10 percent of their work effort in the day, it'll be a really difficult sell and it'll be really difficult to get people to use it."

So many questions our copy could address! With verbatim snippets from a couple dozen calls, I had a list of potential worries about the product's features. I heard anxieties about the time the team would have to spend making the product work. I heard analogies. I heard spelled-out objections. Big concerns about slowing down the team. Interesting insider insight into how large orgs become "report happy" and the tendency toward "busy work." I heard it from every angle—almost everything you would need to fill in the How column across a message matrix.

And in the end, my team and I were able to use what we heard to write a ton of stellar copy for GitPrime. In particular, we were able to plot and write a funnel that nurtured marketing qualified leads to sales qualified leads and sales qualified leads to leads who not only showed up for calls but brought their managers and later signed a contract. Remember, this is part of the work that helped GitPrime generate 337 percent sales pipeline growth in a year. We eavesdropped our way to wins.

"Cool for big companies, Jo, but I don't have a sales team!"

If you don't have a sales team, you likely have a proxy for one—like sales chat, a support team, or the Q&A session at the end of a webinar. Use those. You can also just go ahead and set up 1:1 video calls with prospects.

Be your own salesperson for a little while, listening and endeavoring to move your prospects to buy. For what you'll discover, it's more than worth the time. This is true whether you're selling gumballs online (been there!) or seven-figure tech contracts (been there!).

USING WHAT YOU HEAR

To help clarify what your end goal is when you're Listening, let me show you an example of how my team and I used VOC from the sales calls of our client GitPrime to write their emails. The following email copy was written by the fantastic Liz Painter. It was the first email in a sequence triggered by completing a form requesting a GitPrime demo but failing to schedule the demo. The constraint was scheduling a demo; this email helped to relieve the constraint by taking the time to move the prospect *through* a problem (Beat 4), *through* failed solutions (The Solution Awareness beats), and toward booking a demo.

Note that this copy is for the first half of the email. To read the full email and see more examples, visit copysellingbook.com.

> **From name:** Ben from GitPrime
> **Subject line:** Pull requests gathering dust?
> **Headline:** Unresolved PRs mean code is dying on the vine
> **Body:**
>
> It's the end of a sprint and your team seems to have hit a bottleneck.
>
> You aren't sure what or who's causing the bottleneck, but you know it's a costly problem to have. And it keeps happening. So you need to address it.
>
> But what do you do?
>
> You don't want to assume. You don't want to start down the path of coaching your team as a whole to "up their game." There's a reason the project has stalled. And you need to know what that reason is if you're going to resolve it. And prevent repeat occurrences.

What if you could see what's going on under the hood of your engineering team? What if you could show your engineers exactly what's causing bottlenecks so you can work together to fix it?

Data About Your Engineers Lets You Predict and Prevent Bottlenecks

One of the leading causes of end-of-spring bottlenecks is this: someone on your team commits 300+ lines of code all at once. Engineers who'd normally jump on a PR see that this particular PR is very large. It could take them into the evening to review it.

As a result, the oversized PR sits unreviewed. No comments. No collaboration. No hope of being merged anytime soon . . .

Let's start with the hook, which came from VOC in *Beat 4: Expanded problems and worries.* The hook is this: *Unresolved PRs mean code is dying on the vine.* The second half of that hook is verbatim VOC: "code is dying on the vine." We heard it repeatedly. It was a core problem, mentioned early in sales calls. We then agitated, or brought the problem to life, using a common story we'd heard about product managers discovering bottlenecks too late, usually when a feature release date was nearing. Here are a few of the actual lines we swiped directly from VOC:

- code is dying on the vine
- hit a bottleneck
- who's the source of the bottleneck
- need to see what's going on under the hood

We cleaned up a detailed story we'd heard about how a manager noticed that pull requests weren't getting reviewed and what he found: some engineers were committing hundreds of lines of code at a time, causing senior engineers to worry they'd waste too much time on their code review.

The entire hook and the first two-thirds of the email came from what we heard in sales calls. At no point did Liz Painter or I become senior engineers. We just listened, listened some more, and repeated back what we heard.

And because we had also heard objections to and anxieties about the GitPrime platform, we could match the problem mechanism (unresolved pull requests) with the GitPrime solution mechanism (the Commit Workflow report). Doing so not only resulted in strong demo bookings but also helped leads to show up for the sales call better aware of what the product does and what makes it so effective, which helped to shorten the sales cycle.

HOW TO TELL USEFUL VOC FROM BLAH

Here's the bad news: You're mining to find language that stands out. That's bad news because it's incredibly difficult to know what stands out until you've got experience reading and writing a lot of copy that absolutely does not stand out.

The good news is that there are three laws of sticky copy to help you, and you're about to learn them. But first, when I say "sticky copy," I mean copy that stops a reader and keeps them from wandering away. This is the opposite of what most copy does. Most copy, developed out of guesswork in a boardroom, is so polished as to be anything but sticky. Customers hate polish. Customers love stickiness.

When you're mining VOC, picture two items: Velcro and an ice hockey rink. (I'm Canadian, so writing "ice hockey" physically hurts. It's just hockey.) Velcro is what you want. It makes you stop, even if you don't want to. Things stick to it. It's literally got claws all over it. That's sticky. That's what we want. Compare that to an ice rink, which is slippery. It's polished. You step on it, and you fly away. That's what we don't want. Smooth, polished, sounds like marketing—that's all bad. Copy should be Velcro; copy should not be an ice rink.

The Three Laws of Sticky Copy

Sticky copy is first and foremost unexpected. Secondly, it makes the prospect feel understood. Third, it's unedited. Let me dig into these three laws.

The First Law: Unexpected

It's sticky if it says something in a way you haven't heard before and, importantly, in a way the boardroom or CMO would never dream up. (If your boardroom reaches consensus on a message, toss it.)

Unexpected can mean tone. So to close the loop on an earlier example, when someone in an Amazon review writes, "But if you think you need rehab, you probably do," and no one else is saying anything with such a direct tone, that's unexpected.

Unexpected can mean word choice. If you've watched the excellent TV series *Mad Men*, you'll recall the scene when Peggy Olsen, not yet a copywriter and acting purely as a lipstick consumer, looks at a wastebasket of discarded tissues covered in lipstick and remarks, "It's a basket of kisses." That's unexpected word choice.

The Second Law: Understood

There's an old adage in copywriting: good copy makes me understand; great copy makes me understood. Copy is sticky if I, the consumer, see myself in it. It's aligned with me, not talking at me. It sees me. It respects me, never talking down to me. It knows me.

I'm understood when my lived experience is on the page. I land on a page and instead of hearing a cheerleader telling me the perfect life is right around the corner, I see the phrase "It doesn't even have to be hot out. My armpits are always wet." That is my life. That is my experience. I can visualize my own lived experiences, not glossed over marketing speak, when I read the words. I nod along, and by the end I'm not only ready for your solution but I'm also more deeply in tune with myself.

The Third Law: Unedited

The third law holds that sticky copy makes you feel real feels, tells real stories, and never summarizes the story down to a soundbite. It's unedited. It's raw.

Your customer edits themselves as much as your marketers do. Everyone is in the practice of editing themselves. That's why, in interviews and sales calls, we probe, never accepting the interviewee's first answer as the full truth. But in review mining, in surveys, and in other impersonal forms of listening, we can't prevent self-editing. So we have to look for the most real, honest, and unedited language—and ignore everything that feels edited.

Just because a customer says something does not mean it's good voice of customer data that we should use. The objective is not to have our customers write our copy—that's no better than letting a boardroom write our copy. Rather, we, as trained copysellers, recognize that the most efficient way to clone a customer is to listen to them and swipe their words. But not every word will make the cut. We want unexpected, real, and raw. Everything else we can make up ourselves, and what would be the point in that? That's the old way. It got us nowhere.

• • •

Using everything you learn during the *Listening* phase, you'll be able to complete your message matrices. And here's a bonus. A completed message matrix reads, start to finish, like a long-form sales page or video sales letter. How to use your message matrix will become more evident as you move into *Assembling* and begin to learn about copywriting frameworks.

But right now, you could hand a completed message matrix over to a direct response copywriter, and they could whip up one helluva mailer with it. To ensure they do the job right, however, such that a constraint is relieved, you'd need to first complete a solution design. Let's do that next.

CHAPTER RECAP

- ✓ Listen to leads and customers to find your message and fill each message matrix you've got.
- ✓ Embed a one-question survey, called The Bridge, in your confirmation pages, and then swap in different one-question surveys to fill gaps on your Messaging Matrices.
- ✓ Proxies for your customer are sharing voice of customer data in online reviews, comments, threads, and testimonials.
- ✓ Use both passive and active review mining techniques to find the stickiest language across the spaces where people share.
- ✓ Actively watch sales call replays and track not only VOC data but also patterns in what prospects say across calls, which will give you a fuller picture of the prospect's experience .
- ✓ Apply the Three Laws of Sticky Copy to identify language that will actually work when you use it to write your copy.

CHAPTER 7

Filling In and Using the Message Matrix

"The role of management is to change the process rather than badgering individuals to do better."

W. Edwards Deming, 20th century leader in systems thinking and management practices

If I asked you to write a song for a four-year-old child, what would you write? What would the song be about?

I've asked that question on stages, to audiences that know the topic of my talk is writing copy using voice of customer data. And yet, when I ask that question, I get the sort of answers you'd get in a creative brainstorm:

"It should be about cats!"
"It should be about candy!"
"It should be about their brother or sister!"

There once was a gentleman who wrote songs for four-year-old children. One of the songs he wrote began like so:

"What do you do with the mad that you feel
when you feel so mad you could bite?"

The songwriter was Fred Rogers, or Mr. Rogers to many of us—Peabody winner and calm presence on the public television program *Mister Rogers' Neighborhood.* He wrote that song after a little boy asked him, "What do you do with the mad that you feel?" The song wasn't about cats or candy. It was about feeling mad, and it was phrased the way his audience phrased it: "the mad that you feel," where the adjective "mad" is used as a noun (something that would not make it through the copy approval process). Mr. Rogers listened to what real children expressed, and he turned what he heard into media they would see themselves in.

> **THE 36 BEATS POSTER**
>
> Post the 36 beats on the wall of your office. Download a printable copy of the 36 beats at copysellingbook.com

Your job is the same. But instead of a song, you're writing a sales email. And instead of listening to one person, you're listening to thousands or even millions. Which is why we use multiple message matrices, not just our memory, or a Notes file of interesting-sounding stuff we collect over time.

HOW TO FILL IN A MESSAGE MATRIX WITH WHAT YOU HEAR WHEN LISTENING

You will organize VOC from the *Listening* phase in the "how" column of the appropriate beat on your message matrix. I'm going to walk you through how I do this work manually. But I know that one of the biggest barriers to applying the copyselling system and maximizing your revenue is the manual process of filling in a 36-section spreadsheet. Which is why, at the end of this section, I will add practical insights into using AI to automate piping VOC data into the appropriate beats of the message matrix.

When you're filling in your message matrix, you don't have to go in order. Fill it in as you acquire *What* to say and *How* to say it.

Ask the Question That Gives You a Beat-Specific Answer

In chapters three and four, you learned about the 36 beats to fill in, and in chapter six you learned that one interview or one survey could help you fill in an entire message matrix—but that that's somewhat rare. The most likely scenario is that you (and your team) will populate the message matrix on an ongoing basis, using what you hear across review mining, surveys, interviews, sales call replays, and myriad other qualitative methods of listening. To do that, let's architect core questions that will get the customer to share their unique insight or experience to help us fill each beat. Note that these questions do not represent an exhaustive list; you may have favorite questions or new ones to add to this list, and as long as you get useful VOC from asking them, then you've got my thumbs up!

Expect to see overlap. Expect to struggle to know exactly where to place certain VOC. Expect to capture everything as if it's all gold and then learn, with practice, what's gold and what's just stuff someone said. Expect also problems and desires to surface across the board, which is why the stages of awareness are included in the message matrix spreadsheet—when a customer mentions a problem with a *solution* they're switching from, that problem should be documented as VOC in Solution Aware, and when they mention a problem that they're experiencing without the aid of any competitive solution, that problem should be documented as VOC in Problem Aware.

Beat 1: Core Problem Match

Fill in Beat 1 after you've got a lot of responses in Beat 4. That is, ask the question listed under Beat 4, which follows. You will hear about many problems, all of which you should list in Beat 4. Then, to complete Beat 1, identify the most frequently mentioned problem among those myriad problems, and add that VOC to this beat.

Beat 2: Moment of Highest Tension

Ask this question on a confirmation page or an early interview with a new lead or customer.

What was going on in your life that brought you to look for a solution like ours?

Beat 3: Moment of Highest Pleasure

Ask this question on an exit-intent pop up or in an emailed survey.

What's the perfect outcome that no solution seems to provide?

Beat 4: Expanded Problems & Worries

Ask this question of visitors to your site and leads in early sales calls.

When it comes to [category/problem], what one thing are you struggling most with right now?

Beat 5: The Blame Game

Ask this question to webinar attendees and in sales calls. You are looking for multiple outlets to blame.

Why do you think it's so hard to [outcome]?

Beat 6: Failed Solution(s)

Ask this question in a confirmation page survey, to webinar attendees, and in sales calls.

What have you already tried to eliminate [problem from Beat 1]?

Beat 7: Why They Failed (Unique Problem Mechanism)

Ask this question as a follow-up to Beat 6.

> *You said you tried [Beat 6 response]. Why do you think [they] didn't work?*

Beat 8: "It's Not Just You"

Ask this question in an interview or sales call. Long, detailed, story-based answers are ideal as they will help you write more compelling copy to transform your prospect into a hero.

> *Who else [on your team/in your family] has struggled with [problem from Beat 1]?*

Beat 9: What Might Work Better (Unique Solution Mechanism)

Ask new customers who've used your solution this question in a follow-up customer success call or survey.

> *Now that you've used [named unique solution mechanism], what would you say you like best about it? Why?*

Beat 10: You Need CATEGORY for INDUSTRY, and the Solution Should Champion PERSONA

Ask this question in sales calls.

> *What are you using to [outcome]? Would you describe it as a perfect fit? Why not?*

Beat 11: Why We're the Only Ones Who Can Do This (Category for Industry Serving Persona)

Interview the sales team, founder, and/or product leaders for this beat.

Beat 12: The Category Landscape

Ask this question either of new customers or of leads in a format that allows you to keep their positive attention on your brand even as they think of competitors. Avoid surveys.

If [product/brand] didn't exist, what solutions would you be considering?

Beat 13: Desire & Obstacles

Ask two questions in a row, ideally in a two-part survey on a confirmation page or early in sales calls.

What specific [result] do you want?
What's keeping you from that [result]?

Some categories, like weight loss, are overrun by messages of big, distant desires. In those cases, when a brand wants to minimize wishful thinking and focus on deliberate action for their customers or users, we use this two-part question:

What specific [result] do you intend to achieve?
Why do you believe you haven't achieved that yet?

Beat 14: Competitors All Focus on X (The Old Way)

Ask this question in sales calls, when you've identified what the prospect is considering switching from.

What would you say [competitor name] does to [negative outcome, like "slow you down"]?

Beat 15: Here's What's Wrong with That

Populate this with the more visceral stories the prospects shared as part of Beat 14. If the competitor failing/old way is very specialized, interview experts or do heavier research to unpack what's wrong with the old way.

Beat 16: Here's How That Manifests Badly For People Like Our Persona

Populate this with the more visceral stories the prospects shared as part of Beat 14.

Beat 17: What You Must Leave Behind

Ask this question in a confirmation-page survey or a sales call.

What do you think has been preventing you from getting the [results] you deserve?

Beat 18: New/Next/Novel

Ask this question in a confirmation-page survey or a sales call.

What, if any, [ingredients/features/outcome] in [category] excite(s) you most today?

Beat 19: Product Value Proposition ("The Only")

Ask this question in a survey or interview. If the customer needs help understanding what you mean by value, offer examples that are relevant to your product, but try not to lead.

What value do you expect to get from [product] (that you can't get anywhere else)?

Beat 20: Named Unique Solution Mechanism

The actual named unique solution mechanism comes from your team. How it's described comes from your customers. Populate this beat's "how" column with responses from Beat 9.

Beat 21: High Level Benefits

Ask this question in an existing customer survey or even a focus group with existing customers, if you run those. If you know what solutions they've tried, replace "any other solution you've tried" with the product name.

In your opinion, what do you think [product name] does better than any other solution you've tried?

Beat 22: Value Pillars

This is a good question to ask of both people who are new to your brand and people who are loyal to your brand. Try it in a user test of your website visitors or social media users.

What do you believe our brand stands for?

Beat 23: Differentiated Outcomes ("Unlike Ever Before")

Ask this question in a sales call or when calling brand-new leads or customers.

If you could wave a wand and get the perfect outcome, what would that outcome be?

Beat 24: Vs. Competition

Ask this two-part question when you are talking to a prospect or new active customer about the competition, which they've named and which they are likely switching from.

How did [competitor] come close to delivering [differentiated outcome]?

What do you think prevented [competitor] from delivering [differentiated outcome]?

Beat 25: Proof of How ("The Promise")

Interview your founder(s) and product team to collect this data. You're looking for "secret sauce stuff," not generic statements or pre-approved messages.

Beat 26: Proof of Who

Always be updating this section with testimonials and links to case studies for people/businesses that are like the persona for whom the message matrix is created.

Beat 27: Uniquely Qualified

This is a job for you and the marketing team! List the milestones, in order, that the persona will have hit, by this point, that uniquely qualify them to make this decision. This can get quite literal, including things like "downloaded an ebook on weight loss," "attended a webinar on getting strong," "watched YouTube videos about bone density during menopause." Remember that your objective with this beat is to show your prospect that they are a VIP now—that it is no time for them to turn around or lose momentum.

Beat 28: Big Claims

Survey existing, engaged customers with a dropdown/single-selection question to reveal the #1 concern they had about mentioning your brand or solution as one they wish to invest in; for example, "I wasn't sure I could trust your brand to deliver its promises." Then work to craft a legitimate big claim around the opposite of that concern, thus neutralizing it; for example, "The #1 most trusted weight loss app on the planet."

Which of these nearly prevented you from buying into our brand?
[anxiety A]
[anxiety B]
[anxiety C]

Beat 29: Success Stories, with Risk Reversal

Develop full case studies. Include links to them here.

Beat 30: Use Cases

Ask this question in a confirmation-page survey or when calling brand-new customers.

What's the first thing you're going to use [product name] for?

Beat 31: Goal Amplification

This one is a little trickier, so I'm offering two paths. Choose Path 1 if your marketing team does not have the resources to invest in personalized content, which is true for tiny, resource-constrained businesses and huge, slower-moving businesses. Choose Path 2 if you are invested in personalization, such as with a rich CRM with even richer integrations.

Path 1: Ask this multiple choice question in a new-lead or new-customer survey. Then rank the responses in your message matrix "how" column, with the top response in the "what" column.

When you think about being successful with [product name], what does success mean to you?
[option A]
[option B]
[option C]

Path 2: Ask this open-ended question in a new-lead survey (i.e., when they're signing up for a lead magnet during Problem or Solution Aware). Then pipe each response into the lead's profile as a custom field in your CRM. Later, when the lead has reached Beat 31 on the assembly line, pipe their original response—verbatim—into the email(s) you send them; you can also pipe their original response into an SMS message, in-app messages, or on-site messages.

When you think about being successful with [solution category], what does success mean to you?

Beat 32: Risk & Uncertainty Reduction

Complete this beat with what your brand offers (that this persona cares about!) in terms of guarantees, trial periods, white-glove support, account help, live events, online events, and other risk-reducers. If you have testimonials or reviews in which customers speak to these things, add them, too.

Beat 33: Kill the Status Quo

Trigger this two-question survey—in app or by email—for all users who reach an AHA or high-value moment with your product or service.

How does it feel to [achieve outcome]?

When you think about life before [product name], what would you tell your old self about choosing [product name] to [achieve outcome]?

Beat 34: Offer Optimization & Stacked Offers

List the offers you know that this persona responds best to, as well as the upsells you offer this persona, if unique to them. Ask this question in a customer survey, as a follow-up to a Net Promoter Score survey or in a support capacity, when they've just received good support.

How can we make it easier for people like you to choose us?

Beat 35: Leadership Horizon/Future Proofing

Draw this info from what your business has shared publicly about the horizon and your place in it.

Beat 36: Coach Decisiveness

Ask this question in a new-customer survey.

You said yes to [outcome of product] today. What would you tell someone who's on the fence about choosing [product] right now?

MEGA QUESTIONS FILL MULTIPLE CELLS

You do not need to set up a bunch of surveys or interviews to fill your message matrix. Use the previous list of questions only when you've got gaps to fill. The Bridge, from chapter six, will help you fill multiple cells, as will these questions:

> *What nearly stopped you from buying [today]?*
> *What frustrates you most about the quality of the options in [category]?*
> *What specific result do you want?*
> *When it comes to [category], what's most important to you?*

We haven't dug into customer interviews because it is a wildly huge topic, but know that interviews, especially Jobs to Be Done interviews, can be outstanding for copyselling. Set up seven to ten interviews. And bring all of the questions from this and the previous chapter. Get 'em all answered, in detail, in a couple of days (or one really intense day).

Now Simplify This Work with AI

Start by obtaining a copy of an AI-friendly version of the message matrix template from copysellingbook.com. This template includes specific columns for the source, snippet, timestamp, and more. Alternatively, build a new version in Notion, which is excellent for AI automation.

Then, using a survey platform like Typeform or Tally, set up your confirmation page and other surveys using the questions provided above. Then, using no-code automations, like Zapier or Make, create a series of rules to channel feedback from the appropriate survey to the corresponding set of cells. (This is where Notion becomes very useful.)

You can do something similar with sales call recordings, interview recordings, and larger transcripts, in Chorus, Fathom, Gong, or your favorite software. First, in your sheet, turn each beat into a tag that becomes a trigger; for example, Beat 3 becomes #B3; if you want AI to choose the beat (not recommended), the trigger becomes #B?. Then, in Zapier or Make, add a regex filter that looks for #B(\d+|\?) in text you've highlighted in the software and sends that text to your sheet.

Niche software like Sassy and Dovetail can streamline the VOC organization process. If you're looking for ideas for how to simplify with AI, you can also upload a copy of the message matrix template to your favorite AI platform, then ask it to interview you about what it needs to know in order to help you fill the template with real VOC data. I've repeatedly done this exercise using nothing more than Claude with my templates, prompting, and VOC, and doing so has helped me save entire days of working time.

ONCE YOUR MESSAGE MATRIX IS FILLED, LET'S USE IT!

We'll use a message matrix to organize what we hear in *Listening* so that we can effectively copy-and-paste copy that's nearly market-ready into a framework in a Word or Google document, or straight into AI, if that's your preference. If you've ever used a message map or other message source document in your organization, you already know how to use a message matrix, with a key difference being that a message matrix is very detailed, while most message source documents are quite high level.

Example: Writing a Funnel with a Message Matrix

Let's pretend that we've decided the best solution to a constraint is to acquire new lookalike customers by crafting an ad-driven evergreen webinar funnel that closes on a long-form sales page. We've crafted a solution design for it. We've identified the product we need to sell and the persona we're selling it to. Great. Now what? Now we use the beats to help us deliver the product. This funnel is architected like most funnels:

1. It starts with a series of ads.
2. Those ads drive to a landing page for a free ebook.
    a. Visitors who do not download the ebook are retargeted with ads.

3. On the confirmation page for the free ebook is an invitation to watch a webinar.
    a. Visitors who do not register enter an email automation to drive them to watch the webinar.
    b. Visitors who register are redirected to a page where they can watch the webinar immediately.
4. The webinar runs, with an offer to buy the product at the end.
    a. Visitors who leave the webinar before the offer is presented are retargeted with ads and emails.
    b. Visitors who leave the webinar after the offer is presented and who do not buy are retargeted with ads and emails.
5. The webinar drives to the long-form sales page to accept the offer.
    a. Visitors who buy enter an existing onboarding automation.
    b. Visitors who do not buy are retargeted with ads and emails.

The message matrix answers the question *What gets said in each of those parts of the funnel?* At a high level, assets created for the top of the funnel start at Beat 1, and assets created for the bottom of the funnel end at Beat 36. But then there's all that stuff in the middle. What goes in there?

To answer that question, go to the assembly line. On it, the customer:

1. Consumes the ad and clicks it.
2. Consumes the content on the landing page, desires the ebook, completes the form to get it.
3. Immediately signs up for the webinar.
4. Immediately watches the webinar, start to finish. Clicks to the sales page.
5. Consumes the content on the sales page, desires the offer, buys it.

The ads push hard on Beats 1, 2, and 3. The landing page nails Beats 3, 4, 5, and 6. The ebook backs up a bit, reinforcing Beats 1 through 6 swiftly before nailing Beats 7 to 25, then driving to the sales page. But the prospect never has to read the ebook—they watch the webinar, which reinforces Beats 1 through 6 swiftly before moving through Beats 7 to 29 like a champ. The sales page picks up from Beat 19, reinforces all the messaging of the second half of the webinar (Beats 19 to 29), and moves to Beat 34, where the customer is created with the exchange of their money for our product's value. Brilliant! A totally straight assembly line! What a system!

However. As much as my heart longs for a flawlessly efficient customer creation system, we know there will be offshoots, and we prepare for those. Enter the supplemental assembly lines (SAL)—the ones that catch the stragglers and bring them back to the core assembly line.

The first SAL:

Retargeting visitors who did not complete the form to download the ebook. These people have seen the ads and clicked them, yet they didn't say yes to our ebook offer. We don't have their email address (which matters at the time of this writing), so we focus on retargeting them with ads. But what are the ads about? We can't know without exploring why they didn't say yes to our ebook offer:

- Did they whip through the first ads too quickly, clicking just to click and never reading or watching a thing? If so, they need to go back to Beat 1.
- Did they gloss over the landing page copy because they're a Spontaneous decision maker (see next chapter)? If so, they may need to be retargeted with short, snappy video ads. Alternatively, they may not be a good fit for a funnel with long content like ebooks and webinars at its heart, indicating a new Constraint Identified requiring a new solution design.
- Was the offer not compelling? Retargeting ads could enhance the perception of value for the ebook offer.

Depending on resources, either we create an SAL based on the winningest of these hypotheses, or we create multiple SALs, one for each hypothesis.

The second SAL:

An email automation for those who did not register to watch the webinar. These folks have moved successfully, as far as behavioral data indicates, from Beat 1 to Beat 6 (i.e., they've downloaded the ebook). We want to get them to either read the ebook or say yes to the webinar; both offers will move them to Mid Product Aware, but the webinar will do so in the next sixty minutes while the ebook could sit unread for days, weeks, eternity on their desktop. So we prioritize driving them back to the webinar viewing page.

The email automation starts with Email 1: an email that allows them to download the ebook, but that also prioritizes making the webinar sound like the better use of their time. (In fact, both cover all beats, from 1 to 25.) By Email 1, the customer is, at best, at Beat 6, so we open with Beat 4 or 5, move quickly to Beat 6, then dig into Beat 7, where our webinar swings into action. If this first email ends at Beat 7, the customer should be in a good position to watch the webinar.

Using branching in our CRM, we craft a multi-part automation from this point onward, setting up an automation goal or using if/then scenarios for whether the customer did or did not begin the webinar. If the customer did not begin the webinar after Email 1, then we need to begin the optimization process to better understand what's getting in their way. (See chapter sixteen for more.)

Our email automation ends when the customer has clicked to watch the webinar and when tracking shows that they've actually started watching the webinar.

The third SAL:

Visitors who leave the webinar before the offer is presented. This is a tricky group! How early into the webinar did they leave? What beat were they at when they bailed? With tagging in video hosting platforms, like Wistia, you can set up a new tag for each beat in your webinar recording. With that solution in place, you can trigger a retargeting email or ad for each beat or block of beats.

The fourth SAL:

Visitors who leave the webinar after the offer is presented and who do not buy and who did not make it to the long-form sales page. The SAL writes itself! We're gonna set up retargeting ads and automated emails that hit the points in our optimized offer from our solution design for the webinar. The beat at which the offer was first presented becomes the beat at which we start our retargeting copy. And we move them back to the sales page or to an anchored area further down the sales page—whichever is a better fit for where they are on the line.

The fifth SAL:

Visitors who visit the sales page but do not buy. We can hypothesize that, unless data proves otherwise, this customer is in Most Aware. At this point, our emails and ads dig in from Beat 28 to Beat 36. This can be as straightforward as creating one asset for each beat up to 34:

- *Beat 28: Big claims* is a retargeting ad—video or image—highlighting what makes your product iconic.
- *Beat 29: Success stories, with risk reversal* is a series of emails, each telling a different success story and reinforcing the value of the offer to highlight guarantees and other parts of your optimized offer. If you have video case studies, this beat makes great retargeting ads.
- *Beat 30: Use cases* could be a single email listing out the variety of use cases for your solution that the prospect hadn't even considered or had glossed over when watching the webinar.
- *Beat 31: Goal amplification* drives to a landing page with a calculator or similar tool to help them visualize their lives improving upon purchase. The landing page drives to the sales page.
- *Beat 32: Risk & uncertainty reduction* manifests as ads and emails detailing the optimized offer. Note: if you struggle to write an entire email or more than one ad about your optimized offer, you may need to work harder at optimizing it or at picking it apart in

such a way that prospects can see all of it—not just glazed over summaries.

- *Beat 33: Kill the status quo* is 100% an email! Take your time showing how the old way is not good enough, how this new way is even lower risk, and the better outcomes they're just a click away from getting.
- *Beat 34: Offer optimization & stacked offers* is an email and ads that speak to the offer itself, once again. Although this beat includes the concept of stacked offers, be careful before you write an email or ad about the offer stack—it's more likely to add friction than not. If you hypothesize that the customer actually wants the offer hidden in the offer stack, consider testing an email that showcases the hidden offer, but this too is tricky so be careful.

Beats 35 and 36 are "wind down" beats. This is where some brands start begging with fast-action discounts and similar dances. But I've seen better results by confidently sending a Beat 35 email that inspires the prospect with *what they're buying into* when they say yes to your offer and your brand. Beat 36 is the last mention in this funnel—it's where you send an email that names the stakes of inaction. You may, at this point, offer two calls to action: 1) book a call to talk about what's still unclear for you (the soft yes CTA) or 2) click to officially say no to this offer (the hard no CTA).

• • •

This many SALs can feel like a lot. But that's what technology makes easy! All you and I need to do is keep our customer on the assembly line and watch for places where they fall off—catch them, readjust them, move them back onto the line. If we don't create SALs, we end up with a lot of half-built products stacking up on the factory floor.

"JO, WILL I USE ALL 36 BEATS FOR EVERY CAMPAIGN I RUN?"

If you're not sure where on the line your customer is, assume they're Problem Aware and start at Beat 1. This is important because we need to get them to Beat 4, where the Mega Mean Mouse becomes a thing. Without that mouse transforming into a gigantic gray weirdo, with a creepy tail and yellow teeth, storming down the street in your customers' direction, all your marketing efforts will be more difficult.

With that scary mouse, you can move people really quickly through the beats, as well. If you're literally selling a better mousetrap, you won't need a webinar funnel with SALs. You could do the whole job—all 36 beats—in a sixty-second spot on TikTok.

An abandoned cart email might only hit Beats 25 and 26. A retargeting ad might be focused on Beat 18. A video sales letter might cover beats 25 to 33, driving to an optimized checkout to move them from 34 to 26.

A late-night demo-based TV ad might run from Beats 1 through 7 slowly, then hit 8 through 11 fast. Slowly walk through Beat 12. Rush through Beat 13. Switch to customer videos to talk through Beats 14 to 18. And then spend the rest of the time largely in Beats 19 to 33, cycling through those beats repeatedly to drive them home before finishing with one helluva Beat 34 and lightly adding in Beats 35 and 36.

These are the beats that help you join the conversation happening in your customer's mind and move them toward the next step. The effect is that the performance constraint for the asset in question is relieved.

"AHEM, JO, WHEN CAN I SELL MY ACTUAL PRODUCT?"

When a prospect is Product Aware, you can start offering your product as your call to action (with an optimized offer). That said, the further along in Product Aware they are, the more likely they are to be primed for your product. By the time they're in Most Aware, you should absolutely feel confident in driving your prospect to buy your product.

Those who buy before they reach the very end of the assembly line still need to see the messages that they didn't get to. I recommend you reinforce beats 19 to 36 in your onboarding and retention emails and workshops.

WE CAN HELP

Why complete your first (or second or tenth) message matrix without good guidance? Our team can work directly with you and your team to complete message matrices for your products and personas, using your own voice-of-customer data. To see how to work with us, visit copysellingbook.com.

CHAPTER RECAP

Filling In & Using Your Message Matrix

- ✓ If you're not sure where on the line your prospect is, start them at Beat 1 on the message matrix.
- ✓ Don't hook beats together like boxcars on a train; rather, overlap beats when creating multiple assets.
- ✓ Use supplemental assembly lines to bring customers back onto the line when they fall off.

CHAPTER 8

Designing the Solution

"Think like a fish, not a fisherman."

Copywriting adage

You're now ready for the solution design. This is a short, typically one-page document that synthesizes what we are thinking about the problem and how we plan to address that *in an asset we're going to write.* It will guide our writing and our reviewers' feedback.

A PLAN FOR RELIEVING THE CONSTRAINT

"Showing your work" in writing can feel tedious. The reason you're supposed to show your work in math and chemistry is because one minor miscalculation can lead to a wrong conclusion. But with writing, most of the work happens in your mind long before it hits the page.

. . . She wrote and waited for you, her good student, to say, *"Wait, no, Jo, that's not true at all."*

You're right! It's not true! Thanks to the copyselling system, most of the work happens on the page the whole way through! Solution designs are how we show what we're thinking before we start doing. And to keep guessing at bay, we'll be using a template.

The Solution Design Template

Your solution design is made of five sections:

1. The opportunity statement, where you note the identified constraint;
2. The definition of the customer, called "List";
3. The definition of the goal, called "Offer";
4. The starting beat, proposed hook, and ending beat for the "Copy"; and
5. The solution itself, which is a single statement of your breakthrough idea.

You can download printable copies of the solution design template at copysellingbook.com. You can see the example template below, and I'll show you how to fill it in immediately following, using the example of an engineering service firm.

SOLUTION DESIGN: [ASSET/FUNNEL/CAMPAIGN NAME]

Opportunity statement

Constraint identified	
Our hypothesis	

LIST (Customer Definition)

Persona + their message matrix	
Persona's primary job to be done	
Channel(s) of engagement	

OFFER (Goal)

What we're offering	
Optimized (for List)	
Why the List will love it	

COPY

The beat they're in	
Proposed hook	
The beat to finish in	

THE SOLUTION

My breakthrough idea is this . . .	

THE TITLE

After the word "solution design," add the name of the asset, funnel, or campaign you are working on.

Example: *Corporate website.*

THE OPPORTUNITY STATEMENT

Tell yourself (and your team or AI) why this is important to the business and how you believe the opportunity can best be tapped.

Constraint Identified

As discussed in chapter two, the work we do when copyselling is to relieve performance constraints. These constraints are impeding growth. Which funnel is tanking, and where in the funnel is abandonment highest? What's getting in the way of generating more leads on a landing page? Shouldn't customers return to buy more? Average order value is half what it was last quarter—what's going on? We'll shortlist possible constraints to growth, and then we'll prioritize the best opportunities in that list.

Example: *Underperforming lead generation for a key audience segment, CTOs at Fortune 1000 companies. Too few leads, though organic and paid traffic for segment are on target.*

Our Hypothesis

In your estimation, based on everything you know and the data you have access to, what do you hypothesize is the best way to solve the problem? For best results, fill this in after completing the rest of the solution design. Note that a lot of off-page thinking, meeting, and strategizing will drive this hypothesis.

Example: *A segment-specific dedicated landing page will increase leads for the segment.*

THE LIST, OR WHERE THE CUSTOMER IS DEFINED

Because List is so important, define who is being targeted and where.

Persona + Their Message Matrix

Who is the target audience? This may be a persona, or it may be a variation on your Ideal Customer Profile. Whatever you write in this section of the solution design should match the name at the top of the message matrix you'll be pulling from. If you have multiple personas, you guessed it—you'll need multiple solution designs, one for each.

Pop in the URL for the appropriate message matrix. If it's not housed online, simply be sure to tell people—particularly your copywriter—where to find it. Avoid assuming someone knows where it is. Take two extra minutes to find it and include it.

Example: *Persona C: Anand. Message Matrix on team Wiki, under Marketing Files.*

Channel(s) of Engagement

Email, Meta ad, landing page, webinar—what channels are in play for this solution? Where does this part of the funnel or journey begin, where does it go, and where does it end? If you will engage them on multiple channels, write them here.

Example: *Website—new landing page on primary corporate domain.*

THE OFFER, OR WHAT THE CUSTOMER GETS AND WHAT THE BUSINESS WANTS

Your offer is informed largely by what your business wants the customer to say yes to, in keeping with business goals or targets. But a ho-hum offer produces ho-hum results. So use this section of the solution design to describe a fleshed-out, irresistible offer.

What We're Offering

In this particular asset, what valuable offering is our prospect getting from us that they didn't have before? This may be an ebook, a free demo, an onboarding call, a live info session, a pre-recorded workshop, access to our product university, a trial of our membership community, a discount on our product, or our product itself. What is it? What do they have to exchange to get it—an email address, a product review, an hour of their time, a referral, a payment?

Example: *No change from core offer across site: $129 State of Engineering report marked down to $29.*

Primary Job to Be Done

I cannot express how critical the Jobs to Be Done methodology has been for me, over the last decade, in finding messages that convert and switching people from old solutions to my clients' solutions. This tiny sliver of a field in the solution design is just one of many fields our agency completes on larger solution designs that would overwhelm this book and hinder your progress. So for now, let's keep it chill: simply check the primary job your "list" is hiring your "offer" to do, and include a related line of VOC that expresses that job in their own words.

Example: *Primarily functional—will use report to shape hiring decisions for next fiscal, including agencies to use. Also social—will circulate document among direct reports to inform their fiscal and quarterly planning.*

Optimized (for the List)

You learned about List, Offer, Copy in chapter two. This tiny sliver of the solution design is where you'll document that offer that you've optimized for the customer described earlier and documented in your message matrix. More on offer optimization later in this chapter!

Example: *Bonus checklist on quarterly and annual planning for SVPs and VPs of Engineering.*

Why the List Will Love It

A key part of offer optimization is not over- or under-doing it. A person on the waitlist for a LaFerrari does not need a coupon code to act. A new parent dealing with diaper rash does not need scarcity to act. We optimize our offers for what our list needs from us.

Example: *Because Anand is circulating the report with their team in the hopes they'll actively use it, make it easier for his team to be successful with it. Copy will highlight that this checklist is a great add-on if you're a CTO planning on circulating the report among your SVPs and VPs.*

THE COPY—PARTICULARLY THE STRATEGIC ELEMENTS

The solution design is not where you write copy; it's where you identify what the copywriter needs to know to effectively craft a first draft that, because it's so well informed by a good solution design, will require fewer iterations. Reference the message matrix for this section.

The Starting Beat

Based on what you know about where this asset falls in the customer journey or on the assembly line, what message matrix beat do you believe they're in when they begin to engage with this asset? Write the number in. Your copywriter will reference this.

Example: *Beat 10: You need CATEGORY for INDUSTRY*

Proposed Hook

The starting beat is filled with VOC, in the "how" column. Review that VOC for phrasing that could be a great hook. A hook completes the phrase, "I never thought it was possible but. . ." Go through each line of VOC for the starting beat, and look for a line that completes that phrase. Copy-paste the VOC verbatim into this field. If you can't choose just one hook, narrow down the options to make choosing one easier.

Example: *"We anticipate what's ahead for engineering as a whole—and mechanical engineering in particular—with this industry-critical report." "I'm the CTO for Johnson Controls, and I make key decisions with this report every year."*

The Ending Beat

The ending beat for the customer assembly line is Beat 36, but that is not the ending beat for every asset you develop. Based on the constraint identified as well as the offer, choose the point at which, when the copy is done right, the constraint should be relieved and the offer should be accepted. Consider both the appropriate beat based on the content in question as well as the starting beat for the page or asset that the persona will see next.

Example: *Beat 13: Desire & obstacles*

THE SOLUTION ITSELF

You've hypothesized what will relieve the constraint. Now add color to that hypothesis.

My Breakthrough Idea Is This

Finish your solution design by completing this field (and the earlier noted *Our hypothesis* field). After reviewing everything, what do you think the solution to the problem is? State it clearly. How you complete this field will show how serious you are about the opportunity. You want something that will break through, fully relieving the constraint and bringing in wins worth the effort.

Example: *Embed a video which is the lightly produced recording of a Zoom call between our founder and a current client who represents Persona C: Anand. In the call, both participants look extremely engaged; our founder asks questions based on Beats 10, 11, 12, and 13 so that the client basically creates a video sales letter for this report for other CTOs. Cut in B-roll of stock video or AI-generated video where a leader is distributing a printed copy of the report to three other people in an office environment. (If this works well, further invest in the video so it's more polished and representative of what Persona C: Anand needs to see to opt in.)*

Consider the Bob Principle

Our agency has a term called "Breakthrough or Bust," aka the BOB Principle. It guides everything we produce with and for our clients. When I teach teams to write copy, I teach them BOB. The idea is this:

> *Whatever you write needs to be a total breakthrough or a total bust, and we have no idea which of those things it will be before we validate it in the market. BOB kills any copy or message that is unanimously loved by everyone who reads it.*

The value of a total breakthrough is obvious, but what's the value of a *total bust*? You don't actually want a total bust in the market; you just want some people reviewing your copy, before it's in market, to fear that it's pushing things too far. When everyone on your team loves the copy, that typically means it's not different enough. Safe doesn't bring breakthroughs.

A very good example is the 1984 Apple ad, which Steve Jobs had to sneak out because Apple's board hated it but he loved it. That ad became iconic. Here's a more practical example of BOB from one of our clients. Then-CMO for the scheduling solution Doodle Jared Blank retained us to optimize Doodle's copy on an ongoing basis. One of our projects was to optimize a four-email flow for new users.

Applying the BOB Principle, we recommended Doodle test a sixteen-email flow against the four-email control. Yes, we recommended four times the number of emails. One of my email copywriters at the time, Nikki Elbaz, wrote those sixteen emails, most of which were much longer than the control emails. They were written in a narrative style that requires reading from top to bottom, not scanning. The design was stripped way back. We sent an email almost daily instead of intermittently.

Half of the Doodle team hated our emails and thought they would be a bust. Half of their team loved them and thought they'd be a breakthrough. Our team wasn't sure—some emails demolished better practices in email marketing. Basically, we had a BOB on our hands.

We ran the test. With greater than 95 percent confidence and with sends to tens of thousands of trial users for whom these emails would be highly relevant, we saw our sixteen-email flow outperform the four-email control flow with a **63.9 percent lift** in purchases of Doodle's Pro product and an **18.3 percent lift** in purchases of Doodle's Starter product. And importantly, these emails generated almost triple the unsubscribe rate. More leads hopped *off* the assembly line with our emails. But more leads also stayed on the assembly line all the way to the end of it, becoming paying customers for Doodle.

Exactly zero trial users replied to a single email in the Doodle control sequence. To our BOB variation, the success team got 311 replies. This is a big deal. Emergency meetings were called. The test was nearly shut down. (That's BOB at work!) The fearless CMO Jared Blank worked hard to keep the test running. He was responsible for the, dare I say, *sick* results.

As you work out your solution design, keep BOB in mind. You are looking for an approach that will break through, and such an approach is rarely the stuff that meets so-called best practices.

FINDING THE RIGHT BEAT

The first few times you use a message matrix, you'll find the beat at which to meet your reader by starting at Beat 1 and working your way down the list. For each beat, you'll ask yourself this yes/no question: *Is it reasonable to expect that my reader has already encountered and moved through this beat?*

If yes, move on to the next beat with the same question. When you reach no, that's your starting beat.

You can also use intent or behavioral signals to help you find the best starting beat. Begin by trying to identify the stage of awareness of your reader, not the specific beat. Once you've identified the stage of awareness, you can use signals, data, and even AI to help you zoom in on the beat you hypothesize they are in.

Signals That the Prospect Is Problem Aware (Beats 1-9)

In search, the prospect conducts problem-focused searches without using solution words. For example, "How to fix [problem]," or "Why does [problem] happen." They will use keyword phrases like *struggling with* or *tired of*, without mentioning brand or product names. They will conduct symptom searches, using phrases like *high bounce rate* or *developers going over estimate*.

Behaviorally, they will read your top-of-funnel, problem-focused blog posts. They'll sign up for webinars with problem-based headlines, such as "What to Do When Your Boss Lies to You." They'll engage with day-in-the-life social posts that highlight frustrations. They'll read newsletters featuring stories of people dealing with struggles and challenges. They'll click on links promising insight into why things are going wrong.

Signals That the Prospect Is Solution Aware (Beats 10-18)

In search, the prospect conducts category searches that typically do not include words speaking to problems, challenges, or struggles. For example, "AI-driven marketing automation software." They'll search "Alternatives to [category]," and "Best [category] for [use case]/[user type]," as well as "How to choose [category]." In some cases, if a brand name is synonymous with a category—such as *Tylenol* can be synonymous in American homes with *painkiller*—the search may include a product name. For example, "Alternatives to Tylenol."

Behaviorally, they'll enter your website via your blog posts or landing pages. They'll download special reports on the industry, category, or even key materials. They'll watch videos about the product landscape, such as "How to tell if cashmere is really cashmere?" and "Who makes the best vacuum for pet hair?" They'll download guides and white papers on subjects such as "The State of Project Management Software in 2026." They'll visit directories, like Capterra. They'll engage in subreddits for a broad category, like r/menopause or r/marketing.

Signals That the Prospect Is Product Aware (Beats 19–27)

In search, the prospect conducts searches combining product names with keywords such as:

- [your brand] vs [competitor]
- [your brand] pricing
- [your brand] feature list
- [your brand] reviews
- Is [your brand] worth it?
- Does [your brand] work?
- Alternatives to [your brand]
- [your brand] demo
- How to use [your brand]
- Who is [your brand] best for?

They'll watch YouTube video reviews of your product. They'll direct traffic to your site.

Behaviorally, they'll spend time and clicks, and they'll start exchanging their email address for information. On your website, they'll take time on your product pages and download product-specific content. They'll download PDF case studies and leavebehinds, and they'll watch gated and ungated demos. They'll spend time on your social media. They'll initiate chat and engage in social DMs. They'll engage in subreddits for your brand, like r/substack. And they'll open and read emails that are about your product, like feature walkthroughs and tutorials that drive outcomes.

Signals That the Prospect Is Most Aware (Beats 28–36)

In search, the prospect conducts searches combining product names with buying words, like *coupon*, *discount*, *money-back guarantee*, *where to buy*, and *sign up*. They'll also combine your product name with user words, like *contact*, *implementation*, and *setup*. They may even combine your product or brand name with words indicating last-minute uncertainty, such as, *founders*, *investors*, and *complaints*.

Behaviorally, they'll visit your pricing page repeatedly. They'll forward your emails, which typically means forwarding to a decision maker. They'll book and show up for sales demos. They'll add to cart *more than once* without purchasing. They'll engage with on-site chat. And they'll visit pages like About, Terms of Service, Refund Policy, Legal, and Security. They'll open and click on emails with subject lines featuring the buying words shown above.

Your Marketing Automation Suite Is Made for This Stuff

In addition to using search and user behavior signals, you can pinpoint the best-fit stage of awareness and even the right starting beat using your marketing tech stack. When you write all of your marketing assets using the copyselling system and the message matrix, you always know the starting beat of an asset and its ending beat. Your job is to use your existing marketing automation software and lead scoring systems to ensure the next message the prospect sees from you starts at the beat they're on (or near it) and progresses them through the subsequent beats.

Content engagement scoring shows you which pieces a person has already consumed. Similarly, email engagement scoring shows you which emails a person has clicked on, so you know what messages they've been exposed to in email as well as on the email's landing page.

Your website analytics, tied to your CRM, will show you a person's time spent on site, pages per session, and return visits. You will know that they've read Blog Posts A, B, C, and F; you will know that all of those blog posts, together, move them from Beat 1 to Beat 24; your scoring will reflect that and drive outbound sales initiatives, email automations, and retargeting messages that work together to move the prospect from Beat 24 to Beat 34.

CHOOSING CHANNELS

As marketers, we typically talk *customer first,* but we think and act *channel first.* When planning our next quarter, we set targets for new leads, new customers, retained customers, and added revenue, and then we try to reverse engineer a path to those results with multi-channel marketing.

The first question should not be one of channel selection. Channels are message delivery mechanisms. When you start with channels, it's like a fisherman holding a net, a rod, and a club as he marches past shops and restaurants toward a dock at midday. What's he gonna catch? Whatever's around right now that's chill enough to swim into a net while the sun's high in the sky, shoppers are chatting, and people are skateboarding noisily down the boardwalk. The least evolved fish. The suicidal fish. The carcass of an old fish that died of natural causes, floated past the rod's hook, and skimmed along into the net.

The real question is: *Where* are my next customers, *when* are they there, and *why* are they there?

And it can almost universally be improved with this more accurate question: *Where* were my *last* customers, *when* were they there, and *why*?

We're talking about customer-led growth. It's thinking like a fish, not a fisherman. Mine is not the first book that will advocate for a data-driven, customer-led approach to growth; if you haven't read the excellent *Forget the Funnel* by Claire Suellentrop and Georgiana Laudi, do so right after you finish this book.

When you're completing the solution design field labeled "Where we're meeting them," you're strategically choosing a channel, like *Instagram*, or a series of channels, like *Instagram, drives to lead-generation landing page,* and *drives to one of two segment-specific confirmation pages, one with offer to book a call (SQL) and one with The Bridge (MQL).* If you're not sure where the fish are biting these days, tools like SparkToro are incredibly useful in identifying the best places to target and retarget.

ON OFFERS

Fact: this small section is one of the last parts of this book that I wrote during the first draft, and it was one of the hardest to finalize. That's because it's a remarkably small section for a remarkably large (and critical) subject: offers. After all, your offer is more important than your copy. Remember: List, Offer, Copy—always in that order.

An offer is what you're offering to your prospect in exchange for something that they value. They value their email address, their time, a referral (to a peer, friend, or coworker), money, and more money/repeat business. Likes, comments, and reposts are increasingly used as payment for an offer.

Whatever you're offering in your asset needs to be so valuable that it easily warrants the exchange. If you've crafted a Mega Mean Mouse, the value seems high and the exchange is easier. If you've fleshed out and named your unique solution mechanism, the value seems high and the exchange is easier.

Types of Offers

Every asset you create has an offer, which is the thing your lead is saying yes to in that moment and which is typically not an offer for your product. It's a click to a blog post, the download of a free report, a coupon code for a small offer, or even a call to action to watch a two-hour or two-minute YouTube video.

Each offer should align with your prospect's position on the message matrix. Although there is no hard and fast rule about what offer goes where, in the interest of keeping our customer moving along the assembly line, let me share with you example offer ideas that you could use across the stages of awareness. The offers are divided into low lift, heavy lift, and paid.

	Low Lift (Easy to Make)	**Heavy Lift (Expensive to Make)**	**Paid**
Problem Aware	**Problem diagnosis quiz** *("Are nepo-babies forcing you into community college?")*	**Report on the state of the problem** *("The 5th Annual Report on Barriers to Admission at Ivy League Schools")*	**On-demand course** *("How to get accepted to Harvard")*
	Checklist of common problems *("Which of these are harming your child's chances of getting into Harvard?")*	**Commissioned article for major publication** *("Meet 15 valedictorians who couldn't get into Harvard")*	**In-person workshop** *("The College Application Workshop")*
Solution Aware	**Infographic** *("55 ways to increase your chances of getting into Harvard")*	**YouTube channel** *(Twice-weekly interviews destroy myths on getting into Ivy League schools)*	**Trade show / live event / expo booth**
	Webinar *("The one hack you haven't tried to get into Harvard")*	**Ebook** *("The Innovative Applicant: Why ignoring old ideas is the new way into Harvard")*	**Half-day course** *("The new, novel way to slay your admissions essay")*

	Low Lift (Easy to Make)	Heavy Lift (Expensive to Make)	Paid
Product Aware	**Info session** (*"What is* The Way In System *and will it work for you?"*)	**Demo video** (*"How* The Way In System *replaced 1:1 college coaches to become the new standard in Ivy League application success"*)	**Your product** *("The Way In System")*
	Sales call *("My Harvard Application Gameplay Session")*	**Unique solution mechanism video** *("How 120,000 rejection letters revealed the way into Harvard")*	
Most Aware	**Targeted postcard series highlighting money-back guarantee** *("Success stories with The Way In System")*	**Social influencer promotion series** *("The Way In System is literally the only way in now")*	**Your product** *("The Way In System")*
	Application analysis GPT *("Have you found your way into the Ivy League?")*	**By-invitation-only community** *("The Way In Winners Circle")*	**An upgraded version of your product** *("The Way In System with Live Coaching")*

The best offer matches what your prospect wants. If you start offer development by looking at your completed message matrix, you are more likely to develop useful offers than if you start with a list of offer ideas and try to shove your customers into them.

A checklist only works if your prospect wants and will use a checklist. Same with a coupon code. Same with the word "free." Your offer should always match what your list wants in that moment. Now, how do you make it more compelling?

To Optimize Your Offer, Start with Objections

A million people will have a million ideas on optimizing your offer, and you should make a study of all of them because the more ideas you have, the better. I've made a study of them, and I've found some of my own as well. What I've seen is that the best offers overcome objections to saying yes and neutralize anxieties about saying yes.

Start by writing down the core offer for your prospect. Let's use one from the examples I gave earlier: a webinar called "The one hack you haven't tried to get into Harvard" (an offer for Solution Aware prospects).

Webinar: *"The one hack you haven't tried to get into Harvard"*

What is our prospect's initial objection to that offer? Write it down.

Webinars take a long time with a bunch of talking.

How could we neutralize that objection? We add our neutralization to the core offer.

Webinar: *"The one hack you haven't tried to get into Harvard"*
25 minutes.
The one hack is shared in the first three minutes.

Great. Now what new objection or anxiety did we introduce, or what other objection might they have to the core offer?

Webinars are just trying to sell.

Well, we actually are going to sell. So we could do a few things. We could rename it—make it a free workshop or free group consultation. Or we could say, yes, there will be an offer, but it comes after you've seen the promised hack. And if you aren't floored by the power of the hack, there's no pressure to buy. However, if you try the hack in the first twenty minutes and love it so much you want more from us, then we'll have a special way for you to save on The Way In System that only workshop attendees will see.

> **Free Workshop:** *"The one hack you haven't tried to get into Harvard"*
> 25 minutes.
> The one hack is shared in the first three minutes. If you aren't floored by the hack, there's no pressure to buy. If you are, then you'll get a special way to save just for workshop attendees.

Great. Now what new objection or anxiety did we introduce, or what other objection might they have to the core offer? Write it down.

Hacks sound rudimentary. I don't want hacks.

Okay, you chose the word "hack" because it was in VOC. But maybe it's a poor fit for the audience after all?

> **Free Workshop:** *"The one shortcut you haven't tried to get into Harvard"*
> 25 minutes.
> The shortcut is shared in the first three minutes. If you aren't floored by the shortcut, there's no pressure to buy. If you are, then you'll get a special way to save just for workshop attendees.

Great. Now what new objection or anxiety did we introduce, or what other objection might they have to the core offer?

When there's no new objection or anxiety, we're done optimizing the offer for objections. But we're not done overall. Now we want to move the prospect to an "Oh hellz yes!" response to our offer.

To Optimize Your Offer, Enhance the Perception of Value

Consider your conversion rate for the offers you're running today. Let's say you've got a 2 percent paid conversion rate. That means 98 percent of your "List" didn't convert. Take out a third for bots and another third for randos who were on your site for shits and giggles (or just cannot buy your solution), and you're still left with more than 30 percent of your visitors who did not buy. We cannot overestimate the need to increase the perception of value for every prospect who encounters our brand so that more of them buy.

Alex Hormozi wrote a cult classic, *$100M Offers*, on enhancing the perception of value for your offer. He notes that value is increased when these four things have been achieved:

1. You have closed the gap between this moment and when the prospect will achieve the outcome they want to achieve,
2. You have removed effort for them,
3. You have eliminated any sacrifices they may have to make, and
4. You have increased belief in their ability to realize the value you've promised.

Basically, people want faster outcomes, easier. Which itself isn't surprising. But I love and want to call your attention to both *closing the gap* and *increasing belief in self.*

CLOSE THE GAP

How can you reduce the time it takes for your prospect to realize the outcome promised? Do you have any mechanisms in your onboarding or unboxing to facilitate quicker outcomes? Name them when you're describing your offer.

INCREASE SELF-BELIEF

Hormozi's background in before-and-after transformations for gyms lends itself well to this idea. What might be getting in the way of your prospect believing they can achieve the promised outcomes? What can you do with your offer to reduce uncertainty that your offer will not work for someone like me? We all believe we're the exception to the rule; make it clear that the rule is made by me.

How to Optimize Your Offer: Idea Dump

Hey, sometimes you just need a checklist of ideas! These will not apply to every offer, but one or two could be the cherry you need on top in order to get the yes.

- Reduce the price
- Offer coupon codes
- Offer payment plans
- Offer tiered pricing
- Offer rewards for paying up front or annually
- Offer multiple methods of payment
- Offer trial periods
- Offer extended trial periods
- Offer to buy out a contract
- Offer a complimentary upgrade
- Bundle products
- Add a guarantee
- Double the guarantee length
- Increase the value of the guarantee
- Offer free delivery
- Offer a free gift with purchase
- Reduce the number of products available
- Narrow the time period in which the offer is available
- Offer to complete the switch or migration to your solution
- Offer the services of an onboarding coach for free
- Offer team training on your solution for free
- Add a maintenance plan for free or for a reduced price or related incentive

To Optimize Your Offer, Give It a Mechanism and a Name

In Canada, our #1 coffee shop, Tim Hortons, has an annual promotion called Roll Up the Rim to Win. It's a coupon distribution system meant to drive customer retention. You can win prizes. Most people will win a cup of coffee or a donut, if they play regularly.

Instead of emailing people 10 percent off coupons or running a "Buy 9 get the 10th free," loyalty program, Tim Hortons:

1. **Has a unique mechanism for their offer:** Under the rim of your coffee cup is printed something you won, if anything. You have to roll up the rim when you're done with your coffee to see if you won.
2. **Names their offer:** Roll Up the Rim to Win. (Recently renamed: Roll Up to Win.)

Can you distribute your offer in a way that no one else in your industry does? Can you give that offer a name? A paper coupon is nowhere near as good as a scratch-to-reveal coupon. A limited time offer is nowhere near as good as *The Scratch 'n' Crash 10-Day Attack!* You don't have to create a mechanism and a name for every offer you've got, but what if you did?

FINISH BY EDITING YOUR SOLUTION DESIGN

The solution design template is intended to be one page—no longer—when completed. Big briefs are notorious for increasing confusion in orgs, which leads to multiple iterations on copy and slow review cycles. A tight, well-edited solution design ensures that the only information on the page is information that will shape the solution itself.

Before finalizing your solution design, run it by your team. Make sure everyone's on board with your plan, and ask them to call out areas of confusion, complexity, or oversimplification. They'll later reference your solution design during the copy review and approval process, so now is the time to work out any kinks.

Finish your solution design with the help of AI. Add your solution design document, any files describing the persona(e) you're targeting, and that persona's message matrix to an AI project. Then ask AI to play the devil's advocate. What about the offer might still be wrong? What are some potential flaws in the hypothesis and the breakthrough idea? What else does AI need from you to help strengthen the solution design so it relieves the identified constraint?

When the solution design is finalized, you're ready to move to assembling the copy.

CHAPTER RECAP

Designing the Solution

- ✓ Don't base a great idea on your gut and hope others will recognize its greatness–document your process with a clear solution design that shows how your copy will solve the identified problem.
- ✓ Create a new solution design for each asset (e.g., an email flow, a video sales letter).
- ✓ Develop and optimize your offer for your customer in that moment.
- ✓ Get your team to approve the solution design before you move forward, and use it alongside your copy when you're doing team copy reviews.

CHAPTER 9
Assemble Your First Draft

"Copy is not written. Copy is assembled."

Eugene Schwartz, legendary
direct-response copywriter

Your asset starts with a hook, which is identified on your solution design based on the beat in which you're joining the conversation happening in your customer's head. And with that hook and starting beat, you have enough to start shaping the copy for an asset.

If you hooked your reader at Beat 4 and wanted to move them to Beat 8, because that's the best point at which to drive to your lead magnet, you could copy all the VOC from all five of those beats and paste them into a doc. And what would you have? A mess. Potentially hundreds of cool lines. But no order, no structure—back to the Guesswork Trap.

Instead of that, we use frameworks. A framework will guide what you paste from your VOC and will show you gaps that you'll need to fill with new ad hoc listening.

WHAT DO I MEAN BY FRAMEWORK?

You may have heard of a copywriting framework like AIDA, which is Attention, Interest, Desire, Action—that's the sort of framework I'm talking about. A persuasion framework. A copywriting framework. A copyselling framework. It's a guiding structure.

A framework helps you outline your page, email, ad, or script in a persuasive way. Under each section of the framework, you will organize the best-fit *What* and *How* from the message matrix.

If your framework is AIDA, your copy doc is blank until you add these four words to it:

ATTENTION
INTEREST
DESIRE
ACTION

Under "Attention," you write your hook. Then, under each of the remaining sections of the framework, you begin pasting best-fit VOC from your message matrix. I'm about to show you my favorite frameworks. But first let's answer the question you're about three minutes away from asking: *Jo, of all those frameworks, how do I know which one to choose?*

My answer: Your framework depends on your hook.

FIRST COMES THE HOOK

In your solution design, you identified a likely hook for the asset you're writing. Now we need to categorize the hook into one of these buckets.

Bucket A: Problem hook.
Bucket B: Desire hook.
Bucket C: Promise hook.
Bucket D: Offer hook.
Bucket E: Other hook.

If the hook is in the Problem Aware section of the message matrix, chances are good it's in Bucket A: Problem. If it's about a dreamstate, desire, or value sought, it's likely in Bucket B: Desire. A big claim, big benefit, or promise belongs in Bucket C: Promise. A hook meant for Most Aware prospects who are ready for your offer is likely Bucket D: Offer. And anything else belongs in Bucket E.

Now let's switch to frameworks. Then we'll tie the hook and framework together.

NEXT COMES THE FRAMEWORK

To keep things easy, I associate a single framework with each hook. Here are the five frameworks you can expect to choose from.

The Framework for Bucket A: Problem Hook

My favorite framework is Problem, Agitation, Solution, or PAS. You hook your prospect with the problem they're experiencing. Then you spend time agitating it using real, lived examples of how that problem manifests in their lives. Then you introduce the solution to that problem.

As you use PAS, you'll discover that the "Solution" section of the framework is broad enough to allow you the flexibility to do more than just hop to describing your solution. I like to use "Solution" to explore solutions the prospect has tried that have failed them. (Just like in Beat 6 of the message matrix!) Then I agitate those solutions; what are those solutions doing wrong, and how is it affecting our brilliant prospect? This allows me to use the Problem Mechanism, assign blame to poor-fit solutions, and set our prospect up to receive our solution, including our solution mechanism.

From there, you get to choose the call to action. Do you keep writing, moving them toward product aware and most aware, then closing them? Or do you drive them to a lead magnet that brings them to product aware and then most aware? You get to choose.

Here's a great example of PAS, in the homepage hero section for Basecamp.com.

In April 2025, cofounder of Basecamp DHH (David Heinemeier Hansson) tweeted that the homepage hero ad shown above increased the signup rate for Basecamp by 12 percent.[27] And that happened after years of optimizing the Basecamp homepage, years of driving high signup conversions.

Keep in mind that a problem hook can appear in VOC across almost every beat. So the PAS framework is not limited to the Problem Aware stage. For example, the VOC you find in the How column for *Beat 23: Differentiated outcomes* may be a Problem-based hook. I would expect to find Agitation points in Beats 23 and 24. And Beat 25 would house the Solution to the problem. PAS. You can use it all over the place, anytime your hook is a problem hook.

The Framework for Bucket B: Desire Hook

The best framework for the Desire hook is *Desire, Obstacle, Solution*, or DOS. Like PAS, DOS finishes with the wonderfully broad "Solution" section.

The hook speaks to their desire. Practically speaking, that means you might find a Desire hook in:

- Beat 3: Moment of highest pleasure, longed for
- Beat 9: What might work better (solution mechanism)
- Beat 13: Desire and obstacles
- Beat 18: New/next/novel
- And almost any beat thereafter

The magical part is the "Obstacle" section. Your prospect desires an outcome, but something—an obstacle—is getting in the way. Your solution is the cure for the obstacle.

Desire: They want to get a hair transplant to reclaim the full head of hair genetics took from them.

Obstacles: Fear of winding up with unnatural "hair plugs." Fear of admitting, to doctors and friends, that they have a receding hairline. The idea that their hat is now part of their identity. Hope that no one will care about their bald spot. Hope that they'll stop caring about it. Hope that topical treatment will finally start working. Worries about taking time off work for surgery.

Solution: Two-hour hair restoration treatment under local anesthetic with no scarring and natural "restaurant ready" healing within seven days. Wear that hat if you want to, and take it off when you want to! Start with an easy online submission.

Here's an example of DOS in use (immediately below an AIDA-based hero) on TheHappySleeper.com:[28]

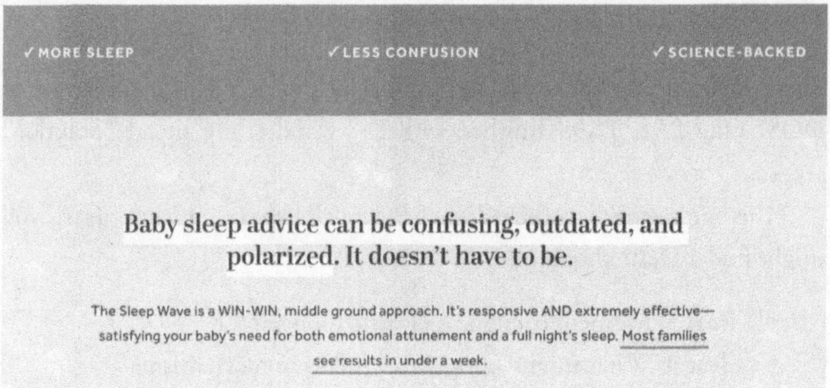

The Framework for Bucket C: Promise Hook

If you're hooking your prospect with a promise in general, a promised outcome, or a big claim, use the 4 Ps framework: Promise, Picture, Proof, Push.

Your headline and/or lede states the promise. (Remember that a great hook typically completes the phrase "I never thought it was possible but. . .") Then the "Picture" section is where you bring that promise to life for your prospect—to me, this really just means arousing, or dimensionalizing, the promise as it manifests in their life. Next, offer proof that the prospect can expect to see your promise realized. And finally, finish with your call to action, or the "Push" section.

A couple key points here:

- A promise is like it sounds—it's a promise. It's an outcome or claim that will turn heads. It's not just a benefit.
- The picture often ends up being two parts. One, how that promise manifests in the customer's life, which is their dreamstate or desire. Two, the solution mechanism that makes the picture and promise possible.
- It's not an accident that "proof" is one of the four Ps. Proof should not be a light smattering of some testimonials. It's a whole section of the asset you're writing. And it must be proof of the promise and of the picture—of everything on the page that came before it.

- Push can be a large section, with an optimized offer and click triggers and any number of messages to make the prospect actually take action. Or it may be a button. I recommend you first write "Push" as a larger section, then edit to its most convincing point.

Here's a classic example of the 4 Ps on a product detail page for a pillow:[29]

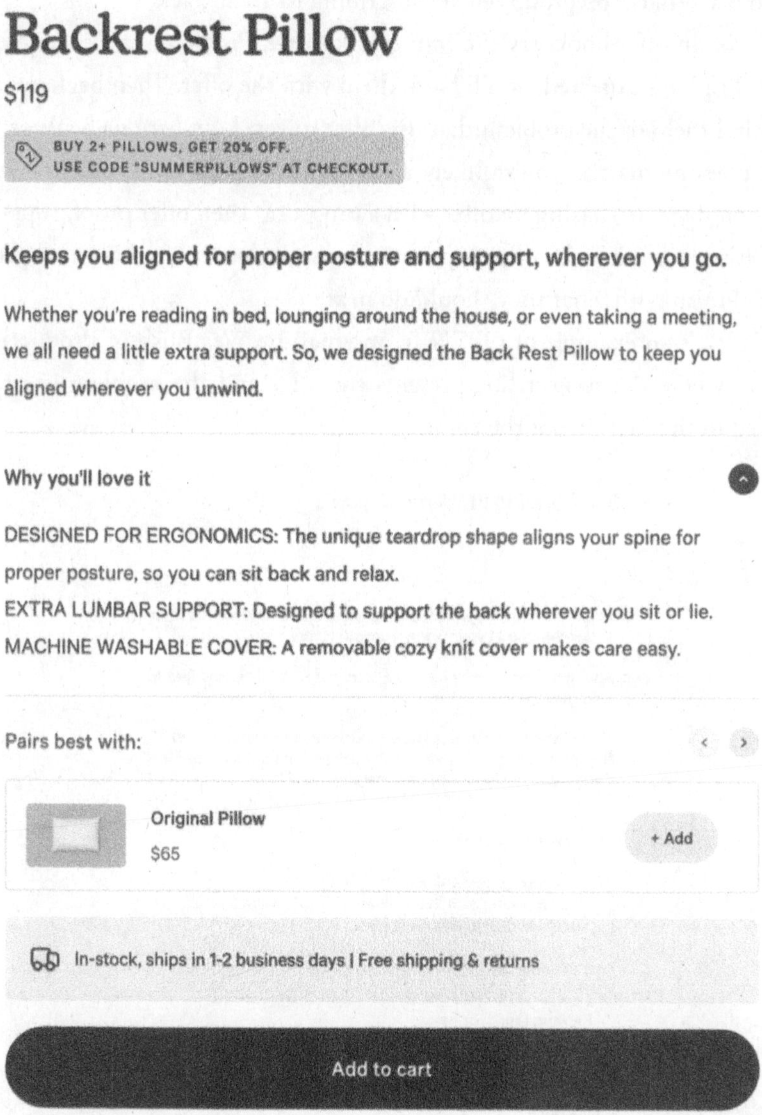

The Framework for Bucket D: Offer Hook

Although I recommend the following framework for pages written for Late Product Aware and Most Aware prospects who are ready to hear your product offer, it can also be used for pages earlier in the journey, when your offer is more targeted at lead generation or lead nurturing. For example, a 128-page special industry report, a five-minute crash course, or even unlocking a bonus WhatsApp group when subscribing to a Substack.

For an offer hook, try the framework Offer, Problem, Evidence, Next, or OPEN. As expected, you'll hook them with the offer. Then back up and remind them of the problem that this offer solves; I say *back up* because, on the message matrix, you've likely already moved past the Problem Aware section if you're sharing an offer with a prospect. Then offer proof, support, or "Evidence" that the offer is great and that it does solve the stated problem. Finish with what they should do next.

Here's an example of OPEN in an email by Wes Bush of ProductLed .com, where the subject line presents the offer and the problem is established in the first line of the email:

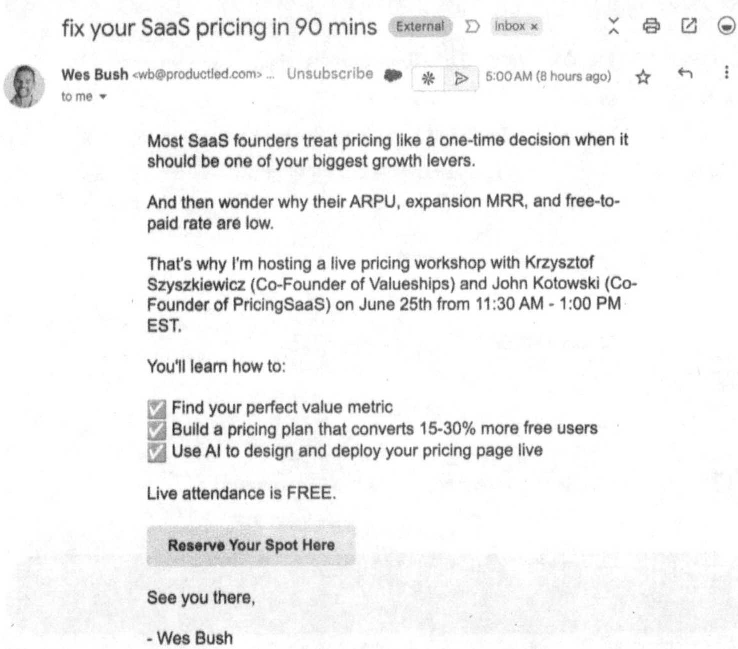

fix your SaaS pricing in 90 mins External Inbox ×

Wes Bush <wb@productled.com> ... Unsubscribe 5:00 AM (8 hours ago)
to me

Most SaaS founders treat pricing like a one-time decision when it should be one of your biggest growth levers.

And then wonder why their ARPU, expansion MRR, and free-to-paid rate are low.

That's why I'm hosting a live pricing workshop with Krzysztof Szyszkiewicz (Co-Founder of Valueships) and John Kotowski (Co-Founder of PricingSaaS) on June 25th from 11:30 AM - 1:00 PM EST.

You'll learn how to:

✅ Find your perfect value metric
✅ Build a pricing plan that converts 15-30% more free users
✅ Use AI to design and deploy your pricing page live

Live attendance is FREE.

Reserve Your Spot Here

See you there,

- Wes Bush

The Framework for Bucket E: Other Hook

The most beloved framework in copywriting history is AIDA, or Attention, Interest, Desire, Action. If your hook doesn't fit into any of the first four buckets, choose AIDA. If your hook fits into any of the first four buckets but the framework I showed you just isn't working, choose AIDA. Basically if all else fails, choose AIDA. You may realize you've been using AIDA all your life without ever knowing it.

In my experience, AIDA's greatest strength is also its worst part: opening with "Attention." *Attention* could really mean anything. A problem grabs my attention; so does a solution; so does a desire; so does a moment of highest tension; so does a claim; the list goes on. But it's the vagueness of "Attention" that so many copywriters like, and who am I to complain when the vagueness of "Solution" in PAS and DOS is what I like so much about them!

Once you've grabbed your prospect's attention, you need to push on it, build on it, make it come to life. That increases your prospect's interest in what first grabbed their attention, hence the "Interest" section of AIDA. If it helps, replace "Interest" with "Deepening Curiosity" and you may have an easier time telling "Interest" from the section that follows: "Desire."

The "Desire" section transforms their curiosity into a desire for what you're offering. This is the section where you begin to share the offer; dimensionalize it so that people desire it; add proof and otherwise optimize the offer so it's even more desirable. Once desire is high, we can finish with "Action," which is as it sounds: the action for the prospect to take.

Here's a classic example of AIDA in a Google ad that surfaces after a competitor keyword search.

Sponsored

Logan & Cove®
https://www.loganandcove.ca › vs-dreamcloud

4 Reasons Not to Choose Them | Buy From a Canadian Business

Make the Right Choice and Buy a Mattress Made in Canada Instead. Shop Logan & Cove® Today! Try Yours Risk-Free for 365 Nights.

★★★★★ Rating for loganandcove.ca: 4.9 - 394 reviews - Return policy: Most items 365+ days

HOOK	FRAMEWORK
Problem	PAS
Desire	DOS
Promise	The 4 Ps
Offer	OPEN
Other	AIDA

These are not the only frameworks you could use. These are just some of the most common and effective.

YOU'VE SELECTED YOUR ASSET FRAMEWORK. WHAT NEXT?

This process is going to be very analogue. First, write the framework in your copy doc. Then paste your hook in, under the first section of your framework. Following that, referencing the starting beat from your solution design, pull in best-fit VOC from the same area. By "the same area," I mean the framework you choose may compel you to pull VOC from a beat or two away. That's okay. Just try to stay in your stage of awareness and advance the prospect as best you can, only moving backward if it's required to move forward—such as if you realize, for your piece to make sense, you have to reference the *How* from a beat that's several steps back.

Let's demonstrate with an example. You're writing a video script for a YouTube ad for Hint o' Mint, a lesser known competitor to Dristan nasal spray.

Your hook is from *Beat 12: The category landscape*, and it's a problem hook based on this VOC: "I hate swallowing pills, but it's like that's the only option if you have a cold."

Because your framework is PAS, you next need to agitate the problem. You find that Beats 12 through 16 all agitate it well, but so does *Beat 5: The blame game.* So you pull in the best-fit VOC from all those beats—even though Beat 5 was back in Problem Awareness. (Hey, if it doesn't work in the final draft, you'll just cut it!)

So now you've established the problem with the category landscape (i.e., it's basically all pills). You've agitated that competitors keep focusing on producing pills because it's faster to get FDA approval even if a pill isn't the right solution to the problem; you blame the FDA and drugstores for a world focused on pills; you keep increasing the size of the Mega Mean Mouse, which is a corporate world in love with pills, to the detriment of those who can't take them easily, or who need faster action than a pill allows.

Finish with the Solution. Now, at this point, we've brought our prospect to Beat 16. We don't want to move them backward—we want to keep moving them forward. So we look for our solution VOC in Beat 16 and onward. We find it in *Beat 18: New/Next/Novel*, where the How column is filled with study data—a *new testing methodology allows the FDA to more rapidly to approve nasal sprays as long as they're formulated and packaged according to The Black Method. This can take years to get right, but Hint o' Mint has only ever used The Black Method and, as such, Hint o' Mint is approved across the US.*

You continue moving through the remaining beats until your video ad script is at the most natural place to drive the prospect to your sales page and close the sale.

EACH SECTION ALSO GETS A FRAMEWORK

Copyselling frameworks aren't just for the asset overall. Within each section of your asset, you can use more frameworks to shape that section.

In the earlier example of Hint o' Mint, your Solution section was, admittedly, quite big. That's common with Solution sections. You can tighten it up by using another framework inside the Solution section. Repeat the process, but this time for the section:

1. Find a hook in the *How* section.
2. Choose a framework based on the hook.

Our hook is in *Beat 18: New/Next/Novel*: "Nasal sprays that meet the stringent requirements of The Black Method are fast-tracked for FDA approval." This line was pulled from an academic study, so it's not particularly hook-y—but its meaning is the hook we need. (See chapter ten for how to improve VOC with formulas.) It fits into the Other Hook bucket, which is where we default to using AIDA.

The result is a copy doc that looks like this:

PROBLEM
AGITATION
SOLUTION
    ATTENTION
    INTEREST
    DESIRE
    ACTION

Now instead of pulling in everything from Beats 16 to 23, we can focus only on phrasing that fits well under Interest and Desire—before driving the viewer to take action on the sales page. Frameworks inside frameworks.

An Easy Body-Level Framework: PCPO

If your hook for a section of body copy is a problem, try PCPO: Problem, Cure, Proof, Offer. This is my favorite framework for body copy on product pages.

The crosshead for the section expresses the problem, which is our hook. In the very next sentence, which is typically the first line of a paragraph, write the cure for the problem. Build on this cure until there's no doubt that the problem is cured. Then prove it—drop in a great testimonial or data point about the problem and the cure, and support that further with an embedded video demo showing the cure in action. Finish with your offer. Here's an example:

Your customers shouldn't notice that your omnichannel experience is omnichannel

Deliver proactive experiences across the channels customers prefer. With AI-powered self-service, including [REDACTED], you can deliver intuitive, multilingual experiences that improve efficiency. Customer success teams see average savings of 3.4 hours per rep per week by proactively engaging customers at scale, in their preferred channel.

Book a demo of your new omnichannel customer experience

THINK IN ONES

When you start pasting VOC into your frameworks, you'll start wondering where it all ends and how much you should paste in. Use the Rule of One to help you decide. A foundational concept in conversion copywriting, the Rule of One tells us to:

- Write for one reader, not a bunch of audiences;
- Hook that one reader with one big idea, not a bunch of little ideas you hope add up to something big;
- Make it believable with one promise; and
- Get that one reader nodding along with you all the way to your one offer.

Furthermore, we want to give everything only one job to do. The headline has one job: grab their attention such that they stick around long enough to read the next line. The next line has one job: keep them reading.

An email from name has one job: get your one reader to look at the subject line. A subject line has one job: get your one reader to open the email. Your opening line, lede, or headline has one job: grab their attention such that they stick around long enough to read the next line. Every line thereafter has the same job: keep them reading by reflecting relevance and building interest. The call to action, or call to value, has one job: get our one reader to click. Is it a qualified click? That's not the job of the call to action. Getting the click is the job. What came before the button is what makes that click qualified.

The email's job is not to sell. The job of the email is to move our one reader along to the next step in the assembly line: the landing page. There the headline has one job: grab their attention such that they stick around long enough to read the next line. The next line has one job: keep them reading.

If you think of giving everything one job to do, all in an effort to get your one reader toward your one offer, then you can better determine what belongs on the page and what doesn't.

WHEN IS A PAGE OR ASSET DONE?

A page, email, video, chat, or ad is done when your copy has earned the *next* qualified click. More precisely, it is done when you've moved the customer from the starting beat for the asset to the finishing beat for the asset, as defined in your solution design. Later, after writing and during editing, you'll cut and add copy, refining it to the point that you will know it is done and ready to test in the wild.

CHAPTER RECAP

How to begin writing your ad, email, or page

- ✓ Start by finding your hook (which should be in your solution design).
- ✓ Then choose the best-match framework for your hook.
- ✓ Fill the framework with VOC from your message matrix, sticking in the vicinity of the starting beat.
- ✓ Use frameworks within sections of your asset-level framework.
- ✓ Control the length of your copy by thinking in ones and considering all decision-making modalities (not just quick-action folks).

CHAPTER 10

Improve VOC with Formulas

"Truth is ever to be found in simplicity."

Sir Isaac Newton, physicist and mathematician,
which you already knew

To further reduce guesswork, we use frameworks and formulas to make VOC punchy, powerful, and persuasive. Frameworks, as you now know, happen at the page level and inside framework sections. The words on the page benefit from everyone's favorite part of copywriting: copywriting formulas.

ALL WRITING ALREADY USES FORMULAS

I believe strongly in formulas. I loved symbolic logic in university because of the formulas; I took four years of Latin because it is an almost mathematical language; I love grammar because it adds science to art; I think you should always spell a word correctly the way I think you should always add two numbers correctly. If you've read anything by Virginia Tufte, you already agree with me.

In the English language, we rely heavily on formulas in the structure of our sentences. The phrases and sentences you easily fly through are based on rules. Consider the IAO Rule. This is nerdy, but you'll love it. The IAO Rule holds that, when two or more otherwise identical monosyllabic words are placed together (a term linguists call "reduplication") but the vowel for the second and/or third word is different ("ablaut reduplication"),[30] the words must be ordered such that the word with the O always goes last and the I always goes first:

Ding dong
Tick tock
Mish mash
Flip flop
Knick knack

The IAO Rule is why we say "clip clop" instead of "clop clip." It's why we zigzag instead of zagzig. It's baked into the English language structure. So too are copywriting formulas baked into the copyselling system.

WHAT FORMULAS DO

If you're doing the work as you read this book, you currently have a big page with raw VOC pasted under headings like "Solution." You use formulas to revise the VOC so that it is no longer raw. Your objective is to keep as much of the VOC as you can—avoiding summarizing—while ensuring that the words on the page are as persuasively presented as possible. That's what formulas do.

The following formulas are for headlines (the line at the top of a page) and for crossheads (the subheadings that introduce sections down the page). Additional formulas for buttons and lists follow below.

Headline and Crosshead Formulas

Rewrite your VOC-based headlines using formulas like these.

Formula A: *If you can [do X], you can [get amazing result].*

Try this one out at the feature level, on a tour page. Or use it to introduce and also complete a demo (bookend the demo with this formula). Examples of this formula in use are:

- If you can add a row in Excel, you can build custom software integrations.
- If you can take a picture, you can share a digital business card.
- If you can drag and drop, you can design a website.

Formula B: *What's the [differentiator adjective] way to [solve problem]?*

Examples of headlines that use this formula:

- What's the gorgeous way to light up your desk?
- What's the less-traveled path to enjoy retirement?
- What's the only way to hold online meetings without a single voice dominating?

Formula C: *[Thing they want] even if [objection/anxiety they have]*

An absolute classic formula! Examples of headlines that use this formula:

- Write compelling sales emails even if you flunked tenth grade English.
- Host a packed online summit even if your list is under 1,000 subscribers today.
- Chat with your website visitors like you're old friends even if they're totally anonymous.

Formula D: *Like a [category or product]. Unlike any [category or product].*

This is one of my favorites to use in crossheads or directly under/over beautiful product shots. It grounds a solution in a known space and then reinvents it, instantly, as the superior leader of that space—so good at what it does, everything else pales in comparison.

- Like a camera. Unlike any camera.
- Like a babysitter. Unlike any babysitter.
- Like a QR code generator. Unlike any QR code generator.

Formula E: *Get X even though Y.*

A few examples:

- Get a promotion even though you just got the job.
- Get an influx of donations even though it's not Christmastime.
- Get fresh, new leads even though your webinar is old and dated.

Hook-Finder Formulas

In addition to "I never thought it was possible but," you should try these formulas to help you find hooks, or ledes, to open your page or to kick off a new section of your copy. Your hook will complete the phrase with these formulas. The formulas themselves do not appear in your copy.

Formula A: *What no one tells you is . . .*

Examples of hooks that complete this phrase are:

- Five years ago, you could have bought this apartment for $88,000.
- A man you looked up to was afraid to make his dream come true.
- The people who live in the rich part of town aren't doctors and lawyers.
- Jefferson had one of the best minds in 1776, but an iPhone is smarter and faster.
- How to win friends and influence people.

Formula B: *You won't regret stopping everything to hear . . .*

Examples of hooks that complete this phrase are:

- You're not you when you're hungry.
- Will you be a checkout clerk or the CEO 10 years from now?
- Does she or doesn't she?
- "I haven't had a glass of water in years."
- No software on the planet will quadruple your leads. Not even this one.

Formula C: *For all the money/time you're spending, you'd never believe . . .*

This is a great formula to use when you've got a strong mechanism in your product or solution. Examples of hooks that complete this phrase are:

- At 60 miles an hour, the loudest noise in the new Rolls Royce comes from the electric clock.
- Do you make these mistakes in English?
- You can switch careers before the afternoon is up.
- A little mistake that cost a farmer $3,000 a year.
- Thousands of businesses have access to this feature but never use it.

Your hook typically appears as either your headline, your subject line, or the opening line (lede) of a paragraph or block of text. And remarkably few brands use hooks. So it may feel unusual to use attention-grabbers like the ones shown here. But doing so is what makes your copy more compelling—and it's a stellar opportunity, given how few brands bother to attempt to hook a prospect.

Now, let's take this one step further because your hook is absolutely critical. Every headline should be a hook. And every crosshead or subhead you write down the page should also be a hook. We are trying, constantly, to keep hooking our reader, most often by continually opening new curiosity gaps. So with that in mind, consider also this headline-slash-hook formula.

Formula D: [Desired outcome] even if [key objection or anxiety]

Let's say you're staring at a crosshead on your copy doc. It's VOC that expresses the outcome your customer got when they used your product: "We tripled our demo bookings." Amazing VOC. But you know that your customers also have a lot of anxieties, worries, and obstacles getting in the way of their success—you see them in so many beats on your message matrix. So you know that it's not enough to state the outcome they want. You have to reduce skepticism and draw them in—hook them—by countering their immediate objection.

So you take the desired outcome VOC, and you grab VOC that speaks to objections to using your solution, and you pop them together with the phrase "even if." Examples are:

- 3x your sales pipeline even if you don't get another lead for the rest of the year
- Stay asleep while 3 AM comes and goes even if your cortisol spikes at 2:58 AM
- Model calm kindness to your second grader even if you're frustrated by their screaming

Fascination (Bullet) Formulas

Not to be confused with a fascinator, which is a strange little hat worn by fancy people—or with the song "Fascination," which is going to be in your head now, you're welcome—a fascination is like a bullet point, but better. It's also known as a curiosity bullet. That's because the whole idea with fascinations is to stack a series of curiosity-builders in list form. Here's an example:[31]

Most bullet lists on SaaS and ecommerce websites are short benefits or feature points; for example, on the Teamwork.com homepage, a series of feature sections are filled with bullet lists that are benefits-focused. Take a look:[32]

> Clients wanting things yesterday? A massive job on the horizon? Key Account Manager suddenly resigned? Be ready for any resourcing challenge.
>
> - See staff availability and workloads at a glance
> - Plan resources for later in the year
> - Easily check if you're under- or over-utilizing your team

You can keep the features and the benefits, but we want to intrigue—not just state facts. Facts are for comparison charts and the back sections of sales sheets. While we're building customers, we have no choice but to fascinate them. That's the job.

So what if we tried to rewrite Teamwork's copy above to use fascinations? Let's try the first block, which we'll turn into this:

Clients want things yesterday? A massive job on the horizon? Key Account Manager suddenly resigned? You'll be ready for any resourcing challenge because only Teamwork gives you:

- A real-time view of who's secretly underbooked.
- Access to the forward-planning move smart teams make today to avoid last-minute chaos in Q4.
- New ways to spot overworked teams before they burn out (and underused ones before budgets do).

These fascinations cover the same topics the original three bullets covered. But they're more intriguing. They speak to a feature or mechanism that can deliver results—not just to the benefits of using a solution. And that keeps people reading.

> **MECHANISMS**
>
> Refer back to chapter four, where you learned about mechanisms as weapons of mass conversion.

Now that we've seen what a fascination can look like in the real world, let's get into formulas so you can upgrade your bullet lists. Keep in mind that, if you can't imagine using fascinations on your product site, you may use them instead for promoting lead magnets, like driving webinar signups and ebook downloads.

Formula A: If X, try Y

X is what the prospect experiences. Y is the feature or solution in your product. (Importantly, don't say how it works!)

- If your copywriters are always missing deadlines, try Reminder Mode.
- If you've never been upgraded to first class, you'll love the bonus section on Aggressive Loyalty Programs.
- If daytime cold medicine leaves you feeling wired, ask a pharmacist to tell you all about the Acetaminophen Anti-Jitters.

Formula B: If X, try Y (+ finder)

X is what the prospect experiences. Y is the feature or solution in your product. And the finder is where they can find Y in your product.

- If your copywriters are always missing deadlines, try Reminder Mode (in the Premier Plan).
- If you've never been upgraded to first class, you'll love the bonus section on Aggressive Loyalty Programs (find it on page 17).
- If daytime cold medicine leaves you feeling wired, ask a pharmacist to tell you all about the Acetaminophen Anti-Jitters (*tap in-app* to chat with a pharmacist).

Formula C: What to do if X

X is what the prospect experiences. In this fascination, you don't mention the solution—you just tease the prospect with the idea that there is a solution to X.

- What to do when your kids don't text you back
- What to do if you've invested half of your nest egg and you're terrified to touch what's left
- What to do to curb your 2 AM cravings

Formula D: The [one/specific] [thing] you should never [do] when [scenario].

Examples of fascinations that complete this phrase are:

- The one packaging sticker you should never ignore when customers are skeptical about your product
- The specific AI prompts you should never use when designing interfaces for healthcare practitioners
- The one button you should never touch when someone else is running a Zoom webinar for you

Fascinations tease. When done right, they'll open a loop only your offer or product can close.

The Best Button Copy Formula

Not to flex too hard here, but you're reading a book written by the person who invented the call to value. Oh, you've never heard of the call to value. Ahem. Cool, no, it's fine. Okay, so here's the deal with calls to value and calls to action.

A call to action—which you've heard of—is the direct action your prospect is to take next. It is commonly phrased as "Learn more" or "Buy now."

A call to value—which you're now going to mention in all your copy review meetings—is the direct value your prospect is going to derive by taking action. Instead of learning more, it is what happens when they learn more, such as "Start my journey as a franchisee."

You'll only need one formula for your call to action or call to value. It's this: Complete the following phrase:

I want to ___________

Whatever goes in the blank is the copy for your call to action or call to value, which is likely going to appear as a button on your page. And this may be the most surprising part: Your button copy should be in the first person. Test it and see!

	Call to action	Call to value
I want to	Download the weight loss ebook	Lose 8 lbs in 30 days
I want to	Watch the bechamel tutorial	See how to make bechamel
I want to	Start my Peloton trial	Try a Peloton workout for free

Importantly, the button copy needs to actually complete the phrase "I want to." So if you find yourself writing "I want to upgrade to the paid plan," stop yourself and revise. No one wants to *upgrade to the paid plan*. What's the value they'll derive when they upgrade to the paid plan? That's what goes on the button.

Bonus: Your button is likely close to a headline or crosshead. Try to plug that headline or crosshead into the "I want to" formula to find your button copy. We've seen button clicks increase significantly by matching the nearest headline with the button copy. For example, if the nearest headline is "You could double your income as a multi-unit franchisee," then the button could be "Double my income."

An alternate take on that formula is this: Complete the following phrase:

I want you to ________

As in, I want you to show me outfits I'll love. Give me free access to the course. Show me a sample report. Years ago, Hiten Shah brought me in to try to beat the very, very strong control for the homepage of CrazyEgg .com. We did beat the control, barely, but one of the biggest takeaways for everyone involved was that the control button copy was wildly powerful. We updated my winning version so that all the buttons used it. The copy was this:

Show me my heatmap

It's a call to value that completes the phrase, "I want you to."

Shouldn't You Always Use a Call to Value?

Calls to value are great up-funnel, but a clear call to action is critical at the point of sale. "Add to cart" is ideal to help people know they're adding the item to their cart. "Complete purchase" is ideal when a user is about to complete the purchase and wants to know that they've bought the thing. As you get closer to the point of sale, like in the checkout or on the payment page, use very clear call-to-action button copy.

THE RIGHT FORMULA HELPS YOUR COPY GRAB ATTENTION AND BUILD INTEREST

Most copywriting formulas are best for direct response mailers or clickbait blog posts—not for the homepage for Bitly, the product detail page for Stream Deck, or the category page for J Crew. What you and I need to do, when we're speaking to a business buyer or a more sophisticated consumer, is pull back on curiosity and balance it with clarity. The formulas I've shared with you in this chapter do just that.

But for any formula to work, you first need this: a childlike enthusiasm about your product.

You need to find—in your voice of customer data and in your own mind—an insatiable appetite for things that make people truly curious about your solution. What workflow breakthroughs will they experience? What unexpected efficiencies will they uncover? What will be their moments of "Oh, cool, I didn't know software could do that"? You've got to get as genuinely excited about your solution as they are. I used to joke that I *had* to write copy for accounting software—"what could be more boring than that har har har"—but the fact was that I had to learn to freaking love accounting in order to write anything that would move people to buy QuickBooks. I had to enthusiastically listen to customers to feel something about accounting. That taught me:

- The day you send an invoice is a really, really good day.
- If your profit and loss report shows more profits than losses, that's cause for celebration.
- What's in your business bank account today might not be there tomorrow, so you've gotta prepare for that—you can't guess at that.
- Accounting means money.
- Smart accounting means more money.
- Money means the nicest house in the nicest neighborhood and a Porsche 911 on your fiftieth birthday.

I wasn't allowed to be bored by accounting software. And you're not allowed to be bored by your solution, either. Find the joy. Find the one person in the crowd who buys into the joy. And write exclusively for that one person, using formulas to amplify a message.

CHAPTER RECAP

How to revise VOC-based draft copy with formulas

- ✓ Rewrite the core of your draft copy using formulas.
- ✓ Be careful not to lose the essence of or the word choices from the original VOC.
- ✓ Make sure your formulas increase the persuasiveness of your copy and amplify the value.

CHAPTER 11
Agitating & Arousing

"Good copy makes me understand.
Great copy makes me understood."

Unattributed copywriting adage

I'm going to start with an example. Let's say you are someone who sweats a lot. You sweat enough that you know the difference between deodorant and antiperspirant, and you can't use either because nothing keeps you dry. Maybe it's not even your armpits that do all the sweating. Maybe it's your face, behind your knees, the palms of your hands. Maybe the soles of your feet get so sweaty you have to wear socks in the summer to keep from slipping around in your sandals.

You hear about a product called SweatBlock. It's supposed to curb hyperhidrosis, which is what you have. So you go to SweatBlock.com and read the hero section of the homepage:

Control your sweat.
And wear what you want.
Stop excessive sweating for up to
7 days with just the dab of a towelette.

There's a photo of a happy woman next to that headline. There's a product shot. There's a button that reads: "Sweat Less. Live More." There's a free shipping callout. And the hero is rounded out by a selection of logos for publications where SweatBlock has been mentioned.

You can understand the product: a towelette that prevents sweating. But do you feel understood? Do you feel seen? Do you see yourself in that copy? Remember that your feet slip in sandals. And then ask, *Do I see myself in that copy?*

STATE AND AGITATE THE PROBLEM

When SweatBlock brought my crew in to optimize their copy, we started way back at Problem Aware. We put the problem on the page, and we agitated it because VOC research surfaced the pain-filled stories of SweatBlock's customers. At the time, SweatBlock had more than five thousand reviews on Amazon, and I pored over each of them manually. What I found was that people had detailed stories to share of their problems—struggling moments in social settings. Time and again, customer reviews for the SweatBlock product included or even led not with the solution itself but with the individual's painful problems. Customer reviews turned hyperhidrosis into a Mega Mean Mouse that always showed up to ruin social engagements.

So I crafted this headline and subhead, based on reviews:

"It doesn't even have to be
hot out. My armpits are
always wet."
Excessive sweating ruins more than clothing. It keeps you
from putting up your hand, from high-fiving friends, from
getting close . . .

And below it, I added a new section: The agitation section, where the problem gets felt.

Agitation, or arousal, is what most pages, emails, and ads are missing. Here's what I wrote for SweatBlock's agitation section:

If you suffer from excessive sweating, deodorant isn't enough. You've likely tried to hide your secret by:

- Never wearing light blue or light gray—black is best
- Wearing a "sweat layer" underneath and keeping a jacket or cardigan handy
- Tucking tissues inside your shirt and trying not to move too much
- Avoiding situations that could trigger nervous sweating
- Wearing sleeveless, colorless tops in the summer (and dabbing frequently)
- Avoiding pointing, and low-fiving instead of high-fiving
- Hugging carefully to keep the dampness to yourself
- Waving with your elbow at your side

I moved almost everything that had been in the hero section underneath this section, using the PAS framework. The control led with the solution; our variation led with the problem. Our variation beat the control easily, generating a paid lift of 49 percent with 99 percent confidence.

AN INTRO TO AGITATING AND AROUSING

Agitating and arousing put on the page all the parts that salespeople prompt, that customers spill, but that marketers and brand managers too often edit away. Agitating pokes at a sore, and arousing stokes a desire. The effect is that the reader cannot ignore their problem.

Consider the framework PAS: Problem Agitation Solution. It's not enough to state the problem and then jump into the solution. First, our prospect needs to recognize the problem. Next, they need to be drawn in so they feel the problem, by agitating it with lived experiences. Only when the problem is unmistakably seen by our prospect can we move on to the solution. The solution itself also uses agitation or arousal.

Every part of any framework you use is likely to benefit from agitation or arousal copy.

Consider the framework DOS: Desire Obstacle Solution. Where would you add agitating or arousing copy in that framework? Under all three parts.

Desire: State the desire. Bring it to life with arousal points.
Obstacle: State what's blocking the desire. Bring it to life with agitation points.
Solution: State the ideal solution. Bring it to life with arousal points.

All of the arousal and agitation points are already on your message matrix, in the *How* fields. The purpose of this chapter is to tell you, in no uncertain terms, to put those points on the page.

HOW MUCH AGITATING OR AROUSING IS ENOUGH?

Start by including more, not fewer, agitation or arousal points in your copy. Under every section of a framework, push on agitation and arousal. Then scale back in editing, validation, or experiment iterations.

Agitation and arousal are how you keep people reading. They help you activate the Sullivan nod in your copy the way a salesperson may do in real life. Summaries are not enough. Great copy brings problems, solutions, features, outcomes—everything that matters to our customer—to life.

CHAPTER RECAP

Using agitation and arousal in your copy

- ✓ Agitate real-life problems in your copy, instead of glossing over them.
- ✓ Arouse real-life desires in your copy, instead of assuming the reader is already imagining ideal outcomes.
- ✓ Use VOC in your message matrix to dig deep into agitation and arousal points.
- ✓ Default to more agitation and arousal points when you first start writing, then edit or experiment to whittle your list down to the most powerful points.

CHAPTER 12
Oh, and Make It Sweaty

"Creativity is just connecting things."

Steve Jobs, Cofounder of Apple Inc.

To write copy well, you need to get *sweaty* about it. Not physically—you can stay seated while writing. I mean *sweaty* in the way that the kids say, "Sweaty." It's what people in the '90s—my people—called being a "try-hard." You're gonna be a sweaty try-hard.

Let go of your ambitions to assemble customers en masse while striving for elegance. The best *performing* copy is not elegant. It's not sophisticated. It doesn't win awards; it wins customers. And that's always been true.

Let's go back to the late 1920s to prove it. Home to visit his parents, a New York copywriter named John Caples placed a large black portfolio on his mother's breakfast table. "I thought I'd show you my book, Mother," he probably said, "so you can see what I do all day." His mother, a Manhattan socialite and the wife of a respected physician, raised an eyebrow.

John had recently risen to fame on Madison Avenue for his direct response ad that had generated masses of leads for a music school. He sat next to his mother and opened his portfolio. He turned to the famous ad and read the headline to her:

> *"They Laughed When I Sat Down at the Piano, But When I Started to Play -"*

Page after page, John walked his mother through his book, which was packed with industry-changing but decidedly unsophisticated ads. When they reached the final ad and he closed the book, his mother had just one thing to say: *"You'd better not show your father this."*

Today, John Caples's ads are regarded as the greatest of all time.[33] The headlines that turned Buzzfeed into a media unicorn[34] were based largely on the headlines for *"They Laughed . . ."* and similar ads that Caples wrote. But his mother didn't, and couldn't, see what her son's copy was getting right. She couldn't imagine that any person, including but not limited to a person of taste, would go in for such a style of advertising. It embarrassed her.

When I was in-house at a tech giant, our division's leader kiboshed my long-form sales page, which I'd written to switch small business owners to our product. He called my copy, and I quote, "fear mongering." He wanted an elegant three-word headline, a pithy supporting line, perhaps three short bullets, and a nice little button. But we had aggressive sales targets to hit. So a fearless marketing manager and I secretly pushed the page live and drove emails to it. And, although I'm not allowed to mention hard numbers, the campaign tidily outperformed the forecast. And by tidily I mean by a long freaking shot.

Copy that converts isn't *just* based on VOC. It's not *just* written with frameworks and optimized with formulas. It's also sweaty AF.

Prepare to embarrass your division's leader (and maybe your mom) with how hard your copy tries.

GET SWEATY WITH YOUR BRAND'S VOICE

Written large on the wall of a boardroom at the Liquid Death headquarters is this line: *"Why should anyone give a shit?"*

For Liquid Death, their brand voice is the reason most consumers give a shit. It's what turned them into a $1.4 billion[35] beverage company that started by selling cans of plain old water. Their brand and its execution are why people love their company. Their brand and its execution are why Liquid Death could break into, and make huge waves in, a very saturated market in 2019, when heavy hitters like Dasani were already filling the market's need for packaged water.

The Lemon Case Study

When Aleksandr Volodarsky asked my agency to write the website for Lemon.io—a newer marketplace for remote developers—he had a kooky idea: the website's copy should sound like it's written for a cult. His exact words to me were, *"We are joking around with the idea of a cult or Freemasons."* And his teammate added, *"We use many ironic references to cults, conspiracy, and the all-seeing eye that helps us find the right people no matter where they are."*

Lemon wanted their brand voice to be *thick*. They rightly saw brand as a key differentiator to attract their target: small to mid-sized businesses in America. A strong brand voice would help make them memorable, given that they were a new entrant, based overseas from most of their prospective clients (they were in the Ukraine), in a very crowded space dominated by known quantities like Toptal, Freelancer, and Upwork.

It was November 2019. We didn't know COVID was around the corner. And we didn't know that the demand for remote developers was about to explode. Nor did we know that the copy we would write for Lemon would not only help Lemon take off and gain traction—but it'd also keep Aleksandr busy fielding emails from fans of his website's copy for years to come. I have more than four years' worth of emails from Aleksandr connecting me with founders who 1) hired Lemon and 2) wanted to hire the folks who'd written Lemon's copy.

So what was the copy?

First, let's look at representative homepage copy from brands that dominated the space Lemon was trying to break into.[36]

Toptal

Hire the Top 3% of Freelance Talent
Toptal is an exclusive network of the top freelance software developers, designers, finance experts, product managers, and project managers in the world. Top companies hire Toptal freelancers for their most important projects.

Freelancer.com

Hire expert freelancers for any job, online
Millions of small businesses use Freelancer to turn their ideas into reality.

Gigster

This is gigster. We build and manage distributed teams like no one else. It's a whole new approach to creating software that will make you rethink what your company is capable of.

Codementor

Project-based freelance work

- Find experts for on-demand code review
- Build features for your existing product
- Turn your idea into an MVP

Upwork

The talent you need.
The flexibility you want.
Upwork expertly matches professionals and agencies to businesses seeking specialized talent.

You can see why Aleksandr saw an opportunity to differentiate based on brand. I have a hard time identifying anything resembling brand in the copy his competitors were leading with on their homepages.

We followed the Copyselling system for their homepage before we layered in brand voice elements. We started by auditing the competition, interviewing the Lemon team, and conducting deep voice of customer research; we synthesized that into a solution design; we found our hook in VOC and selected a framework (in this case, we used AIDA); we slotted raw VOC into the framework, then optimized it with formulas and better practices. We were clear on the problem mechanism ("Valley of Product Death") and solution mechanism ("Secret Sect of Devs"), even if they weren't called that yet.

> To see the original copy live on the website, go to copyhkr.com/lemon

Only then did we layer on the heavy brand voice. And here's a selection of what we produced.

> **Behold! The almighty devs you've been looking for**
> Why squander time and money on developers who aren't perfect for your startup? Let Lemon match you with engineers that can transform your vision into reality—diabolically fast.
>
> **Find your startup's**
> **Chosen One**
>
> 1. You find yourself treacherously close to the Valley of Product Death.
> 2. Confess your product needs by chat on Lemon.io.
> 3. A benevolent Lemon account manager reviews our secret sect of devs.
> 4. Your Miraculous Match developer is named and offered to you.
> 5. Unto the world is born the greatest iteration of your product.

Their UI design brought the branded copy to life.

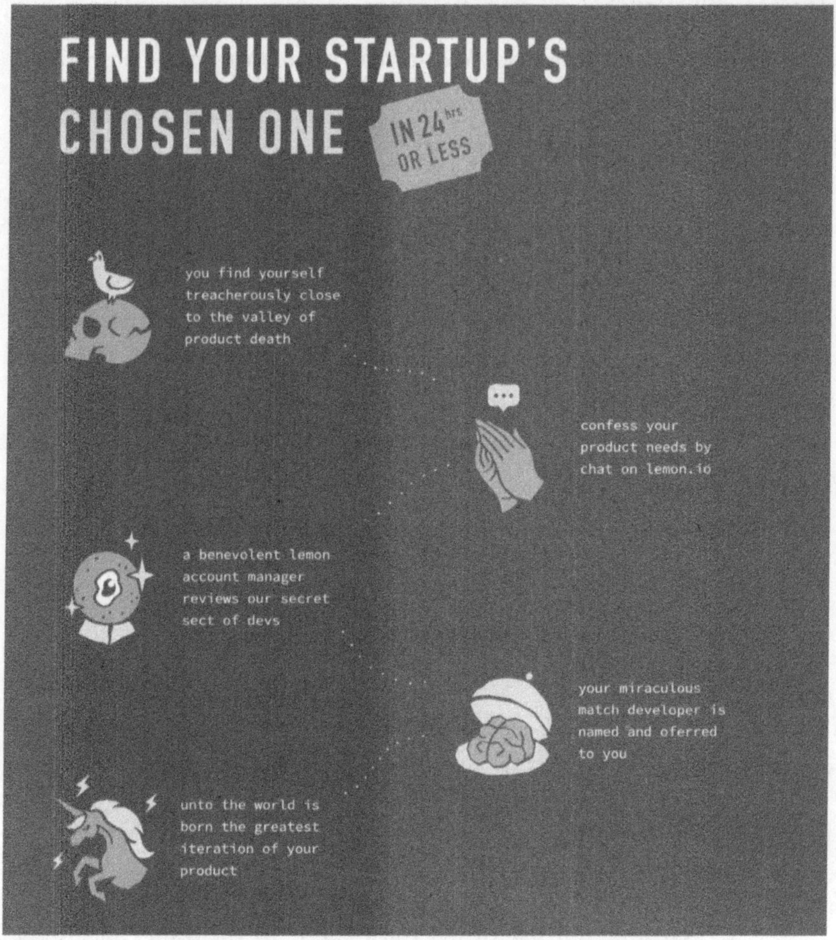

This voice helped Lemon grow its monthly revenue from $180,000 in 2019 to $1,400,000 in 2023.[37]

Avoid Neutral Copy

A strong brand voice is the beginning. That's the artfulness that can bring conversion copy to life. And you'll usually find that voice in VOC. Plus, it can perform much better than voiceless or voice-neutral copy. We tested two headline and button combos on a shopping site. The control was voice-neutral:

Clothes you'll love
perfect for your shape
and style

Button: Sign up now

Variation B was voice-rich, based on how the brand's audience of women spoke about dressing their bodies:

Big bum? Thick waist?
Not so perky boobs . . . ?
Find outfits you'll look
fab in—just as you are

Button: Show me outfits I'll love

Variation B drove 124 percent more clicks to sign up, with 99 percent confidence.

Here's another example worth sharing from KOHA Pet (kohapet.com), a brand that is competing in the saturated category of natural or raw pet foods. Voice is a differentiator for them.

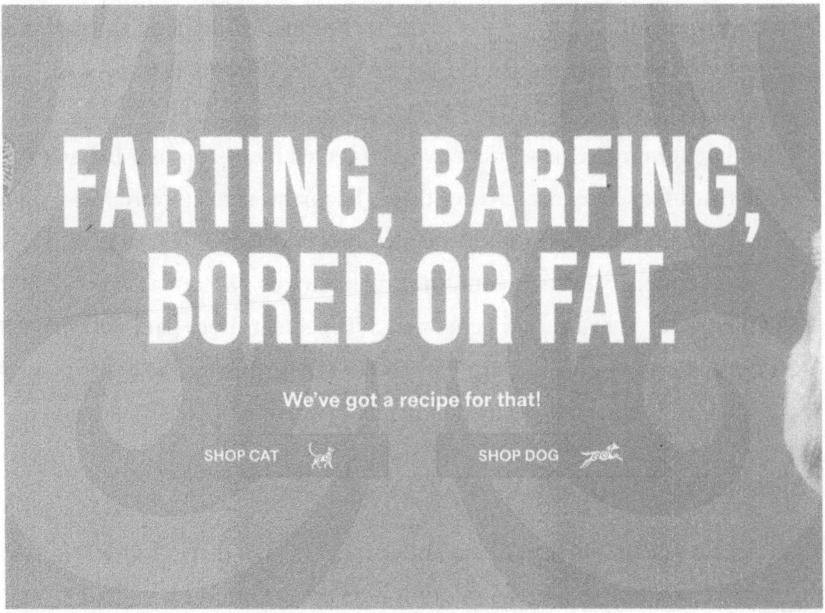

It's not just about grabbing attention—it's about interrupting patterns. Think of how mindlessly we go through life. You put your shoes on the same way every morning, mindlessly. But did you know that studies show[38] when you go on vacation, you may actually put your shoes on *differently* without realizing it? Did you know that a hypnotist shakes your hand in an unexpected way in order to put you in what's called a transderivational state, making you more open to suggestion? Did you know that an offer phrased as "300 pennies for eight cards . . . which is a bargain!" sold twice as many cards as when the offer was phrased "$3 for eight cards"?[39] If you can break a pattern, you can break into the mind. Neutral is the enemy.

12 MORE TECHNIQUES TO MAKE YOUR COPY SOUND AWESOME

Ahem. Hello. Hi. Welcome to the part of the book you thought this whole book was about: copywriting techniques. As in, specific, word-level instructions on how to make your copy *get read* and *resonate*. There are perhaps 777 such writing techniques. Instead of listing a bunch of them, let me walk you through high-leverage techniques, illustrated through the case study of an email sequence I wrote for SaaS brand Wistia, targeting digital marketers.

For background, this sequence was triggered by in-app user behavior. It was the third sequence in a series of three. Its goal was to convert a trial user, who had been nurtured through the previous two sequences, to paid. Both the control and my variation contained eight emails. We ran a two-way split test. The result? My variation generated 350 percent more paid conversions than the control, to greater than 95 percent statistical significance.

Personalize Naturally

You've got a person's first name, company name, blood type? Use it inline, the flow of a sentence, not as a salutation or other noticeable callout.

NOT	BUT
Hi %FIRSTNAME%, People are watching your video.	Good news %FIRSTNAME%! People are watching your video

Here's how I used personalization out of the gate in the first email in the winning Wistia sequence:

It's not revolutionary. A lot of great techniques are not revolutionary. It's just important not to eff them up, which some advice taken out of context can do. So if you're already using personalization inline, bravo! Keep doing it!

Only Ask a Question You Know the Answer To

Let's say you're writing the call to action on a homepage. You write this crosshead above the CTA form.

Ready to book a call?

What's wrong with that question? It's that you want a "yes" but the prospect could just as soon be thinking, "Mmm, no, not really." And now you get to watch that prospect drop off the assembly line.

Rewrite every question so that the reader answers the way you want them to. That often means not using a question at all. Instead of asking if someone's ready to book a call, we'd be better off speaking to the value of the call.

Get clarity in a 1:1 call.

That doesn't mean you should never be okay with a "no" answer. In the below Wistia email example, the opening line of the body copy reads, "Fantastic, right?" The user at this stage is likely to answer the way we want them to: "Yes." If a user happens to answer "No," that didn't mean they were saying no to Wistia; they were more likely to simply dread having someone watch a video they starred in or produced.

Good news [illegible]!
People are watching your video

Fantastic, right?

Now here's a question...

Don't Linger a Millisecond Too Long

Remember when we spent a bunch of time in chapters eight and nine talking about hooks? Even still, chances are good that someone on your team will forget all about hooks when it comes time to write. Enter the Battlefield Principle, a way to talk about hooks without screaming: *"Where the Helsinki is the hook for this thing?! How many times do I have to tell you to open with a hook?!?!!"* Ahem.

The battlefield principle is a non-Latin way to say "in media res"—as in, start in the middle of the action. Instead of walking people up to the battlefield with slow copy, drop them into the middle of the fray. No warm-up copy. No cool-down copy. We want to move them into the action stat and advance that action rapid fire.

NOT	BUT
The sniffles started at 8 AM. By lunch, she had a full-blown coughing fit. But it wasn't until dinnertime that her sinuses were so congested she could barely breathe while chewing her ravioli. It was time for Dristan.	She gasped for air between bites. It was time for Dristan.

In an example Wistia email, we dropped them into the action ("people are watching your video"), matched where they were at in two words ("fantastic, right?"), then jumped to the next line before they could take a breath ("now here's a question"). Straight into the next moment. Only then can we start to slow down, spend more time talking with them.

Good news !
People are watching your video

Fantastic, right?

Now here's a question...

How can you put your new video data to work for you?

You may be wondering: *What's the good in knowing that, say, 10% of people are playing*

We used bolding and line breaks to enhance the sense of action—a staccato, snap-snap-snap effect. We even increased the font size for the opening line a tad because bigger fonts feel easier, the way reading a large-font book feels easier, to reduce the sense that reading this email is going to be any level of *work.*

Connect the Dots for Them

If you've read Steve Krug's excellent classic *Don't Make Me Think*, you know this one. Never leave it up to your prospect to figure things out themselves—it's your job to connect the dots for them. Doing the opposite is why most websites don't work. A relentless focus on meaningless crossheads, three-column layouts, and very few words of substance means the visitor has to just figure everything out.

Instead, spell it out for them. Do the math on the page. Support it with a calculator widget so they can do the math if they want to (e.g., if they're a logical decision maker).

For Wistia, the first email in the control was about video analytics. It endeavored to teach the user how video analytics are useful. It listed three benefits and then offered more information in a video. This all seems perfectly good, doesn't it? Take a look.

WISTIA

Your video is live!
Let's see how it's doing...

Party time! Your video is live. Ready to dive into some data?

Analytics help determine if your videos are helping you achieve your business goals. Wistia stats will explain **who is watching your video, how they're interacting with it,** and **how to improve your video ROI.**

In this short (1:39) video, **Jeff tours the Wistia analytics you'll see as visitors start watching your videos.**

Three benefits—the rule of three! That's something in copywriting, right? And drive to video—people love video, and Wistia's a video platform, so it's a good match, right?

It was perfectly fine, but it was putting the weight of connecting the dots on the visitor. We knew it was important for trial users to understand (and use) Wistia analytics in order to become sticky paid users. So I spelled out the insights analytics could give them:

How can you put your new video data to work for you?

You may be wondering: *What's the good in knowing that, say, 10% of people are playing my video and 90% are not? Or that viewers are dropping off 2 mins into a 10-min video? Or that some people are rewatching a particular part of a video?*

That data will make your life so much easier. For example:

- If only a small percentage of people are clicking to watch your video, either a) autoplay the video or b) customize its thumbnail to a frame that makes people want to click
- If viewers drop off after a few minutes, a) customize your controls to hide the play bar (where the timeline is) or b) make shorter videos
- If viewers are rewatching a segment, add a Turnstile email collector in the middle of that oh-so-interesting part... and turn views into leads

You can do all of those things in mere seconds in Wistia...

I want to try those ideas out - take me to my Wistia videos now

OR

Show me more about video analytics in Wistia (1:39 video tutorial)

BTW, as you keep using Wistia, data about your viewers and what they watch aggregates. So you'll be able to see which viewers prefer which videos. And make data-driven decisions about the content to create next.

It takes time to connect the dots. But it's what actual prospects need from us. We connected the dots repeatedly in the winning Wistia emails. Here's how we did it in the very next email in the flow.

Getting 18% more views is pretty major. Videos that used to get 100 views a day now get 118 views a day. In a month, that's an extra 500+ views. And it only takes something like 11 seconds to make this very simple but very powerful change to your videos...

Sounds really easy - I want to change my video player color now

And again in the email after that.

> **It's a really elegant content gate in Wistia.** Here's how it turns your marketing and demo videos into Lead Collection Machines:
>
> 1. Prospects land on your page.
> 2. They see your video front and center, not squished next to an ugly form.
> 3. They click play.
> 4. They watch.
> 5. And then, just at that moment when you're about to reveal an incredible data point or the climax of a killer story, ***voila!*** The Turnstile appears...
>
> You can add a Turnstile at the beginning of a video. At the end. Or at an exact point on your timeline.
>
> And anywhere you embed the video - on any page or any site - you can collect leads.

Always connect the dots. Without lingering a millisecond too long.

Engage Curiosity with an "Empty Suitcase"

At some point in my undergrad life, someone told me that the word "this" or "that" standing on its own—with no noun to follow it—was called an empty suitcase. The word "this" tells the brain that a noun is coming—*this car, this house, this vampire*—but then no noun shows up. An empty suitcase. The semblance of a thing, with nothing inside.

Empty suitcases open loops. People need to keep reading to close the loop. Our brains require closed loops. So using an empty loop at any point in your copy, from your headline to the language around your call to action, can compel the reader to keep reading in order to close the loop. AKA clickbait.

Here's how we used an empty suitcase in the second email in our winning Wistia sequence. Note that we quickly closed the loop. We were being safe. You could experiment with how far you can take things before you have to close the loop for your particular reader.

WISTIA

We saw 18% more people click "play" when we did this Joanna

We customized the color of our video players.

Format Your Copy as Broetry

For ads, emails, and social posts, try broetry.

That's when you write short lines.

Like this.

With spaces in between.
And sometimes lines stacked close.
So it's a little block of copy.
Just like this.

And then you write another line.

And never wrap the sentence.

You can write an entire email, ad, or post that way. Or you can use it sparingly. When you want to ease people into your copy, format the opening lines like broetry. Short sentences. With line breaks. Made easy to scan and read.

We saw 18% more people click "play" when we did this Joanna

We customized the color of our video players.

That's all it took to get nearly 20% more views of our videos.

The Wistia video player defaults to grey. Which is nice. But grey.

So why stick with grey when you can go with hot pink... or dollar-bill green... or, well, Wistia Blue? Take a look:

Double Down on Visual Specificity

As the classic (although admittedly troubled) fictional character Don Draper said, *"The greatest thing you have working for you is not the photo you take or the picture you paint. It's the imagination of the consumer. They have no budget. They have no time limit. And if you can get into that space, your ad can run all day."*

One way into their imagination is the photo you take and the picture you paint—that is, the use of specific visuals. Double down wherever you can on specific visuals. Get specific in your copy, and then support that specificity with an image that basically repeats what the copy said. Repeat to reinforce. Repeat to reinforce. Repeat. To. Reinforce.

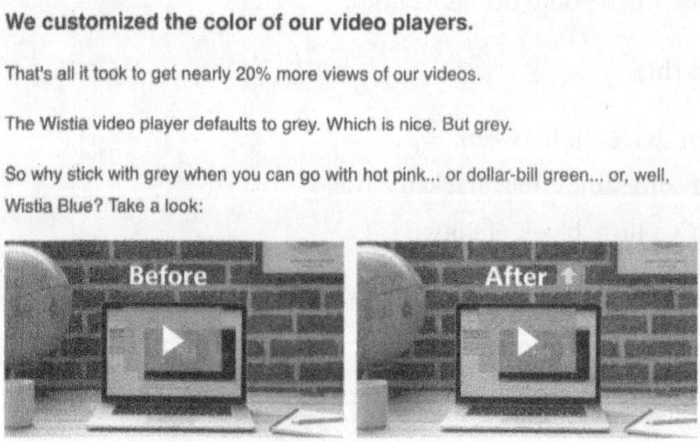

Get Conversational (Even For B2B)

There's this strange idea that B2B stands for "boring to boring." In reality, your B2B points of contact, influencers, and decision makers are all real, living, non-boring people. Accountants go sky diving; CMOs go on tequila tours; SVPs of technology take their senior engineers and product managers on afternoon hikes to clear their minds. People in roles are still people.

Try simulating a natural conversation between your brand and the person. In email and ads, this is easier because there's a one-to-one quality. Start, as always, by hooking your reader. Draw them into the conversation you'd love to have with them. And then have that conversation, like we did in the third email in the winning flow:

> **What if you could double your leads without doubling your PPC spend...**
>
> ...without doubling your content production...
>
> ...without doing anything more than switching on Wistia Turnstiles?
>
> When we stopped using on-page lead-generation forms and started using video turnstiles, **we went from a 6% conversion rate to an 11% conversion rate.** That's nearly double the leads. Without any extra effort.
>
> "Sounds great," you say, "but what on earth is a Turnstile?"
>
> This, my friend, is a Turnstile:

> **It's a really elegant content gate in Wistia.** Here's how it turns your marketing and demo

Align the New with What They Know

You may have heard that the film *Alien* was successfully pitched as "*Jaws* in space." The creators of *Alien* aligned what their investors knew (*Jaws* is a blockbuster featuring a deranged shark) with their new idea. We can do the same in our copy to help people understand something they need to understand to convert.

In the case of Wistia, we helped our audience—digital marketers—understand the *new idea* of adding buttons to their video, something you could not do in competing platforms at the time, with the *known* best practice of adding buttons to other marketing assets, like pages and emails.

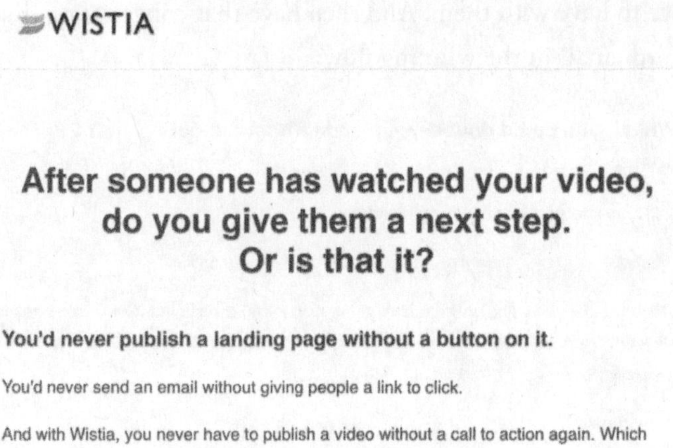

WISTIA

After someone has watched your video, do you give them a next step. Or is that it?

You'd never publish a landing page without a button on it.

You'd never send an email without giving people a link to click.

And with Wistia, you never have to publish a video without a call to action again. Which

Seed Ideas to Create Better Customers

Studies show that increased consumption of a product increases revenue. Your company benefits from people actually using your product. But oftentimes people need more *ideas* for how to use your product. If you're in SaaS, think of all those features in your product that you love but that only the most active users actually use. If you're in ecommerce, think of the best products sitting dusty on the shelf because they're so niche they don't surface in keyword searches—but they're incredible products. Give people ideas for how to get the most out of each purchase they make.

The bullet list and bonus tip here give just a quick selection of ideas that were pulled from VOC data, ensuring they're likely to resonate with Wistia's reader.

You'd never publish a landing page without a button on it.

You'd never send an email without giving people a link to click.

And with Wistia, you never have to publish a video without a call to action again. Which means that all the work (and time and money) you put into creating and promoting your videos will no longer go unrewarded.

Get your viewers to take **any** of these actions at **any** point in a video:

- Click a custom text or image CTA: *"Get the whitepaper"*
- Click an annotation link to learn more about a topic: *"Curious about this topic? You should watch this video too"*
- Enter their info to get something: *"Type your email to keep watching - plus, we'll send you a $10 coupon"*

Dead-end videos are bad for business.

Add a CTA or a Turnstile to your videos now

BONUS TIP: If you're using the same video on more than one landing page, you should customize your CTAs for different audiences. To do this, upload a few copies of your video to Wistia, then customize each one. Copy A gets a PDF download... Copy B gets a free trial offer... Copy C gets a live demo...

Try a Value Waterfall

Flood your copy for Late Product Aware and Most Aware readers with what I call a "value waterfall." This is where you list a massive dump of features or benefits or outcomes in list form, not to get the prospect to read them but to create a clear visual that overwhelms the reader with just how much value they're about to lock in when they convert.

In an email designed to convert the well-nurtured Wistia user to buy, we used a value waterfall made of twenty-four paid features. We peppered in the benefits for key features that we wanted to draw their eye to; a longer bullet in a list of shorter bullets gets noticed and read.

To remove that banner and focus your viewers 100% on you:

Switch to our 25-video plan for just $25

When you upgrade to our very budget-friendly Wistia 25 plan, you'll enjoy so much more than full control of your video branding. You'll also get all of the tools, video analytics, and core integrations that make Wistia loved by more than 225,000 brands like yours. You'll get powerful features like:

- Trend reporting to see what your viewers are watching most
- Video heatmapping
- Audience insights: see your whole audience plus details about "identified viewers" (like the company they work for)
- Video hosting for greater speed and stability
- Customizable thumbnails
- Customizable player colors
- Autoplay options
- Replay options
- Commenting options
- Custom controls: hide or show a play button, a play bar or volume control → great for video sales letters
- Video captions
- Calls to action
- Annotation links
- Turnstiles → capture email addresses for leads
- Social bar: hide or display Twitter, Facebook and other share icons
- Inline video embedding
- Popover video embedding
- SEO metadata in embedded videos
- Links to share videos from specific times on the timeline
- Customizable fixed sizes for embedded videos
- Responsive video sizing for embedded videos (so videos resize to fit any screen)
- Project defaults: apply customization specs for one video to all videos in that project... with a single click
- Video-level data like engagement, total plays, play rate, and CTAs
- Integrations with MailChimp, Aweber, and a dozen more CRMs

And, of course, there's no limit on the number of viewers. And you've got 200GB of bandwidth to use each month, with more available as you need it.

Get it all! Upgrade now

Downgrade, upgrade, or cancel anytime.

When It's Time for the Offer, Focus on the Offer

Throughout the Product Aware and Most Aware beats, you are likely to find yourself popping the offer into your copy alongside messages from the message matrix. But eventually your prospect is just ready to consider the offer. Eventually, we stop selling.

If you've created a Mega Mean Mouse, highlighted your unique solution mechanism, and otherwise nailed all the beats on the customer journey, just write about your offer. Make it easy to buy. Put the offer in front of them, confident that you've guided them to this point, and let them buy.

When you do, remove all competing buttons, images—everything. Frontload headlines with what I call *money words*, like "save" or "get." Repeat the most valuable part of the offer on the CTA. Add value adders, or click triggers, near each button to increase its chances of getting a confident click.

It may surprise you, but you're officially done with the writing stuff. If you've been doing the work as you read along, you may have pages filled with a framework featuring VOC that's been refined using formulas and better practices. But that page is probably still pretty long. And it doesn't look at all like you thought it would.

Yup, you did it right. Copy that converts never looks like anyone expects it to.

Now, to be fair, I can't see what you wrote. It could be an absolute disaster. Or it could be a masterful work of revenue-generating genius. Both are possible at this stage. Editing and validation will make it all better. So let's dig into editing now.

CHAPTER RECAP

Oh, and make it awesome

- ✓ Don't be sophisticated or unnecessarily minimalist with your copy—be a sweaty try-hard who'd embarrass a socialite with how uncool your efforts are.
- ✓ Flesh out and use a powerful brand voice.
- ✓ Use techniques like the Battlefield Principle to revise your VOC-heavy copy so it's more readable and engaging.

CHAPTER 13
The Seven Sweeps

"A good editor is someone who cares a little less about the author's feelings than about the reader's experience."

Dinty W. Moore, American essayist, editor, and professor

Edit out the extra. Edit in the awesome. That's how we take our copy from a first draft to a near-final draft. We read through it and cut everything that will not move our prospect efficiently along the customer assembly line, and we add in the "awesome" extras that we may have overlooked during the writing process—such as:

- Callouts that speak to the secret value of our offer
- Crossheads over our testimonials
- Little touches that make our messages stick better, like light rhyming

Editing is a skill unto itself. I started as an editor, I'm a tough editor, and I invite you to be tough, too. If you don't personally like something, ignore your feeling. If your teammate doesn't like something, ignore their feeling. But if something gets in the way of your prospect advancing, pay attention to that—and edit it.

THE SEVEN SWEEPS

Finish your first draft by sweeping it for editing opportunities. My friend Ryan Schwartz and I developed the Seven Sweeps around 2018 after commiserating about how the wrong editing process can mean sacrificing everything interesting to the gods of pith. It's true that you want to use the exact number of words required for the job and not one more; however, copyselling typically takes more words than creative directors, designers, and other reviewers, *who are not trained conversion copywriters*, want. As Josh Billings, friend of Mark Twain, once said to the famous author: "The difference between the almost right word and the right word is really a large matter—it's the difference between the lightning bug and the lightning." We don't want to edit out critical stuff for the sake of keeping things succinct.

So Ry and I developed the Seven Sweeps to protect copy from aggressive red lines. The Seven Sweeps are used for editing. I'll define each sweep so you know just what you're looking for during the editing process. But first let me explain the concept of a sweep, especially a series of them.

WHAT IS A SWEEP AND HOW DO YOU USE IT?

A sweep is a fast-moving line-by-line review of the copy you've written. When you sweep your copy, you highlight parts that you should revisit after you've completed the full sweep. You do not make edits as you go.

The seven sweeps are ordered one through seven intentionally. You start with the first sweep (which is the clarity sweep), and you read through your copy, asking each line, sentence, block, and the whole asset this question:

Is this clear?

The question is simple, making it easy to answer yes or no. If you read a line and answer no, then you highlight the line and continue on with your sweep. If a word is unclear, highlight it. If a sentence is unclear, highlight it. If a paragraph, button, or bullet is unclear, highlight it. Then continue sweeping down the page.

After the clarity sweep is done, you return to each of the highlighted areas and edit them to improve clarity. Sometimes this is a line-level edit; other times you may realize, say, that the bigger concept you thought you were expressing with an analogy is totally clunky now that you're reading it, and the analogy needs to go away. Or the voice of customer data that seemed so perfect doesn't really work when it's standing on its own as a crosshead.

When you have made your clarity-specific edits, you continue on with the next sweep. When that sweep is done, you then return to the sweep that came before it. Always go back to the steps that came before the sweep you just completed. You do this all the way down the Seven Sweeps, always returning to the sweeps that came before in order to ensure that an edit you make to fix, say, specificity doesn't, in turn, compromise something more important on the list—like the voice and tone. Importantly, clarity trumps all. The clarity sweep happens seven times during the seven sweeps.

#1: The Clarity Sweep

Ensure the message is easy to understand. It's memorable. It speaks to our reader in clear terms they see themselves in, with no ambiguity.

#2: The Voice and Tone Sweep

Can you hear the brand's voice? If not, reread it and try to pinpoint the places where the brand voice falters, perhaps because of word choice or unusual formatting. Highlight the problem areas.

What about the tone? In most cases, tone hides behind voice. But your tone can be urgent when an offer is ending; confident when your reader is lacking confidence and needs to borrow yours; humble when something major just happened for your brand; or even optimistic when you're releasing important news that shifts your customer's future.

This isn't a book on brand voice or tone, so here's a quick tip on how to think of voice versus tone. Think of your mother. How does her voice sound? You can probably hear it pretty clearly. Now, how does that voice sound when she's got "tone"?

#3: The So What Sweep

Evaluate whether the copy clearly communicates the value proposition and why the reader should care. Identify any unsupported claims or assumptions and ensure they are backed up with evidence. Ask each line, "So what?" If the next line doesn't make the so-what clear, highlight it.

#4: The Prove It Sweep

Does a line need proof? If it's a claim, a benefit, or an outcome, it does. Highlight anything that needs proof but doesn't have it. Proof can come in many forms, as we've discussed.

#5: The Specificity Sweep

Use vivid language to bring your message to life and create a stronger connection with your reader. You're being specific not just to replace vague words with strong imagery. Rather, specificity helps your prospect see themselves on the page. It holds up a mirror.

An example of specificity I've heard is this: instead of using the word "book" in your copy, use an actual book title, like *The Adventures of Huckleberry Finn*. That's fine advice on overcoming vagueness and creating word pictures. But we want to hold up a mirror. When we do, is our customer reading *The Adventures of Huckleberry Finn* . . . or are they listening to *The Let Them Theory* on Audible? Hold up a mirror that reflects who they actually are in that moment, not just a less-vague version of a random person.

Not every line needs to be filled with specifics. If your reader needs to see it, touch it, hear it, smell it, taste it, *feel* it, or experience it, use specificity to help them.

#6: The Heightened Emotion Sweep

The heightened emotion sweep asks each section of your copy, *Is this making me truly feel something that I need to feel in order to move forward?*

Is the problem section of your page deeply agitating the problem such that I feel it so powerfully I can't imagine not resolving it? If not, highlight it. Is the solution section stirring up a desire for the perfect outcome, as soon as possible? If not, highlight it. Is the offer lacking appeal because you were afraid it was coming on too strong, but now it reads like you're just trying to get people to download a random ebook? Highlight it.

#7: The Zero-Risk Sweep

Zoom in on the offer section of your copy. You've optimized the button so it's a call to value (yay!), but does your prospect feel confident that they know what's on the other side of the button—or might they feel hesitant about clicking it? Have you propped up your offer to make it sound great, but you forgot to mention that there's a fourteen-day trial or that no credit card is required? If there is a credit card required, when does it get charged—and what warnings will I get before it's charged? If there is a money-back guarantee, what's it called? (Give everything a name!) How do I ask for my money back? How long does it take to process?

Copy typically gets a little longer when you do your sweeps. That's okay. This is intentional editing that focuses on what customers need to hear, not just word count.

And remember: we always finish with the Clarity sweep. So if you've added anything confusing or unnecessary during the other six sweeps, that final Clarity sweep will give you the chance to delete or refine it.

CHAPTER RECAP

Edit using the Seven Sweeps

- ✓ Finalize your copy by sweeping it in a "laddering" motion—never start a new sweep without revising the sweeps that came before it.
- ✓ Always highlight areas of opportunity across a full sweep before going into the copy and correcting those highlighted areas.
- ✓ Begin and end with the Clarity Sweep.

CHAPTER 14
Validation

"The meaning of your communication is the response you get."

Gregory Bateson, pioneering communication theorist

You've got a solid draft in your hands. So, is it any good? Is it likely to work in the wild? The proof that your message or copy works comes from external validation: Does it relieve the constraint and, in turn, generate leads or sales at scale? Does it convert?

External validation comes later.

First, we need internal validation. For this, I offer you two rubrics. The first is called PARR, and it will help you identify if your copy is fundamentally set up to relieve the constraint. The second is called ASSET, and it will help you identify if the copy you've written is good enough that it merits external validation.

THE PARR RUBRIC

Your copy needs to pass the PARR Rubric in order to stand a chance of relieving an identified constraint. The PARR Rubric is all about the foundations of the copyselling system—have you applied them, and have you applied them well?

PARR stands for Primed, Aligned, Routed, Relieved. When you review your copy against this rubric, give yourself a pass-fail score for each criterion. Failure is not an option.

Primed means you have reason to believe that your prospect has the context for this copy to resonate for them. Basically, is your prospect primed for this message? Based on intent signals, does this message start in the right beat for the prospect? You'll give yourself a *pass* if you know that you're joining the reader at the appropriate beat in the appropriate stage of awareness. You'll give yourself a *fail* if you're not sure you're joining the conversation already happening in your prospect's head.

Aligned means your message and market are in alignment—you're speaking your prospect's language. Does your copy authentically mirror what your prospect is going through, in their own words? Did you use voice-of-customer data to write the copy? And does your brand align with them (and never against them)?

Routed means you're moving your prospect forward on the "assembly line" systematically. You know the beat they're in, and you're moving them intentionally through the subsequent beats toward the appropriate beat, where your stage-appropriate offer is made. In conversation with your team, you can map exactly how this copy moves the prospect closer to purchase while respecting where they are on the assembly line.

Relieved means you've directly addressed the prioritized growth constraint from the solution design. Your copy solves a measurable business problem—it does more than *sound good.* When published or sent to the persona in question, you believe the copy will demonstrably relieve the constraint.

When you earn a pass across the PARR rubric, you're ready to move into measuring the likelihood that your copy, as written, will actually sell.

If you don't pass PARR, your copy does not stand a chance—no matter how brilliantly written it may be. So pass PARR first.

	Fail	Pass
Primed		
Aligned		
Routed		
Relieved		

THE ASSET RUBRIC

The ASSET Rubric helps you identify if your copy will sell. It stands for Architected, Striking, Swiped, Enhanced, Tight. When you review your copy against this rubric, give yourself a green-yellow-red score for each criterion. Green means you've addressed it perfectly; yellow means it could use improvement; red means you have not addressed it effectively at all. Move all yellows and reds to green before moving on to external validation, the next step.

Architected means that your copy is structured to persuade. You've written it using a proven persuasion framework (e.g., PAS), and if you've interpreted that framework slightly differently it's because the data or system told you to—not because the framework felt inconvenient. Note that this is the easiest criterion on which to earn a "green" score because you either used a framework (green) or you didn't (red).

Striking means your copy grabs and holds attention. It stops the scroll. It's clearly different from what others are saying. You've got a great hook. And your copy keeps your persona reading, nodding along with you, line by line. Placeholder language and marketing speak is nowhere to be found—you've used interesting language that you found in VOC or VOS. You've applied agitation and arousal techniques to make problems feel urgent and solutions feel compelling.

Swiped means you've swiped on-page copy from customers, prospects, your sales team conversations, your founder—you did not develop it by sitting at your desk, blindly asking ChatGPT to come up with a draft, or by sitting in a brainstorming session with marketers. When you look over your copy, you can highlight actual voice-of-customer data from your message matrix. If you aren't sure which of your phrases are VOC or VOS, you've earned a yellow or red score on this criterion.

Enhanced means you've applied proven copywriting techniques, including formulas, to transform assembled VOC into copy your CMO and CFO alike will high-five you for writing. You've cut the word "and" as often as humanly possible, ensuring crisp messages, not rambling lists of stuff. You've eliminated high-friction words; varied sentence lengths; added specifics; and connected the dots. And you've done it all without losing the authenticity—and power—of the original VOC.

Tight, aka *toight*, means just what it sounds like: you have kept that copy tight! For all the VOC you waded through and the beats you've had to hit, you've landed on copy that efficiently moves your prospect forward on the assembly line. Your copy drives toward one optimized offer with a clear call to action; distractions are nowhere to be found; the next step is obvious and compelling. You should never use two vague words when one crisp one will do.

	Red	Yellow	Green
Architected			
Striking			
Swiped			
Enhanced			
Tight			

EXTERNALLY VALIDATING WITH YOUR AUDIENCE OR A LOOKALIKE

Remember when Pepsi hired Kendall Jenner to offer a Pepsi to a police officer in the middle of a riot? And the world cringed. That is why large brands have focus groups and why all brands should engage in basic external copy validation before just dropping something into the wild.

External validation is where you ask a small percentage of your audience to point out anything they notice in your copy that feels off. You ask them to do this before you put your copy out into the world. This gives you a chance to correct an identified problem or to choose not to correct it because you're willing to accept the risk. (Totally fair.)

What External Validation Can Show Us

External copy and message validation identify our blind spots. A simple validation exercise can surface insights like:

- The headline you thought was encouraging comes off as ableist
- That emoji you're using means something totally different to Gen Z
- The name you gave your Unique Solution Mechanism means "organ donor" in Mandarin
- Indeed you should have killed some commas like Jo told you to because no one can remember what your product's value prop actually is

Validation can also tell you—like the word suggests—that everything's fine. That your copy is clear, memorable, and ready for public consumption. Of course, if everyone gives it the thumbs up with no notes, that may be a sign that it's bland. Sorry! Remember "breakthrough or bust" from earlier in this book? Remember John Caples's story with the disappointed mother? No notes means try again.

How to Validate Your Copy with External Groups

We use online five-second tests to run clarity-focused validation experiments. If you use any SaaS that offers five-second tests, you can typically use the questions they provide right out of the box.

We flash a screenshot of the copy in question, such as the hero section, and then ask people to answer a question. We're trying to see what we may be blind to.

If you think you're blind to confusing product messaging, ask:	You just saw a screenshot for DesignLabs. Based on what you saw, what does DesignLabs do?
If you think the primary benefit of using your solution is unclear, ask:	You just saw a screenshot for DesignLabs. Based on what you saw, why should a designer use DesignLabs?
If you want to identify if your unique solution mechanism is sticky or memorable, ask:	DesignLabs is built with a special feature that automates 3D rendering. What is the name of that feature?
If your brand voice is best described as "energetic" and you want to ensure the new copy you wrote is energetic, ask:	What word would you use to describe the feeling you got when you read about DesignLabs?

Because five-second tests are not very expensive to run, you may find yourself refining your validation question or questions over a series of tests. I know I have. And because every new group of user testers is different from the last, it's important to be somewhat flexible with your expectations. This is an imperfect science. Use it for the shortcut it is, not as a perfect replica of your ideal audience, reading every word on the page, processing it, and reflecting back the exact insight you need to run a billion-dollar campaign. It's just people pointing out a blind spot or two.

Should You Make a Change, or Not?

In more than a decade of copy validation experiments, I've only ever made modest tweaks to the copy based on user feedback. If the copy is clear enough that they can repeat back what it expressed, and if they don't mention anything odd (e.g., the copy is tone deaf), then the copy is ready for real-world validation. That is, it's time to launch the copy or run the experiment.

It's important to note that I fundamentally disagree with asking people what they think of the copy. *Do they like it? Would they buy? Would they tell their friends? Would they trust this brand? What would they do differently?* Call me a snob, but a user isn't qualified to answer any of those questions. That's okay. It's not their job.

In validation, the value a user adds that is worth acting on is this: they have pointed out something we were blind to. I recommend you only consider making changes to your copy based on user feedback if they have pointed out something you were blind to and if you have reason to believe that will affect its performance in the market.

Let users prevent a catastrophe. Otherwise, launch it and learn.

WHAT ABOUT TEAM OR INTERNAL COPY REVIEWS?

I was trying really hard to get out of this chapter without mentioning copy reviews. Every team reviews copy. People who don't know a thing about copy review copy. I've had comments on my docs from finance people with no training in copywriting but with a "really great idea" for how we could word a sentence. And I got to sit there and negotiate all the feedback. It sucked. Please don't do that. That's how you end up with frazzled copywriters and copy docs titled BFCM_EM_Cart-closing_Final-FINAL2-FINAL ACTUALFINAL-V16b. Which is how you end up with deeply mediocre copy. Because eventually your copywriter gives up and learns to just do whatever everyone says.

Before anyone in your organization reviews a line of copy, validate it using everything you've learned in this chapter thus far.

When it's time for the team to review copy, book a copy review meeting. This is a disciplined meeting. All copy approvers and contributors need to attend actively; for those who can't attend, reschedule the meeting or remove that person from the review process for the asset in question. In this meeting, you'll review no more than three hundred words: about four emails, one homepage, a social media video script, or a section of a sales page.

The lead copywriter on the asset runs the meeting. One person, who is not the lead copywriter, takes notes. (You can find a copy review meeting guide at copysellingbook.com.) After the meeting, circulate actions the copywriter will take against notes, next steps, and the deadline for final copy.

Five Rules for Reviewing Copy

What's the most commonly used word in a copy review? "Like." So when you strike the words "like" and "don't like" from your copy reviews, as is the first rule of reviewing copy, you'll be surprised by how quiet things get! Teams are used to saying what they like and what they think the copywriter should try—and then waiting for the copywriter to give it a shot right there, live, right in the doc. Instead, we want to focus our reviewers' notes on the purpose of the copy.

Will this copy help us build a customer more efficiently, with greater success? Will this copy help us relieve the performance constraint?

Those two questions make up your primary concern when reviewing copy. Here are five rules to help you get there.

Rule 1: Avoid mentioning your preference unless you're explicitly asked which of a selection of options you prefer.

Rule 2: Our only emotion is for our customer. Leave personal feelings out of copy reviews.

Rule 3: Use data for good. We may have tried something like this before, and it didn't work then, but be careful not to kill a good idea today because data indicates it wasn't a good idea yesterday.

Rule 4: Focus notes on accuracy, legality, and brand.

Rule 5: Gives notes, not edits. If you're not a copywriter, don't write copy.

Share those rules at the start of your copy review meetings. In the beginning, it's going to be kinda tough. For everyone. Even and especially your copywriter. You'll have to learn to trust your copywriter; they'll have to learn that they're being trusted and, as such, they can't rely on the team to tell them what to do. But when that breakthrough happens, your copy stands a chance.

And remember the Breakthrough or Bust (BOB) principle. The copy that's most likely to generate results is the copy that your team cannot agree is either totally perfect or totally wrong. If your team is divided when reviewing the copy, take that as a signal that you may have BOB-worthy copy on your hands.

CHAPTER RECAP

Validate before you launch

- ✓ Get a small group of users to help you pinpoint any blind spots in your copy before you go to market.
- ✓ Ask simple, pointed questions using five-second tests.
- ✓ Don't use user testers as a proxy for your actual audience–you won't truly learn what that market thinks until you launch your copy or your copy experiment.
- ✓ Control the copy review process, and focus it tightly around the problem the copy is intended to solve rather than personal preferences.

CHAPTER 15
Optimizing Copy for Performance

"Whoever gets closer to the customer wins."

Bernadette Jiwa, author of *Hunch* and *Story Driven*

"How do I keep even more customers moving along the assembly line?" That's what optimizing is for, and that's what we'll cover now. During optimizing, we watch how our copy performs in the wild, we listen and learn, and we continue iterating.

Sometimes what we learn in Writing & Optimizing reveals a whole new constraint, requiring a new solution design and kicking off a new project. For example, in an email automation, analytics could show you that a segment of your list is unsubscribing from the flow in alarming quantities, and that insight drives awareness of a constraint specific to that segment, as well as the need for a new solution for that segment.

START WITH ANALYTICS WHEN OPTIMIZING YOUR COPY

Optimizing copy isn't about tricks. It's about relieving constraints to enhance efficiency. Sexy, right? So sexy. Systems are the best.

Earlier in this book, I recommended that you give every element and then every asset one job to do. A headline's job is to hook the reader and keep them reading. A button's job is to drive a confident click. An email's job is to drive qualified traffic to a landing page. And so on. Every element, and every asset made up of those elements, has one job to do.

So if we see in our analytics that a copy job is not being done or done well, we look first to which asset or element is responsible for that job and also to the element or asset that appeared before it. Consider a few of the most basic jobs on a homepage.

- If the bounce rate is high, the headline is possibly not doing its job.
- If the bounce rate is high, the ad that drove to the page is possibly not doing its job.
- If the click rate is low, the call to action is possibly not doing its job.
- If the click rate is low, the copy establishing the offer is possibly not doing its job.
- If video plays are low, the video thumbnail is possibly not doing its job.
- If video plays are low, the crosshead introducing the video is possibly not doing its job.
- If people stop watching the video after twelve seconds, the hook may be doing its job but what follows the hook is possibly not doing its job.

(Note that, because we're focused on copy optimization, I'm not mentioning technical challenges that could impact performance. For example, slow page load.)

Where performance is not what it should be, there we can identify constraints. We'll then seek to relieve those constraints with our copy optimization work. And if you're totally not sure—if everything's wrong or everything's right and the leads or money are not flowing in—then follow the age-old rule: start optimizing closest to the offer.

BRING IT BACK TO LIST, OFFER, COPY

Optimizing largely relies on moving through the copyselling system on repeat, each time identifying different constraints. A key piece of the system to refer back to, during *Writing & Optimizing*, is *List Offer Copy*, first mentioned in chapter two. When I'm optimizing copy with a client, I walk them through a simple triangle-shaped diagnostic that typically looks like this:

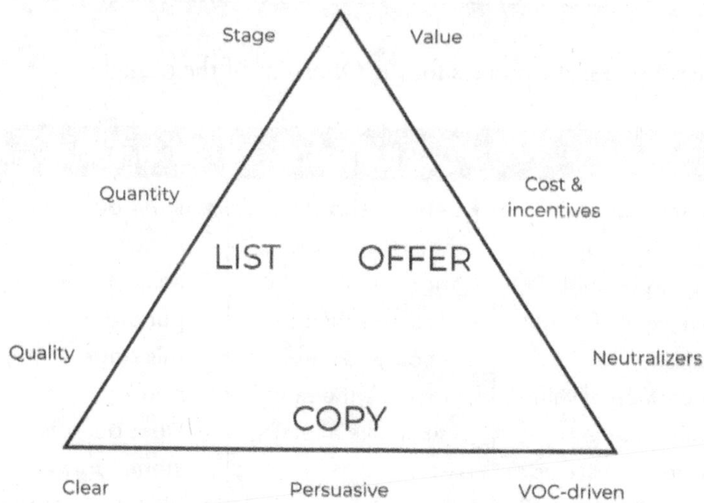

I explain each word to them as a refresher, and as I do, I ask them to give me a quick red-yellow-green analysis for each item. For example, *Is list quality green (good), yellow (fine), or red (a constraint)?*

Quality	Quantity	Stage
• Is it our ICP / the persona at our ICP? • Are they motivated? • Are they capable of action? • Is this the right segment? • Should we narrow this segment further? • Is it too narrow? • Did they come from an ideal referral source, or did we buy the list?	• Are enough people seeing our copy? • Are there more people where that came from? / Is it increasing over time? • If we pushed this asset to more quality leads, do we believe we'd see better results?	• Are we matching the stage they're in and moving them forward on the message matrix? • Did they sufficiently move through the stage before this one, priming them for this message? • Are they new enough to us for this message to feel fresh? Are they too old or stale?

Then I repeat the process for the Offer side of the triangle.

Value	Cost & incentives	Neutralizers
• What is our offer, and is its value obvious enough? • Have we sufficiently increased its perception of value? • Is the value proposition stated clearly in the asset?	• Are we showing the price at the right time? • Are we adding enough context to make the price seem like a total steal?	• Does our offer neutralize the anxieties we know our prospect has at this stage, for this offer? • Does our offer stomp down objections or render them obsolete?

Value	Cost & incentives	Neutralizers
• Have we made it clear they can achieve promised outcomes speedily? Can we make it clearer? • Do they see their dream state in our offer? • Are we connecting the dots for our prospect or asking them to?	• Are we balancing time, social, and emotional investments required with outcomes that are disproportionately awesome in comparison? • Have we left incentives off the page erroneously? • Can we heighten scarcity, urgency, discounts, extended access, bonuses? Do we need to add these?	• Are we incorporating offer optimizations that are not actively neutralizing the concerns of our List?

As expected, only when we've addressed List and Offer do we address Copy. And to be fair, the three words I write along the bottom of the triangle change all the time . . . usually based on an assessment I've already done. That said, the words I most commonly write are *VOC-driven*, *persuasive*, and *clear*. I'm basically asking if they're red, yellow, or green on parts of the system, including the message matrix, persuasive frameworks, and the Seven Sweeps.

VOC-driven	Persuasive	Clear
• Does the vast majority of copy come straight from the message matrix? • Is the message matrix filled with VOC, VOS, and VOP . . . or has someone added old marketing messages to it? • Did we find our hook in VOC? • When did we last update the message matrix? Is our VOC outdated?	• Was it written with a framework? Is the framework a mismatch for the hook? • Are we agitating or arousing enough? • Is it enhanced by formulas? • Do we move through each beat, taking our time and never skipping beats for the sake of "keeping it short"? • Did we get sweaty enough, or did we try to go elegant? • Are we using low-friction words? Are we accidentally falling into poor word choices?	• Is it easy to read and consume our message? • Are we specific enough that we can draw pictures in our customers' minds using our words, or are we losing power with vague, summarized copy? • When we make a claim, is it clearly supported by proof? • Is our voice too heavy? Is our tone off?

By the end of the exercise, we will have identified red elements, yellow, and green. Anything red gets prioritized in the optimization process.

But just because we're prioritizing fixing what's red doesn't mean we're abandoning the yellow and green parts. If something is green it means it's working, and we should try to do more of it. For example, if you're green on List Quality because you've got a strong referral partner, you can "do more" by getting more strong referral partners. If something is yellow, it's not quite working, so let's do it better. Let's say our perception of value for our Offer is better than it's been in the past but we can do more with closing the gap between saying yes to the offer and seeing results. Great—do Offer Value better.

When the Offer Is Red

I'm going to assume you cannot just go around changing the offer whenever you want to. Some campaign offers are established three quarters before the campaign even goes live. So instead of optimizing your offer, let's optimize how your offer is messaged on the page.

First, identify your offer in your copy.

The offer is located wherever you have a button or a link to click. If you look at a button on your page or a link in your ad and go, um, no, there's no offer there, then we've found ourselves a constraint! There may not be an offer. There *should* be an offer. If you can fix this, you'll likely see a win.

To fix it, refer back to your solution design. Copy the optimized offer from the solution design and just paste into the copy doc. Turn that into both a crosshead that speaks to the value of the offer and supporting body copy that shines a light on the mechanisms that deliver the value.

Next, scan the offer area for friction-filled words.

Does your call to action begin with "Get" (a low-friction word) or "Download" (a high-friction word)? If your offer's free, do you use the word "Free" enough? If it's a new offer, like a recently published industry report, do you use the word "New" enough? In *Mad Men*, mentioned earlier, there's a scene in which Betty Draper is in a commercial for Coca-Cola and the producer takes the cap off the bottle, removing all sense of life being remotely more difficult with the product. What caps have you left on your bottle? Take them off!

If you mention price, do you have to, or can you save that information for a click down-funnel? If you have to (or wish to) keep the price on the page, how can you make the price seem smaller? Across experiments, marketers have shrunk the perception of price by:

- Introducing a more expensive option next to it,
- Leading with more cashflow-friendly payment terms, like weekly payments instead of monthly,

- Clearly highlighting the features inside the offer, or product, that make it more valuable,
- Making intangible services tangible,
- Making digital products seem physical (e.g., show an ebook cover in an ereader), or
- Physically altering the size of the font for the price so it's smaller.

When our agency optimized emails for a high-ticket ecommerce brand, the introduction of Klarna payment plans absolutely exploded conversions. Can you introduce payment plans? Keep in mind that, with offer stacking (see chapter four), you can score a sale with a lower payment plan upfront and then, in the seducible moment of the post-purchase experience, introduce an upgrade offer to move them into a different plan or to pay the full price now in order to either lock in savings or secure a bonus, such as a free consultation or tchotchke.

We like to make the value we offer much, much bigger. Which is great. But consider also making your ask feel much, much smaller. Whenever you can make something big that your prospect has to do feel smaller, you are likely to increase conversions by doing so. Consider your thirty-day free trial. I'm sure a lot of VOC supports you keeping, and messaging, those thirty days of luxurious freeness. However. Thirty days is an absolutely enormous commitment for a person or business to make, even to a solution as good as yours. What if you continued to offer a thirty-day free trial, but in your actual offer area on the page (or in the email), you shrink the commitment term? What if instead you focused them on the next seven minutes? How will your new customer know, in the next seven minutes, that they've absolutely made the right decision and they should continue on with the thirty-day trial? Do you offer a fast-action feature? For example, if you sell courses, what lesson will they watch first, and how will they know in those first seven minutes that they've made the right decision in trialing your course?

And lastly, does your button copy reflect the value stated in your offer section's crosshead? Already lightly covered in the last chapter, headlines and buttons work well together. When you're optimizing button copy, find the most high-value part of the offer section crosshead, and use that language in your button copy. So if your headline is this:

> Send AI-optimized cold emails to
> 100 proven leads **every minute**
> (without hurting your sender reputation!)

Then your button copy is this:

> Send 100 emails a minute

If Your Offer's Optimized, Your Next Step Is to Go Big

Big swings teach more, faster than small, incremental copy changes do. So when ecommerce brand Huel reached out to ask me to help them optimize their homepage, I went for a big swing—not a few tweaks. Once you've established a winning variation, then you can start swapping elements in or out to drive better performance.

My optimization process begins, of course, with Listening. But my Listening activities are different for optimization jobs. Here I prioritize the following three tactics:

1. An audit. This is just me versus the page. I turn on Loom and start reviewing the control. This audit is based on everything you've already learned in this book.
2. Researching like a prospect. Quite simply, I do a Google search of the brand name and follow the links for the top five to ten results on the search engine results page; more recently, this means also using ChatGPT or a similar LLM, like a prospect would. This surfaces Reddit threads, articles written by journalists, affiliate pages, and more. Then I read 'em all and take lots of notes.
3. User tests. Using UserTesting.com, I set up five competitor studies and five standalone studies for the asset in question. For Huel, that meant an exploratory study of Soylent's homepage versus Huel's homepage and a study of Huel's homepage in isolation (i.e., without asking study participants to also look at Soylent).

I start with an audit because that creates research questions, which I can eventually narrow down to a hypothesis. Every optimization project should start with a hypothesis. Note: my enduring hypothesis is that people do not convert because they do not read your copy because your copy is not worth reading.

The questions I ask in user tests are informed by what I saw in the audit and what surfaced when I was researching like a prospect.

OPTIMIZING HUEL'S HOMEPAGE

Huel is a complete meal in powdered or bar form. It's about four hundred calories, and replaces breakfast, lunch, and even dinner. I knew what I thought of that, and I knew quite a lot about the category Huel was in because I was super active on Hacker News when Soylent, like Huel, first launched to the Hacker News community (and blew up!). But what did people today, in that moment, think of a solution like Huel? User tests would tell me.

User tests are an absolute gold mine. Consider this small selection of snippets I pulled straight from users:

"What kind of nutritional value does this have . . . from a nutritional, calorie, and macros level"

"I'd use this if I was in a situation where I wasn't able to eat lunch or something"

"Huel's packaging is dull and boring"

"Soylent comes in a convenient bottle"

"Flavor boosts don't sound good"

"What does it cost on a per unit basis?"

Multiple users took interest in Huel as "actual food" instead of a "meal replacement."

And when I was researching like a prospect, I found masses of insights. One person, who tried living on Huel for a while, wrote this:

"Humans are social animals. If you think you can get away with drinking what looks like brown sludge in an office environment without having questions asked and fingers pointed, you're wrong. The hardest thing about going all Huel might actually be this; people will go on nights out, they will be invited to company dinners, and they will definitely be asked questions about the weird thing they're doing instead of eating proper human food like everyone else. I worked from home for the duration of this little experiment, which was my true unfair advantage. No one in the office needed see me chug [liters] of the stuff. Even given this leg-up, I had a hard time turning down social events. My wife definitely looked at me funny with a dash of concern for the first month."

A common problem arose: People were hiring Huel because they were tired of cooking. They used phrases like:

"Have just plain grown tired of the cooking game"
"I get tired of leftovers more easily and hate to waste a huge amount of food."
"I also wanted to up my own lunch game, so tired of frozen meals and lunch meat."
"My kids are tired of sandwiches and cold lunches."
"I was REALLY tired of frozen meals or boring sandwiches and soups for lunch."
"I'm a truck driver and got tired of cold deli sandwiches and the few restaurants that I can park in."
"Tired of eating a yogurt or a microwaved box meal."
"I am tired of eating junk food."
"I was getting tired of packing lunches"
"For those who are trying to eat healthy, and are tired of plain, boring sandwiches."
"Tired of diet gimmicks"
"I get tired of food service in work places."

By the time I was done Listening, I'd developed a series of assumptions that I used in my solution design. These included:

- "complete food" as copy is garbage
- Soylent seems more people-y
- The ingredients are a big deal
- We should focus on one meal to replace, probably lunch
- We should stop trying to get bros—they like Soylent
- The price-per-meal is very affordable

Some of my favorite VOC was:

"It's food-food."
"wilted salad takeout"
"I leave it in my car"
"It's like no it's just food"

And soon, a new page started to take shape. Following everything in the copyselling system—message matrices, frameworks, formulas—I arrived at a page that led with the customer and put every word in the customer's own language. I showed ingredients because they said they wanted to see them. I reduced anxieties about skipping dinner because they said their wife looked at them funny and because we know dining is social. And I introduced an optimized offer section.

The result was a statistically significant increase of 49 percent more paid conversions. To see the winning copy, which is too lengthy to show here, please visit copysellingbook.com.

A FINAL NOTE ON OPTIMIZING YOUR COPY

I cannot say enough about moving your prospect quickly along the assembly line without letting them fall off. This is straightline sales at its most literal and possibly its most scalable. The more time a person spends on your assembly line, the more chances they have to fall off.

I like getting leads in, and I like getting sales in. Others will teach you other things, and they're possibly very right about those things. But for me—for you, I think—and for this system, if you're truly intent on growing your business, be intent on painstakingly crafting and improving your assembly line.

Email more, not less. Emphasize the value, don't shrink. And sell solutions to painful problems—wildly better traps for a Mega Mean Mouse.

CHAPTER RECAP

Optimizing Copy for Performance

- ✓ Start with analytics and look for constraints based on giving every element and asset one job to do.
- ✓ Optimize your on-page offer if you're not sure where to start optimizing.
- ✓ Big swing overhauls are often more effective than modest copy tweaks.

CHAPTER 16
Copyselling Is a Team Sport

"Everyone on your team is a copywriter."

Joanna Wiebe, hi that's me
how are you today

Now that you've got the copyselling system at your fingertips, your team needs it, too. It's not enough for one person to understand that copy is your scalable online salesperson. You can't be the only one who gets this stuff. Neither can your copywriter. Every single person who writes, reviews, and/or approves copy at your business has to get it. As a reminder of what my friend, the growth expert Matt Lerner, likes to say: *"Anyone with the power to fuck up your growth has the power to cause it."*

Your team members can get in the way of growth. And they *will*, if you or your copywriter come in with this whole new way of writing emails, ads, and pages and your team members don't know anything about it. They'll ask why the email is so long, why you've got this trademarked name for part of a feature that wasn't even in the brief, where this strangely phrased line came from, and why you're not sticking to the four core messages everyone agreed on in Q1. They are just trying to get their job done well and on time. You can't blame them for resisting something new that they know zilch about.

So right now, let's make a business case for training your team on copyselling. Think about one part of your customer's journey you most want to optimize—the site of the biggest, most immediate constraint to growth. Let's say it's the primary landing page you drive high-value paid traffic to and the email flow that follows it, driving to book a call. So you've got:

1. Ads
2. Landing page (lead generation)
3. Email flow
4. Book a call page
5. Confirmation page

You have acquired the skills to optimize your copy across all parts of that flow. Let's imagine you can increase conversion for that flow from 1.9 percent to 2.38 percent—a 25 percent increase. Now let's say you're working on that flow with two other people, Suzy and Mo. They veto or challenge most of your new copyselling techniques. Your conversion lift drops to 10 percent, and the flow is converting at 2.09 percent because ol' Suze and Mo didn't know what you know.

You hand them each a copy of *The Copyselling System* and have a book club every Friday for the next four Fridays. By the end, you've all got the skills to bring in 25 percent lift, and you're each contributing stellar ideas that work together, with a compounding effect. Now your flow's conversion rate is 3.71 percent. To keep the dream going, all you have to do is distribute Suzy and Mo to more flows. The people they're working with will also need to know this Copyselling stuff so they stay out of the way and—better yet—help improve conversion rates. With seven people now upskilled in copyselling and generating 25 percent lifts, your 1.9 percent average conversion rate pops up to 9.06 percent.

Admittedly, there is work required to get big lifts. Your team has to take a steamship to Uruguay, locate the mystical Blood Cherry Ruby, hold it up to the sun while facing north during a lunar eclipse, then perform advanced parkour to reach a Barnes & Noble, where *The Copyselling System* is available for purchase. It's a lot to ask, I know. But these are the things we do for the businesses we believe in and the customers we wish to serve.

• • •

I hope you know I'm thrilled that you spent this time with me. You let me rattle on about words not as poetry or art but as engineerable sales tools. You trusted me enough to buy this book. I hope you trust me even more now that you're done reading it.

I love to hear from entrepreneurs and fellow marketing types. If you struggle to implement anything I've shared here, please reach out. If you want more examples, please visit my website. If you want me to help you and your team more directly, please email or DM me.

Blessings,

Jo

P.S. My publisher notes that you can get bulk book discounts (for your team or school) by contacting them directly.

CHAPTER RECAP

Make copyselling a team sport

- ✓ Champion the copyselling system internally.
- ✓ Get copies of *The Copyselling System* for your team.
- ✓ Establish weekly meetings to discuss integrating the system into your work.
- ✓ Continue ensuring buy-in to the system so you see compounding rewards.

RESOURCES

DIAGRAM OF THE COPYSELLING SYSTEM

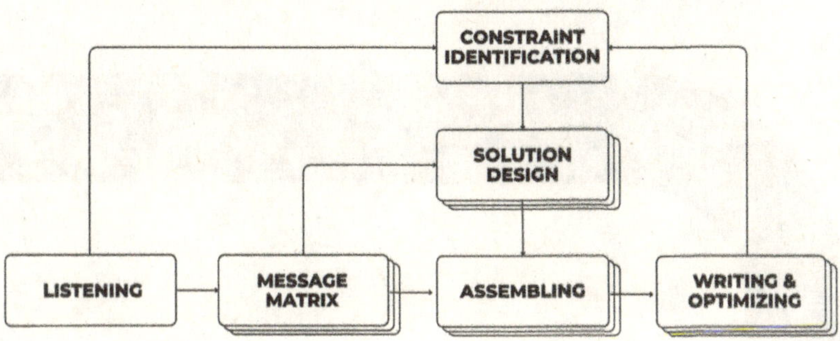

POSTER OF THE MESSAGE MATRIX

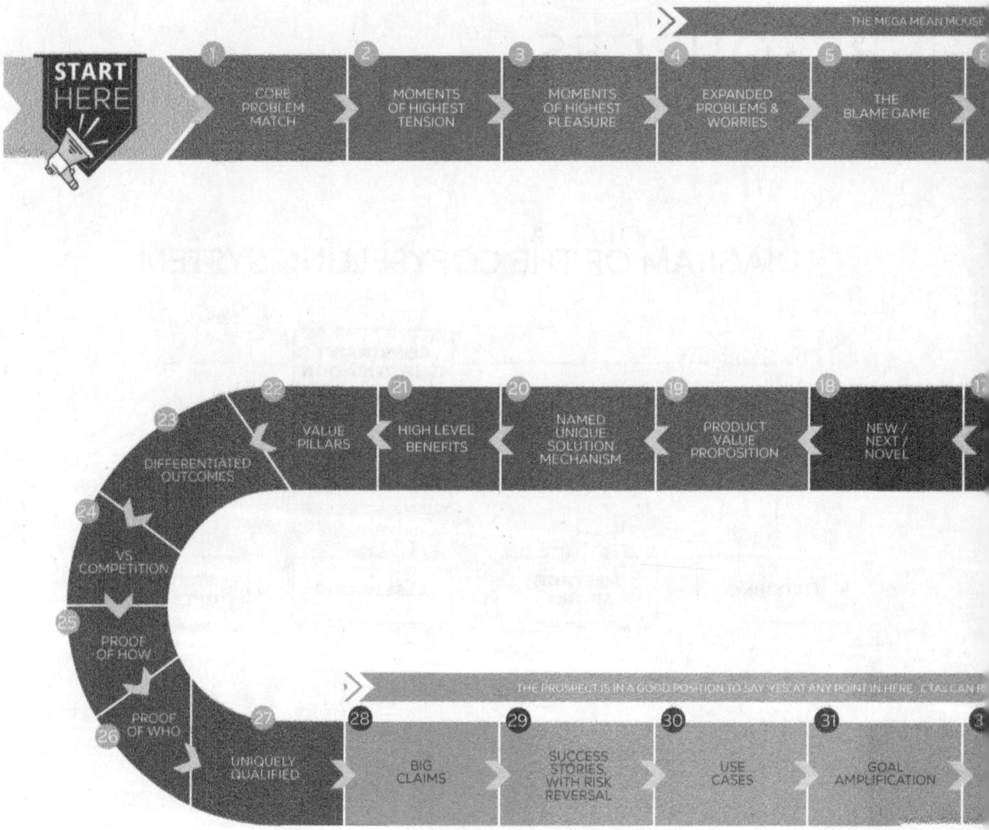

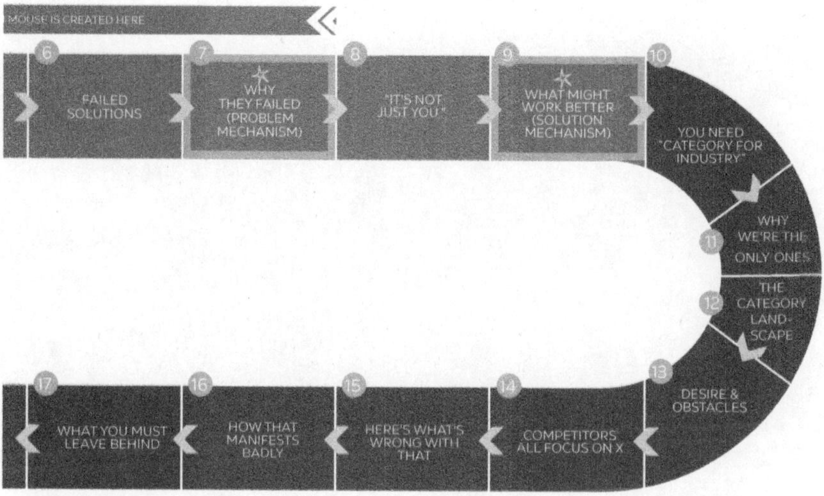
MOUSE IS CREATED HERE
6
FAILED SOLUTIONS
7
WHY THEY FAILED (PROBLEM MECHANISM)
8
"IT'S NOT JUST YOU."
9
WHAT MIGHT WORK BETTER (SOLUTION MECHANISM)
10
YOU NEED "CATEGORY FOR INDUSTRY"
11
WHY WE'RE THE ONLY ONES
12
THE CATEGORY LAND-SCAPE
13
DESIRE & OBSTACLES
14
COMPETITORS ALL FOCUS ON X
15
HERE'S WHAT'S WRONG WITH THAT
16
HOW THAT MANIFESTS BADLY
17
WHAT YOU MUST LEAVE BEHIND

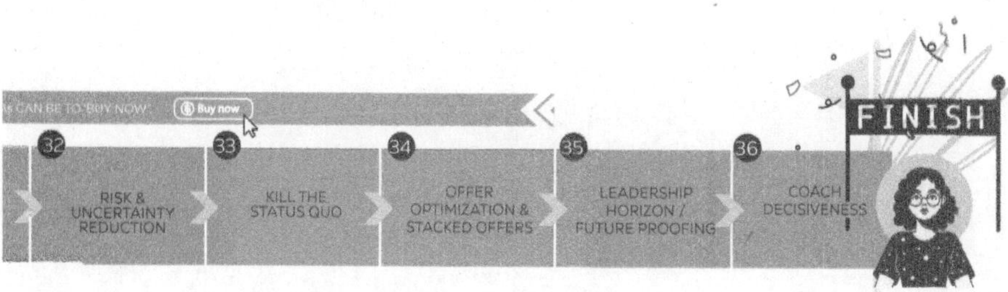
CAN BE TO 'BUY NOW'.
Buy now
32
RISK & UNCERTAINTY REDUCTION
33
KILL THE STATUS QUO
34
OFFER OPTIMIZATION & STACKED OFFERS
35
LEADERSHIP HORIZON / FUTURE PROOFING
36
COACH DECISIVENESS
FINISH

NOTES

1. Data collected (websites reviewed) January 25, 2025, at 7:40 AM Pacific.
2. Data collected (website reviewed) February 1, 2025, at 12:32 PM Pacific.
3. Lance Spaude, "Death of an Organizational Man: An Advertiser's Resistance to the FTC and the Creative Revolution in Advertising in the 1960s." *Oshkosh Scholar*, Vol VII (2012): 35–50. https://minds.wisconsin.edu/bitstream/handle/1793/70991/OshkoshScholarVol7Complete.pdf?sequence=1&isAllowed=y#:~:text=advertisement%20for%20the%20German%20carmaker,DDB. https://minds.wisconsin.edu/bitstream/handle/1793/70991/OshkoshScholarVol7Complete.pdf?sequence=1&isAllowed=y#:~:text=advertisement%20for%20the%20German%20carmaker,DDB.
4. Jakob Nielsen, "How Users Read on the Web." NN/g Articles & Videos Page, September 30, 1997, https://www.nngroup.com/articles/how-users-read-on-the-web/.
5. Cited January 12, 2025 at https://www.statista.com/statistics/1378808/most-visited-states-us/. I for one have been to Nebraska several times and loved it.

6. Thomas H. Klier, "From Tail Fins to Hybrids: How Detroit Lost Its Dominance." *Economic Perspectives* Vol. 33, 2nd (2009): 2–17. https://www.chicagofed.org/publications/economic-perspectives/2009/2qtr-klier.
7. AIMAM, "Evolution of Car Tariffs: A 125-Year History of Trade Wars, Economic Shifts, and Power Plays." Global Law Today Technology, Innovation Page, April 10, 2025, https://www.globallawtoday.com/technology/innovation/2025/04/the-evolution-of-vehicle-tariffs-a-125-year-history-of-trade-wars-economic-shifts-and-strategic-power-plays/.
8. The Samba Archives Page, https://www.thesamba.com/vw/archives/info/salesfigurest1.php.
9. Team TBH, "A Case Study on Volkswagen's Think Small Campaign," The Brand Hopper Case Studies Page, July 24, 2024, https://thebrandhopper.com/2024/07/24/a-case-study-on-volkswagens-think-small-campaign/.
10. The copy was finalized after multiple iterations by the late, great Julian Koenig. The headline was the brainchild of the lesser-known but amazing Rita Selden. "Dominik Imseng on Great Copywriting," YouTube video, posted by Dominik Imseng, March 15, 2023, https://www.youtube.com/watch?v=ytzpX3AWEVE.
11. Ibid.
12. Paraphrased from Claude C. Hopkins, *Scientific Advertising* (Chicago: independently published, 1923).
13. See the study here: Joanna Wiebe, "We used these 3 copywriting principles on a home page. And doubled ecommerce revenue. (Case Study)." Articles Page, June 7, 2016, https://copyhackers.com/2016/06/copywriting-principles-sweatblock/.
14. Wynter, "How Wynter helped Appcues improve their conversion rate by 73% with messaging that resonates." Wynter Case Studies Page, May 4, 2022, https://wynter.com/case-studies/appcues#:~:text=A%2FB%20test%20results%3A%2073.
15. Talia Wolf, "Messaging optimization: The #1 item that needs to be on your 2025 CRO plan." LinkedIn, October 31, 2024, https://www.linkedin.com/pulse/messaging-optimization-1-item-needs-your-2025-cro-plan-talia-wolf-wto1f#:~:text=Messaging%20optimization%20is%20what%20helped,uplift%20in%20organic%20Search.

16. Jennifer Havice, "Use Voice-of-Customer Research to Boost Conversions." CXL Blog, CRO & Testing Page, June 21, 2020, https://cxl.com/blog/voice-of-customer/#:~:text=Simply%20telling%20visitors%20who%20these,weeks%20and%20reaching%20statistical%20significance.
17. Meka Asonye, "0-$5M: How to Identify Your ICP—Lessons from Vanta, Clay, Retool." *First Round Review*, May 15, 2025, https://review.firstround.com/how-vanta-clay-retool-found-icp/.
18. Kevin Sanchez Farez, "Scrub Daddy's famous sponge was rejected by a Fortune 500 company and forgotten in a box for years. It's now a $220 million empire." *Fortune*, February 2, 2024, https://fortune.com/2024/02/02/scrub-daddy-founder-interview-shark-tank-success-story/.
19. As per Basecamp's website, documented in May 2025.
20. Detailed study, with side-by-side images of pages, here: Joanna Wiebe, "How I Optimized the Crazy Egg Home Page." Articles Page. February 12, 2014, https://copyhackers.com/2014/02/optimized-crazy-egg-home-page/.
21. Jared M. Spool, "The Search for Seducible Moments." Center Centre Articles Page, November 8, 2022, https://articles.centercentre.com/seducible_moments/.
22. Data for B2B sales opportunities, as reported by CSO Insights and Gartner, among others. Source A: https://www.csoinsights.com/, Source B: https://www.gartner.com/.
23. Meka Asonye, "0–$5M: How to Identify Your ICP—Lessons from Vanta, Clay, Retool." *First Round Review*, May 15, 2025, https://review.firstround.com/how-vanta-clay-retool-found-icp/.
24. Ibid.
25. Jared M. Spool, "The Search for Seducible Moments." Center Centre Articles Page, November 8, 2022, https://articles.centercentre.com/seducible_moments/.
26. Credit to Jared Blank @ Gobbledy for this example in his April 2, 2025, newsletter.
27. Originally via DHH, Twitter post, April 23, 2025, 3:10 AM, https://x.com/dhh/status/1914939888056619070. Further discussed, with Jason Fried, in this LinkedIn thread: https://www.linkedin.com/feed/update/urn:li:activity:7327753962487537665/.

28. Sourced June 22, 2025, from the homepage of thehappysleeper.com.
29. Sourced from Casper.com on June 22, 2025.
30. Explained well here: Mark Forsyth, "The language rules we know—but don't know we know." *BBC*, September 8, 2016, https://www.bbc.com/culture/article/20160908-the-language-rules-we-know-but-dont-know-we-know.
31. Sourced from: Elena de Francisco, "The most powerful weapon to make people listen (AND buy everything you offer)." *The Expat Copywriter* (blog), January 27, 2021, https://www.elenadefrancisco.com/the-most-powerful-weapon-to-make-people-listen-and-buy-everything-you-offer/.
32. Sourced from https://www.teamwork.com/.
33. The Creative Hall of Fame notes this ad as one of the most quoted in advertising history: Creative Hall of Fame, "John Caples: 1973 Creative Hall of Fame Inductee." Inductees Page, https://creativehalloffame.org/inductees/john-caples/.
34. At the height of its popularity in 2021, Buzzfeed (NASDAQ: BZFD) had a market cap of $800 million USD, as per https://stockanalysis.com/stocks/bzfd/market-cap/ (sourced April 3, 2025).
35. Valuation based on Series E funding round in March 2024, which doubled its prior valuation. Secondary market data in late 2025 suggests a valuation closer to $1 billion.
36. All copy captured during 2019 audit of websites in question.
37. Revenue estimates as per Lemon CEO Aleksandr Volodarsky in email exchange with Joanna Wiebe in July 2025.
38. Charles Duhigg, interview by Terry Gross, "Habits: How They Form and How to Break Them." *Fresh Air*, National Public Radio, March 5, 2012, http://www.npr.org/2012/03/05/147192599/habits-how-they-form-and-how-to-break-them.
39. Bushra Azhar, "The Quick and Dirty Guide to Turning Your Website into a Persuasion Powerhouse." Articles Page, April 22, 2014, https://copyhackers.com/2014/04/website-persuasion/.

INDEX

ABOUT THE AUTHOR

The original conversion copywriter, Joanna (Jo) Wiebe is the founder of Copyhackers, where marketers of all stripes learn to become the most profitable people in the room. Since 2005, she's worked with tiny brands and Fortune 100 companies to replace guesswork with strategically engineered messages that are proven to convert leads into customers and customers into referrers. Her popular Copy School programs have helped more than 5,000 copywriters worldwide become bankable assets to the brands that are lucky enough to hire them.